This Restless Prelate

DEDICATION

To the memory of Dr John Cashman, late Assistant Archivist of the Clifton Diocese, whose enthusiasm for Bishop Baines was infectious and my brother, Alan Gilbert B.D., priest and teacher, whose life inspired many and whose early death left a great void.

This Restless Prelate: Bishop Peter Baines 1786–1843

Pamela J. Gilbert

GRACEWING

First published in 2006

Gracewing
2 Southern Avenue
Leominster
Herefordshire HR6 0QF

ISBN 0 85244 592 X
ISBN 978 0 85244 592 1

Typesetting by
Action Publishing Technology Ltd, Gloucester, GL1 5SR

Printed in England

Contents

Acknowledgements

I am grateful to the Bishop Emeritus of Clifton, the Rt Rev Mervyn Alexander, for permission to use the Clifton Diocesan Archives during the years in which they were at Bishop's House. I have received a great deal of help from the Diocesan Archivist, Fr Dr J. A. Harding and the Assistant Archivist, Dr Kenneth Hankins, during my research at Clifton and I am very appreciative of all their kindness.

I also owe a debt to Fr Philip Jebb, O.S.B., the Archivist at Downside, for all his help during the many visits I made there, and to Fr Anselm Cramer, O.S.B., the Archivist at Ampleforth, who went to a great deal of trouble to obtain the information I wanted and to show me round the places of interest connected with Bishop Baines.

I am grateful, too, to the former archivist of the Jesuit Archives at Farm Street, Fr T. G. Holt, S.J., to the staff of the City of Bristol Record office, the City of Bristol Reference Library, the City of Bath Guild Hall and Prior Park College. I also received valuable information from Dr Christopher Stray, Lecturer in the Classics Department of the University College of Swansea on the work of Dr Feinagle and from Miss Toni Eccles, Secretary of the English Catholic History Association on Wardour Castle.

Dr Sean Gill, Senior Lecturer in the Theology and Religious Studies Department at The University of Bristol was kind enough to read through the first part of my manuscript and to make valuable comments, and I am grateful to him and to Gill and Ian Love who helped me with the computing.

Finally, this work would never have materialized if it had not been for the inspiration of Dr John Cashman, late Assistant Achivist of the Clifton Diocese, who was a Baines enthusiast and encouraged me to start my research.

The publisher would like to thank Dr Rory O'Donnell FSA of English Heritage for his help and for constructive comments with regard to the architectural background of Bishop Baines' work and ministry.

List of Illustrations

Introduction

Peter Augustine Baines was a product of the English Benedictine Congregation as it existed around the year 1800. It was, on account of the French Revolution and the Napoleonic Wars, a Congregation in crisis: its numbers depleted and by the time of Baines' departure from Lamspringe in 1803 without any Continental houses or for that matter anything resembling a monastery; there were only mission houses and two fragile small communities at Ampleforth (from 1802) and Acton Burnell (transferred to Downside in 1814). Nor was the strength of the Congregation to be found in numbers but in the gritty determination of its members to survive.

The English Benedictine Congregation had been revived at the beginning of the seventeenth century and had become the third force on the English Mission alongside the much bigger and better resourced Jesuit and secular missions.[1] Englishmen had made their monastic profession at various Italian and Spanish monasteries and by 1619 the Spanish-professed English monks had come together 'to be called the English Congregation, so that being thus united it would be continued and restored, and if there is any need of it, newly erected'. The English Benedictines saw themselves as the continuation of the Pre-Reformation Congregation through the links of the early seventeenth-century monks with the Abbey of Westminster renewed under Mary Tudor.

By 1633 most of the English monks then professed had joined the Congregation. What distinguished the English Benedictine Congregation was its missionary apostolate. Its organizational structure, which was to remain in place until the end of the nineteenth century, reflected this purpose and owed more to the spirit of the Counter-Reformation orders like the Jesuits than to the traditional monastic order. Collaboration and frequent elections to posts of responsibility were marked characteristics of the new Congregation. The overall superior of the Congregation was the President General elected by a General Chapter which met every four years. Monks on the mission came under the immediate jurisdiction of the Northern or Southern Provincial, also elected officials, and those on the Continent under the prior of the various English communities. Monks on the mission worked as chaplains in Catholic households and increasingly, in the eighteenth century, in Catholic centres of population; Bath, with its large transient population of Catholics, was perhaps the most important of the Southern missions, Liverpool, with its growing seaport the Northern equivalent. In the seventeenth century several monks died for their faith, and three of the forty English Martyrs of the Reformation canonized in 1970 – John Roberts, Alban Roe and Ambrose Barlow – were members of the Congregation.

At the time of the French Revolution there were three English Benedictine monasteries for men in France, and one in Germany. St Gregory's at Douai, a great centre of English Catholic activity since the foundation of the English College there in 1568 by Cardinal William Allen which allowed its students to study at the University of Douai, was founded in 1606 and by the end of the eighteenth century had a school with an impressive set of new buildings. The patronage of St Gregory suggested the Congregation's call to follow in the footsteps of the Gregorian Mission of the late sixth century. Baines' own monastic name, Augustine, had a similar resonance. The priory was strategically sited on the boundary between French and Spanish culture and in easy reach of England. St Lawrence's Dieulouard, near Nancy, in Lorraine, was also on the borderland between French and German traditions, and had been opened by 1608. The third community, dedicated to St Edmund, King of the East Angles, was in Paris. Founded in 1615 it benefited from the rich theological life of the French city. The nuns of Cambrai, whose community life begun in 1623 also formed part of the Congregation and were often its spiritual centre. The teachings and writings of Dom Augustine Baker, who died in 1641, gave some religious coherence to the Congregation's activity with their emphasis on a contemplative prayer which was ideally suited for life in the English Mission. The French communities were small and impecunious, priories with superiors elected for only four years at a time, minor players in the life of the French Church which, in the seventeenth and eighteenth centuries, was at the height of its intellectual and institutional influence.

The Abbey of SS Adrian and Denis at Lamspringe, in the vicinity of Hildesheim in Northern Germany, was not like the three other long-standing houses for men in the English Benedictine Congregation.[2] It was German rather than French. It was closely integrated in the life of the local church and its superior was a significant local personage. It was an abbey rather than a priory and its abbot cut a suitably baroque figure in his splendid abbey church, opened in 1691, and in the spacious monastery buildings of the mid-eighteenth century. It gave many of its monks to the English mission but unlike the other English monasteries it had a sizeable resident community. Its school pupils were brought up in an atmosphere of refined magnificence and in a place which more than anywhere else had the feel of what a great English monastery of the Georgian period might have been like if there had not been a Reformation, a taste of a Catholic English Baroque that was not to be.

Lamspringe, founded under the patronage of the Bursfeld Congregation, occupied a site that had been monastic since the ninth century, and was opened in 1643 as part of the final settlement of the Thirty Years War. Lamspringe had oscillated between Catholic and Protestant control since the Reformation. The monastery was undoubtedly English: its church commemorated the great founding fathers of English monasticism as well as the Stuart dynasty and the church had its own major relics in the body of St Oliver Plunkett (not beatified or canonized in the Lamspringe period) who was executed in 1681 just ten years before the opening of the church. The community and students were exposed to the spirituality of Augustine Baker. It remained part of the English Benedictine Congregation throughout and at one stage, in the late 1790s, it was the only surviving monastic house within the Congregation.

In 1803 Lamspringe went the way of the French houses and was suppressed as part of the destruction of the old order in Germany and its restructuring in the wake of Napoleonic military success and Prussian ambition. The community was by then without an abbot. The last abbot, Dom Maurus Heatley who had been involved in prolonged conflicts with both the Congregation and his own community, had died early in 1803. The monks were pensioned off by the Prussian government and the remaining scholars sent off to England where they formed the basis of a small school at Ampleforth just opened in North Yorkshire. Augustine Birdsall, perhaps (with the young Baines still a schoolboy) the most energetic of the young monks, attempted to revive the community on English soil at Broadway in Worcestershire where he acquired a property in 1828. This community survived Birdsall's death in 1841. Birdsall's Broadway venture, which included a church and a school, was not in the league of Prior Park but his accumulation of debts, ambitious plans and sense of destiny paralleled Baines with whom, in his capacity as President General of the English Benedictines, he did battle.

The English Catholic Community in the first quarter of the nineteenth century was in a state of general crisis. The French Revolution had not only dispersed the Benedictines but had led to the closure of the substantial network of Continental colleges which had provided pastors for the English mission. England was not without Catholics but it had, not for the last time, a serious shortfall in clergy at least of the native variety; clerical statistics at this time are complicated by the great number of French exiled clergy resident in England who were also victims of the Revolution. Lack of personnel, lack of money and a continuing tradition of anti-Catholicism were accompanied by what appeared an institutional and administrative vacuum at the heart of the English Catholic Community.

The self-government practised by the Benedictines and the Jesuits, themselves at this period following the suppression of the Society in the late eighteenth century in a state of suspended animation, existed on parallel lines to that of the secular clergy who were under four missionary bishops or Vicars Apostolic, appointed from the end of the seventeenth century onwards, whose powers were limited. The new challenges presented by the early nineteenth century would need new strategies and Baines was a pioneer of the new age. Prior Park was the focus for all his endeavours.[3] Baines was a man of vision and energy, as this important new study suggests, but his alternative view of things was restricted not only by the English Catholics' lack of material resources but also by the surprising resilience of the old order and especially his own English Benedictine Congregation.

Dom Aidan Bellenger, OSB

Notes

1 For an overview of the contribution of the Benedictines to the English Mission since St Gregory the Great see D. Rees (ed.), *Monks of England*, London, 1997.
2 See A. Cramer (ed.), *Lamspringe, an English Abbey in Germany*, Ampleforth, 2004.
3 For a new historical survey of Prior Park see P. Cornwell, *Prior Park College, The Phoenix*, Tiverton, 2005.

1

The High Flier

The Return to Prior Park 1841

> Four beautiful horses were harnessed to the Bishop's modest and unpretending carriage, which awaited his arrival about a mile from the city of Bath on the London Road. In this he was conveyed at a rapid pace through the city. At the commencement of Prior Park Road, two leaders were added, and the whole cortège mounted the hill at a spanking pace until they reached the lower entrance gates, where a numerous body of professors and students met him, and in spite of the Bishop's remonstrances, the horses were taken out, and he was drawn by the whole assemblage to the foot of the splendid flight of steps leading to the mansion.

Bishop Baines would have revelled in such a moment. He loved pomp and ceremony and the adulation of all. It was a characteristic which led him into extravagance and self-aggrandizement, but also raised his own profile and that of the Catholic Church. For nearly twenty-five years, Baines had been a colourful figure in the area and the *Bath Weekly Chronicle* devoted a full page to the coverage of his return to Prior Park after a long absence, knowing that whatever the Bishop did was news.

The reporter continued in the flamboyant style of the day:

> if we consider the occasion – the return of a beloved father to the midst of his flock, of a Bishop to a college of his own forming, surprise will not be felt when I tell you that tears of joy flowed plentifully. The Bishop's feelings would not allow him to do more than utter a few words of gratitude and thanks for the reception given to him. The college was brilliantly illuminated at night, and this evening I understand there is to be a splendid display of fireworks.[1]

The magnificent ceremonial was a moment of glory for Baines in the midst of the disintegration of all his ambitions. He had returned from Rome, where he had been summoned by the Pope to explain his controversial pastoral of the previous year, 1840; he had come back to Prior Park, where he had established a seminary, a school and the foundations of what he hoped would be a Catholic university, but the future of the establishment was uncertain, weighed down by debt and controversy. Two years before his premature death in 1843, Baines appeared to be at the nadir of his fortunes, and yet on that night in the spring of 1841, he delighted in all the ceremony that had been prepared for him and, always the eternal optimist, he looked to the future with hope.

Early days in Lancashire

It was all a world away from Baines's birth and early years. He was born at Pear Tree Farm in Kirby on the outskirts of Liverpool. When Bishop Burton of the Clifton Diocese visited it in 1918, it was still in a rural area, and he described the farmhouse as 'small and neat and unpretentious'. The huge pear tree, which gave its name to the house, had only recently been cut down.[2] Baines's father, James Baines, sometimes referred to as Baynes, was a tenant farmer, as were many others of his fellow Catholics who farmed land belonging to Catholic landlords in West Lancashire. John Bossy claims that before the Industrial Revolution there were more Catholics in this rich agricultural area, bounded on the north by Lancaster, in the south by the Mersey, and in the east by a line running through to Wigan and Warrington, than the remainder of the north put together.[3] It was an area which had seen little change in hundreds of years, and had maintained traditions of life which included loyalty to the Catholic faith.

It was an area, too, in which numerous numbers of the Catholic gentry had survived, minding their estates, getting on tolerably well with their Protestant neighbours and providing a source of livelihood to those who lived on their estates. In rural areas they also made it possible for their tenants and labourers to continue worshipping in the Catholic faith, for many of these gentry had built chapels attached to their houses, and employed chaplains who also served as priests in the local communities. Catholic communities of this kind were to be found all over the Lancashire Plain, from Cottam Hall near Lancaster in the north down to Crosby Hall and Ince Blundell in the Liverpool area.[4] James Baines's family came from Claughton, south of Lancaster, where most of them farmed. There had been priests in the family, however, as far back as the seventeenth century, when a John

Baines was baptized in 1653 by the priest at Cottam Hall, the seat of the Haydock family, and was ordained priest at Rome in 1678. He returned to the English mission in 1681, and assumed the name of John Kendall. About 1703 he took over a barn near the Hall as a chapel and started the mission of Cottam independent of the Hall. After his death he was succeeded by a relative, Henry Kendall, probably an uncle of James Baines, who was born in 1740.[5]

Little is known about James Baines's early life, but later family reminiscences reveal something of his character. He was plainly, as his son Peter was to be, a lover of the good life, even if this meant living beyond his means. For some years he was heavily in debt and in danger of being sent to prison. He loved to excel in everything he undertook, and hated not to come first, a characteristic which was to lead to his unfortunate death in a riding accident. A few months before this accident, one of his sons, Thomas, described how James Baines 'has gotten on the last October meeting of the agricultural society a silver cup, presented to him for showing a bull! He is often ready to talk and swagger about such things . . .'[6]

By the 1780s James Baines had left Claughton, where two of his brothers, John and Thomas, lived; he moved down to Kirkby, then just outside Liverpool, and took up a tenancy in Aintree at Pear Tree Farm. He married Catharine Tasker, who came from Aughton but had relatives in the Liverpool area. She was a deeply religious woman, who became the steady rock in James's life. They were soon raising a large family of five daughters and five sons; all the daughters married early, either to tradesmen or farmers, while four of the sons, James, Barnaby, William and Thomas also went into farming or trade.

The other son, Peter, born in 1786, was the great exception. He was baptized at St Swithin, Gilmoss, then only a small chapel. In 1918, Bishop Burton recalled[7] seeing the old loft there, where mass was said before the penal laws and studying Baines's birth certificate[8] in the nineteenth-century church, since rebuilt. From an early age, Baines's parents realized that he had the potential to excel, and they sent him at the age of ten to the Benedictine school of Scholes, Prescot, five miles from their home. This was the temporary residence of the exiled Benedictines of Dieulouard, who had come from Lorraine in eastern France, where they had lived and worshipped since the seventeenth century. At the beginning of the French Revolution, Dieulouard was so far from Paris that the monks were remote from the events in the capital, but by 1793 life was becoming more and more difficult and the prior was threatened with arrest. He managed to escape to Ostend and from there to England, where his monks eventually succeeded in following him.[9]

School Days at Lamspringe

The Benedictine community of St Laurence had lost their permanent home in France owing to the war and relied on wealthy Catholic families to give them temporary refuge. By the time that the community arrived in Scholes they had already had two homes in England, and were destined to move on again in 1797. James and Catharine Baines must have thought that the future was so uncertain for the Benedictines of Dieulouard that it would be better to send Peter to a school that appeared to be more settled. French schools, once the automatic choice of Catholics with means, were now out of the question. They decided upon the English Benedictine school of SS Adrian and Dionysius at Lamspringe in the region of Hanover, an area not yet involved in the French Revolutionary wars. It must, though, have been a formidable undertaking for a boy of twelve to leave home and to travel to a country so near the area of conflict. It must also have been a drain on James Baines's financial resources, and the whole family including uncles and aunts, and numbers of friends, appear to have guaranteed money for Peter's education. This could have placed a strain on family relationships, particularly as the other sons grew up and had to earn their own living, but later correspondence reveals little jealousy or animosity against this brother whose education they continued to finance.

Peter Baines was at Lamspringe for four years and the abbey must have had a great influence on him in his formative years. It was a noble building, one of the largest baroque churches in northern Germany, with nine altars and a fine organ. The abbot had once been a prince of the neighbouring territory and held his own court with powers of life and death. Although he had long lost such powers, he was still regarded as an important person in the area. The power of the office was increased by the fact that only two men had held the position between 1730 and 1802. Abbot Rokeby rebuilt the monastery and its school between 1730 and 1761, so that the young Baines studied in much less spartan conditions than he would have known in many monastic schools.

Rokeby was succeeded by Abbot Maurus Heatley, who presided over the community for forty years. He maintained a large, prospersous monastic community, but by the time Baines started at Lamspringe, the rule of the abbot was coming to be regarded as too autocratic. A strong movement developed among some of the religious and older students against Abbot Heatley in particular. There were also signs that some of them, imbued with the spirit of the French Revolution, were questioning the need for the centralized power of an abbot in the monastic community at all. The chief spokesman of this group was Austin Birdsall, later to become Baines's antagonist.[10]

Baines must have been affected by this movement and the feeling of resentment among older students. Fr Dionysius Allerton, his Professor of Canon Law and Prefect of Studies, was exceedingly rough and arbitrary, and always sided with the Abbot, so Baines would have heard the other side of the controversy in a very forceful way. It may be possible that this experience was the source of Baines's disillusionment, so that in later years he did not seem to sympathize with the Benedictine way of life. He never returned to Lamspringe in future years, nor recalled it with the nostalgia which Fr Birdsall was to feel. Birdsall came back to Lamspringe in 1828, twenty-five years after it had been suppressed, and recorded:

> The church is very little changed, indeed not at all changed. The odds and ends that lie about the sacristy would lead you to fancy that it was but yesterday that the monks had left it. The vestments, the chalice and the cruets in the church, the pictures, the statues, nay the stalls and the seats in the choir are all the same as we left them with the exception of the four great pulpits or desks for the choir books at which the juniors used to stand ... I said mass in the church at the High Altar on the Sunday morning early, when a great many of the poorer sort and they also the elder ones who had known other times attended and by their countenances showed that those other times were present to their recollections. As I went out of the church, they stood in silence with uplifted eyes and folded hands and many of them not without tears, forming a kind of avenue for me to pass. I knelt during High Mass in the Abbot's seat, and as Mr Towers I find had kept up amongst some of them the vain and groundless notion that some day or other we should re-enter its possession, some of them asked me if it were really true that we were going to return.[11]

Baines seemed to have no such memories of Lamspringe, but he certainly imbibed a taste for splendour and ecclesiastical magnificence, which was to last him all his life; he formed also a relationship with his future opponent, Fr Austin Birdsall, which was later to prove unfortunate. Birdsall was made Prefect of Studies in Baines's last year at Lamspringe and, even after Baines became a bishop, was inclined to address him as an erring pupil rather than his ecclesiastical superior. This made a potentially difficult relationship between two proud and obstinate characters even more tempestuous.

On the credit side, Baines's four years in the Benedictine community at Lamspringe gave him a broad education, a love of music and the fine arts, and a good prose style in English which was to influence his writing and public speaking. In Latin, too, a fragment of his prose, on the death of Cicero, shows that he was accomplished for his years.[12] He remained a creature of the eighteenth century, a well-rounded man of letters.

His studies were rudely interrupted in 1803, when Lamspringe was overrun by Prussian troops and the community scattered. A few German monks remained in the neighbourhood in the vain hope that they would be able to regain their monastery, but Peter Baines and his fellow English students departed for the perilous journey home to England.

The novice at Ampleforth 1803–1809

By this time the Baines family had left Kirkby and moved to Ince Blundell near Crosby. Presumably the lease of Pear Tree Farm had ended and James Baines was not able to rent it again on favourable terms. Instead he was able to rent land from Henry Blundell, who owned the Hall and most of the surrounding land at Ince. Blundell was held in very high esteem as a landlord and a benefactor to the Catholic Church, giving contributions to the erection of St Nicholas's chapel in Liverpool and to other religious and educational undertakings. He was to prove a good landlord to James and his son, Thomas, and gave the family a security they had not known before.[13]

Peter Baines remained home at Ince Blundell for several months, while the family debated what should be done about his further education. Plainly it was no longer possible to send Catholic boys to school on the Continent, and the only alternative was the schools run by the exiled Benedictines, who had fled to England from Douai and from Dieulouard. The former, the community of St Gregory, had not yet found a permanent home, but the latter, the community of St Laurence, had recently found a permanent home at Fr Anselm's house at Ampleforth in the Vale of York, and it was here that James and Catharine Baines finally decided to send their son in 1803 as a novice.

By this time Peter Baines was sixteen years old, well advanced in his studies at Lamspringe and full of self-confidence. At some stage before returning to England, he felt that he had a vocation to the priesthood. There is no evidence, however, that he ever felt a particular calling for the monastic life, regarding his training at Ampleforth as a means to an end. Later, in fact, he was to criticize those who made clear distinctions between regular and secular priests. As a schoolboy he had been greatly moved by the beauty of worship and the ceremonial of the great abbey at Lamspringe, but there he had not been subject to the rigour of the full Benedictine Rule, which he was to find at Ampleforth when he began his novitiate in 1803. Rising early in the morning, he would attend matins and lauds followed by four short offices throughout the day, and ending with the evening office of vespers and the bedtime office of compline. It is likely, though, that the timetable of offices was modified at Ampleforth, as at other monasteries with schools, to accommodate the demands of work; further hours were devoted to lectures, private study and prayer. He was always to find such a disciplined life difficult.

The novitiate had been established at Ampleforth to accommodate Baines and two other very promising students from Lamspringe, Edward Benedict Glover and Alban Molyneux. Baines had known Edward Glover since childhood days in Lancashire, and the two of them had travelled together to Lamspringe. All three were clothed at Ampleforth in May 1803 and were shortly afterwards joined by a fourth, Gregory Robinson from Bath. He was considerably older than the other three, having done a medical training and served for some years as a ship's surgeon. These four were to become the first fruits of the new foundation at Ampleforth, which gradually expanded over the next few years. At the same time the school was re-opened to take a growing number of pupils, and the whole community grew to such an extent that two extra wings had to be added to the original building.

Early in his novitiate Baines displayed his extreme self-confidence, which might be described as arrogance. In a letter to Bishop Sharrock, the Vicar Apostolic of the Western District, he complains about the Prior of Ampleforth, the Revd Thomas Appleton. Baines may have had some justification in his criticism of Appleton, as Benedictine records later recorded that, although the Prior was a strict and religious man, 'his rough and ready ways combined with a sour temper were not subject to give satisfaction to others.'

It is understandable, too, that Baines with his growing taste for the good life should have disagreed with Appleton's harsh philosophy, but few students would have dared to write to a bishop in the following terms:

> We have for some time past been surprised at an assertion of the Rev Thomas Appleton that every action we perform is either an evil or a virtue and that no action whatever is indifferent. Last Sunday ... he again strongly enforced that whatever is taken in meat or drink that is superfluous, or whatever was beyond neces-

> sity was a sin; he expressed the same with regard to conversation and amusements. On the same day in his discourse he emphatically maintained that the rich man after he has supplied himself with the necessaries of life is bound by the law of God to dispose of the remainder of his wealth to the poor, or to other charitable purposes for the honour and glory of God.[14]

Bishop Sharrock's feelings upon receiving this letter from an unknown student at Ampleforth can only be imagined. Not surprisingly he did not reply to Baines directly, but wrote to the Revd Thomas Appleton to relate what had happened. We learn this from another letter written by Baines to Bishop Sharrock on 19 August 1805. In this he seemed to be quite bewildered as to how he had managed to incur the Bishop's displeasure. He related somewhat pathetically:

> A week ago Mr Appleton ordered me to go into penance without acquainting me in what I had transgressed. The next day, when I waited upon him to request to go out of penance, he asked me what I had written to you, and at the same time charged me with having accused him. He then ordered me to go back again to get off by heart the degrees of humility. I have been now a week confined to my room, and as I am obliged at the same time to pursue my regular studies and teach my school, I make but little progress in the penance enjoined me.[15]

Humility was a virtue which Baines was to find difficulty in acquiring, and this was not helped by the reverence given him by his family in Lancashire, who followed his progress, thanked him for his advice and found the financial means to support him. His younger brother, Thomas, was now helping his father on the farm and so busy that there is a veiled rebuke in his letter of 26 June 1807:

> I find your very obliging letter on Monday last, but as you want so speedy an answer, and me a poor inditer, that you have scarcely given me time to compose a sufficient answer to your request: but however I shall do as well as I can. You may be sure dear Brother, that I have a sincere love and affection for you in every way, as I have for myself, and you may depend that I shall follow the advice you have now given me, and I am much obliged to you for it . . .'[16]

His father wrote to him on the same date, showing his concern that Peter had everything he needed:

> if you want anything within reason be not afraid to ask for it for God has been so good as to put it in our power and we wish to make good use of which he has put into our power. We have sent you a £5 note and paid for carriage and safety for it – do hope you will send word when you have received it as soon as pos . . .'[17]

Thomas was not beyond pulling his brother's leg, though. On one occasion he included his own letter with his father's, so as to save expense (Peter would have to pay the postage when it arrived): 'I know you do not like to part with more money than you can help: excuse freedom my dear Brother . . .'[18]

It was the year before Peter Baines was ordained priest that his father was killed in a riding accident. He accepted a challenge from an acquaintance to race him on horseback across the sands to Great Crosby for a shilling wager. His mare's feet stuck in a line of quicksand and she threw James Baines right on to his head. His death was typical of the impetuosity of the man, a feature to be so prominent in his son.

Peter Baines did not come home for the funeral, his family agreeing with him that 'it would be attended with expense and lots of time and we think there is no necessity for it'.

Yet they must have wanted his support on such a sad family occasion, and other relatives and friends must have wondered at the absence of the son on whom his father had lavished all the money he could spare, so that he might realize the great hopes he had of him. It was not the only time that Baines was to show a lack of feeling for his family and friends, and one wonders why a man who could win over many by his charm and enthusiasm, and inspire lifelong devotion in the few, could yet lack something in basic humanity.

Thomas wrote to him on behalf of their mother and himself: 'We received your very kind letter on the 14th inst and am glad to hear that you resign your will to the will of God and willingly, which we will resolve to do in like manner by the grace of God . . .'[19]

Thomas now took over the farm, as the other unmarried brother, James, had just left home to start a warehouse near Preston. As the lease on the family farm was soon to run out, Thomas was worried that he would not be able to afford the increased amount, but eventually he and his mother decided to renew it for another six years. 'It is a little above double to what it is now, but we did not like to leave it.'

In the following year, 1810, there were further worries that the Baines family might lose their farm when the landlord, Mr Henry

Blundell, died, and the will was disputed by his heir. Peter Baines was obviously concerned about this, but a friend from Ince Blundell, Hugh Spencer, wrote to assure him that there was no danger of Charles Blundell, the new owner, selling the estate. Baines was worried about this, not only for the welfare of his family, but because he was still dependent on financial support from home to see him through his studies.

By 1812 Thomas had taken over the farm for a twenty-one-year period as a tenant wholly, and was to pay his mother £50 a year. She was to move back to Kirkby, to a house built for her on land adjoining the house of her son, Barnaby, and wrote to Peter to tell him about her plans. 'I have always wished for a small place I could call my own in case any change might take place amongst my children; there I may see my child or friend and be troublesome to no one. I hope in your next you will give me your opinion of the present plan.'[20]

Priest and teacher 1810–1817

Peter Baines received a settlement of £220 from the family and was by this time financially independent. He had also been ordained to the priesthood in 1810, given teaching responsibilities, and by 1814 was Prefect of Studies at Ampleforth. His great interest was to be in education and he soon became accepted as headmaster of Ampleforth school as well as acting as tutor to the students in the seminary.

His prospectus for the year 1814 shows that the range of subjects covered at the college was wide-ranging and imaginative. At a time when Eton taught little but the Classics, Ampleforth also offered Hebrew, French, History, Geography, Natural History, Ornithology, Botany, Algebra and Geometry.[21] Baines became an admirer of Professor Fenaigle, who followed the Mnemonic method and used mental images to help students to remember a sequence of facts. His theories were not new but, more than his predecessors, he adapted his sytem to the needs of educators, providing special techniques for learning each subject. He also advocated regular examinations in public, and Bishop Baines was attracted by this idea. Such events conducted with great ceremony would bring to Ampleforth not only partents, but many other members of the public. He made several trips to London to stay with the Professor and while he was there in March 1812, his friend Gregory Robinson, now Prior of Ampleforth, wrote to him from Ampleforth: 'Before you leave London I would wish you to obtain from Mr Fenaigle a grammar of as many languages as he can give you conveniently without trespassing too much upon his time – a grammar of the French I particularly wish to have . . .'[22]

In April Baines was still in London and Robinson wrote to warn him that the President of the Benedictines, Dr Brewer, was getting restless about his long absence:

> If you are not careful you will bring me into a scrap with the Dr. By a kind of Jesuitive, telling part of the truth and concealing a part, I informed the Dr that you would be from home two or three weeks. You must clear up the matter as well as you can, without bringing me into a hubble.[23]

Baines was never afraid to be away from his work for long periods if he felt that it was important for him to be elsewhere. (This was a practice which was to disturb Bishop Collingridge, when Baines became his coadjutor.) He remained in London a little longer before returning to Ampleforth and inviting Professor Fenaigle to visit the college. The professor wrote to him on 13 July 1812:

> I bring a great deal of work with me; you shall be more convinced that it is my firm resolution to make your college the first perfect pattern of a school. I shall stay with you as long as it shall be necessary and convenient. I have already a number of drawings for the History; and made very good preparation for the most difficult parts of Chemistry and likewise Botany and long very much to see you all . . .[24]

The use at Ampleforth of Fenaigle's system in developing the Art of Memory and thus leaving time in the curriculum for a much wider range of subjects aroused favourable comment. Baines received a number of enquiries on the subject, such as a letter from a Mr Seckerson on 29 November 1815:

> . . . in a note it is remarked that the school in which you preside has long been conducted in that system (Fenaigle's Art of Memory) with great success. The father of several boys and solicitous to give them every advantage which can be derived from an improved system of education, I hope to be pardoned for the intrusion into your time and attention.[25]

Baines was equally concerned with his students' cultural and leisure activities, and was in correspondence with a Mrs Goadby about obtaining a dancing master for the college. Mrs Goadby recommended a Mr Hargitt and assured Baines, 'Mr Hargitt from his attention to my instruction and his usual industry and perseverance in his practice will no doubt be able to answer the purpose required of him.'[26]

Drawing and music were considered equally important and Baines mentioned in his diary that he had assisted in discussions about the appointment of drawing and music masters. He also wrote to a Mr Constable, who had offered to put up money for 'a new ball place' to be built at the school. Mr Constable was inclined to think that 33ft in length and 13ft in height for such walls was rather a small scale, but 'I sincerely hope you will be satisfied.'[27]

The smallest details were of concern to Baines, assuring fathers considering sending their sons to Ampleforth that the boys had a healthy diet, little sickness and that every precaution was taken to prevent the spread of infection. He assured them, too, that good discipline was maintained without the use of the cane, except in the last resort. This was at a time when flogging was a daily occurrence in public schools. The decision practically to abolish the use of the cane had been taken by the senior boys themselves.

On the other hand Baines was traditional in his approach to testing. Following Professor Fenaigle's teaching, he believed in the importance of yearly examinations, not only for testing the students' progress, but also in advertizing the achievements of the school. Numbers of parents and influential people were invited to witness the examinations, which were given orally. He noted on 5 October 1814 that the examinations were attended by numbers of people in the audience, e.g. Mr Middleton of Middleton Lodge, Dr Lawson, Mr and Mrs Fairfax, Charles and the two girls etc. At the end of the day there were celebrations of the kind that Baines loved, with fireworks being discharged on the terrace.

Not everyone was enamoured of Baines's method of conducting examinations, one complaining that the arrangements were impudent and unjust and that the boys had not been given sufficient examination, while Prior Robinson complained that Baines was constantly entertaining the gentry. These criticisms did not worry Baines, who knew that his school was becoming more popular and increasing in numbers.

Among his contemporaries a few admired Baines for his great energy and his intellect, but the majority were critical. They complained that

> Like Bottom the weaver he had a desire to play all parts. On account of this he has been accused of discontent and ambition. But

> it was hardly ambition in the strict sense of the word. He was quite capable of laying down the office of Sub-prior or Professor of Theology to become head gardener or cook. He became distinctly unpopular, for his brethren were uneasy with a man who was never satisfied with a thing unless he had done it himself.[28]

Baines's diary for this period certainly demonstrates his constant desire to be involved in a great variety of occupations and interests. On 19 September 1814 he records 'digging the foundations of a cow-house and stall'; on 26 November, he was helping to plant trees and in December he was pleased that he and his helpers had been able to get the cows into their new cow-house and the pigs into their new sties. Earlier he recorded that the new gardener had arrived and that 'Mr Armstrong had come to assist in staking out the new plantations of trees',[29] showing that everything that went on in the confines of the monastery concerned him.

When the lake near Ampleforth froze in hard winters, Baines delighted in taking to the ice and showing off his skating prowess to admiring students. The winter of 1814–15 was particularly hard, the snow often falling all day in December, and the lanes around Ampleforth up to three feet in snow. This did not deter Baines from going out on horseback and visiting or preaching in neighbouring villages.[30] He appears to have been a popular priest in the missions, often being asked to preach or officiate at mass. It was a foretaste of the renown he was to gain as a preacher throughout the country and later in Rome.

While at Ampleforth Baines also gained a liking for the high life, using his charm and ability to get to know well-to-do families in the neighbourhood. He was a frequent visitor to Gilling Castle, about four miles from the college, where the Fairfax family had lived for generations. He maintained his contacts with them long after he had left, staying with them in February 1830, when he was reported to be 'settling some affairs betwixt the family'.

His superiors at Ampleforth were suspicious of all these activities and surmised that he was trying to undermine their authority, and their suspicions were justified when Baines suggested that their policy hindered the progress of his students. He was determined that they should not be distracted from their studies by other activities at the college, even if these pertained to the spiritual life. On 10 March 1815 he wrote to Dr Brewer, the President, with a scarcely veiled threat:

> I have been told it is the intention of Mr Robinson to put the three

> first year students into the habit at Easter. Your Reverence will excuse the liberty I take in requiring that this ceremony may be deferred till after the next public examination ... you must be aware that the success of that examination depends principally on the first boys. You must be equally sensible that to interrupt their studies by giving them the habit, obliging them to make the usual retreat, giving them rooms, engaging their time and attention with religious and choir duties, taking them in fine from the regular school duties and exempting them partially if not entirely from any jurisdiction will completely unhinge their minds and render it quite impossible for them to prepare for the exhibition. So certain am I in my own mind that another failure must be the consequence of putting the boys into the habit before the examination, that I have come to the unalterable determination not to preside at the exhibition or be in any way responsible for its success should the proposed arrangement be carried into execution.[31]

It is not known how Dr Brewer reacted to this letter, but the lack of tact on Baines's part, even though he had some right on his side, did not increase his popularity, nor did his criticisms of Appleton, Robinson and Marsh, the three priors he worked under. An example of his scathing criticism of Robinson, despite the fact that he had always counted him a friend, is to be found in a letter to Fr Alban Molyneux in 1813:

> There has been a total and unaccountable change in Mr R. since the commencement of his priorship. He has now become a complete Mr Appleton from head to foot, from the heart to the greatest of his views and activities – clothing, food, behaviour towards the religious are Mr A exactly ... amongst the other things we have to complain of is Mr R's unaccountable treatment of strangers. Some of our Knaresborough friends have not fared better than the others and must I think be dissatisfied with the treatment they receive.[32]

This sort of criticism, justified or not, made some feel that Baines was becoming too arrogant, too sure of the rightness of his own views. The feeling was increased by the knowledge that he had been writing letters to the Prior of Downside, advising him about the relocation of his monastery, although his advice had not been sought. He tried to convince the Prior that it would be better to move to premises near Bath than try to expand the present premises near Downside:

> If you had a proper building you would beat us by much on account of the neighbourhood of Bath and the great distance from any other college. Your present position is a bad distance from Bath . . . you are also rather too far distant from good stone. Is it not possible to purchase a small piece of land near Bath (the distance of a mile or two at the most) on which you may erect a house? You might keep your present house at Downside, and either let it or keep a hind [a steward] upon it, who will live in the house. It will serve you also as a kind of country house to go to sometimes in vacations etc. I am so fully convinced of the advantages of you having a good house, or rather a good and convenient college near Bath, and so entirely persuaded that you might have one of the finest and best establishments in the Kingdom, that I cannot help feeling particularly wishful that you should lay aside the idea of patching your old place at Downside, and do something to the purpose.[33]

Here Baines must have wondered whether he was perhaps presuming too far, as he goes on to say, 'but I find I am again making too free with my advice'.

This kind of advice, generally unsolicited, was resented by many of Baines's colleagues in the Benedictine order and, although he retained some warm admirers, the majority could not have been sorry when, in 1817, Baines asked to leave Ampleforth and be appointed to one of the English missions. This was not an unusual decision, as many Benedictines left Ampleforth and went to work on the Benedictine missions throughout the country. It was normally a joint decision agreed upon by the Superior of the Abbey and the President, who must have realized that Baines had talents above the ordinary. Yet even if they had doubts about him, it would have been difficult for them to refuse Baines, with his dominant personality which brooked no obstacles. He was sent to the Bath mission, the centre of the Catholic Church in the Western District. He was now thirty, the age which he was later to say was ideal for a priest to enter the missions; he had found the life of a monastery restrictive, being always more of a man of action than one of contemplation. He hoped that Bath would give him greater scope for his talents, and the chance of playing a wider role in the life of the Catholic Church.

Notes

1 *Tablet*, 24 April 1841, quoting from *Bath and Cheltenham Chronicle*.
2 Clifton Diocesan Archives (CDA), Bishop Burton's Diaries, 1918.
3 John Bossy, *The English Catholic Community 1570–1850* (London, 1975), pp. 91–5.

4 Ibid. and also F. O. Blundell, *Old Catholic Lancashire* (London, 1941).
5 Lancashire Registers, *The Fylde*, vol. 1, pp. 107ff. Catholic Record Society (London, 1915).
6 CDA, Bishops' Letters, Thomas Baines to Peter Baines, 15 January 1809.
7 CDA, Bishop Burton's Diaries, 1918.
8 CDA, ibid. and also Prior Park Files 5–15.
9 E. L. Taunton, *The English Black Monks of St Benedict*, vol. 2, pp. 219ff (London, 1941).
10 Ibid. pp. 307ff.
11 Ampleforth and Downside Archives, Allanson's 'Lives of the English Benedictines'; unpublished material for the English Benedictines, circa 1858.
12 Ibid.
13 F. O. Blundell, *Old Catholic Lancashire*, p. 71.
14 CDA, Bishops' Letters, Peter Baines to Bishop Sharrock, 2 August 1805.
15 Ibid. 19 August 1805.
16 Ibid. Bishops' Letters, Thomas Baines to Peter Baines, 26 June 1807.
17 Ibid. James and Catharine Baines to Peter Baines, 25 August 1807.
18 Ibid. Thomas Baines to Peter Baines, 15 January 1809.
19 Ibid. Thomas and Catharine Baines to Peter Baines, 23 April 1809.
20 Ibid. Catharine Baines to Peter Baines, 8 February 1813.
21 Ampleforth Archives, EX01.
22 CDA, Bishops' Letters, Robinson to Baines, March 1812. See also Bryan Laver, 'Gregor Fenaigle, Mnemonist and Educator', *Journal of Behavioural Science* 15 (1979).
23 Ibid. 4 April 1812.
24 Ibid. Fenaigle to Baines, 13 July 1812.
25 Ibid. Seckerson to Baines, 29 November 1815.
26 Ibid. Goadby to Baines, 2 August 1815.
27 Ibid. Constable to Baines, 27 December 1815.
28 Ampleforth Archives, 'Recollections of Fr Abbott, priest at Ampleforth'.
29 Ibid. BX26, Baines's Diary, 1814–15.
30 Ibid.
31 CDA, Bishops' Letters, Baines to Brewer, 10 March 1815.
32 Ampleforth Archives, A267, Baines to Molyneaux, 17 August 1813.
33 CDA, Bishops' Letters, Baines to Prior of Downside, 10 September 1814.

2

The Young Missioner 1817–1823

The Bath mission

The Bath mission to which its new priest came had seen a gradual rise in the number of Catholics since the seventeenth century. The Elizabethan and early Jacobean recusant rolls contained only ten Bath names, and fewer for the surrounding villages. Numbers were augmented by well-to-do Catholics who, in spite of the penal laws, were allowed to visit Bath for the sake of their health. There is evidence that some used the opportunity of travelling and meeting other Catholics to further the cause of their religion.[1]

The Benedictines were associated with Bath from the late seventeenth century, and by the 1700s had centred their mission and school on a lodging house, known as the Bell Tree House. This arrangement was not unique in Catholic England, but was particularly appropriate in Bath where there was continual coming and going of visitors to the Spa.

The Bell Tree House must have been large, as several visitors with their servants were able to be accommodated. It was also the residence of the Vicars Apostolic of the Western District between 1742 and 1786 for whom special rooms were reserved.[2] A long room was set aside for divine worship on the second floor and there was also accommodation in the house for the priest. Masses and other services were conducted with considerable ceremony and rich vestments were used, 'one of mohair crimson with silver lace; another of Purple adorned with open silver lace, the 3rd of black'.[3] This was many years before the repeal of the penal laws giving Catholics greater freedom of worship, but the designation of the Bell Tree as a lodging house must have disguised some of the religious activities which went on within its walls.

By the middle of the eighteenth century the Bath Catholics were beginning to feel confident enough to advertise openly in the printed visitors' Guides to Bath, and there is no evidence of action being taken against them by the authorities. Ralph Allen, the owner of Prior Park, who was once mayor of Bath and a magistrate, entertained Catholics such as Alexander Pope and Martha Blount at his house, but is reported to have thought it inadvisable for his coach to be seen waiting outside the Bell Tree chapel for the latter; instead, the coachman was told to wait for her some distance away.[4]

By the 1770s the Bell Tree House was beginning to be considered too small for the growing Catholic population, besides having disadvantages due to its dual purpose. The new priest, Dom Bede Brewer, raised a subscription to build a new chapel and residence for himself and an extension building which would be used to yield an income in place of the Bell Tree House. These were built in St James's Parade on the west side of St James's burial ground. The buildings were so heavily damaged in the Gordon Riots of 1780 that the Catholic community was forced to return to the Bell Tree House.

By 1786 a new Catholic chapel had been opened in Corn Street. The author of the Bath Guide later described how 'The chapel in Corn Street is well furnished with seats, has a gallery with commodious pews; a fine altar, with an elegant painting of our Saviour over it. Here is Divine Service every Sunday at seven, nine and eleven.'[5] The building could not have been large enough or was unsatisfactory in other ways, as by 1809 the chapel was transferred to Orchard Street, where there was also room for a school, and apartments for letting.

It was to Orchard Street that Peter Baines came in the late summer of 1817. Only ten minutes' walk from the Pump Rooms and the Assembly Rooms, and even nearer the abbey, the centre of Anglican life, Orchard Street was a world away. Several of the buildings straggling round the cobbled streets into Pierrepoint Place belonged to the Catholic Church. They were dilapidated and in urgent need of repair and renovation; one of the houses and parts of others were let or sublet in a maze of tenancies. Even the rooms over the chapel were let out to beggars.

The new Catholic priest, Peter Baines, surveyed the scene on that August day in 1817 and was not impressed. Characteristically, he determined to change everything no matter what the expense. He was soon making plans to convert the rooms above the chapel into a school, and to let the rooms at 5 Pierrepoint Place to more suitable tenants. He put a Mrs Hippisley in charge of the lodgings in the house, and she also opened a shop on the ground floor in which she sold Catholic books and devotional articles. The shop raised the tone of the street and was a constant source of interest to the new priest, who often wandered in to buy books and prints.

The chapel needed so much alteration that Baines left it for another year, and concentrated on renting a house to provide a new presbytery for himself and any additional priests. He chose 2 Pierrepoint Place, a large and more substantial house than the former presbytery in Philip Street, and within a few yards of the chapel.

Fine tastes and little money

He took a great deal of interest in furnishing his new house, recording in his diary for Thursday, 11 September:

> Went to sale at Lincumb House – bought two bronze candle sticks and a shade lamp, £1.1. also a reading screen 12s; And on Saturday, 13th September, went to look at furniture at Green Park Buildings and Montpellier. Bought a dining Pembroke table £6; On Monday, 15th September, bought at a house in Seymour Street two chairs at a guinea, and 2 Grecian couches for 11 guineas and at a sale, 48 Pultney Street a lootable, [apparently a circular card table for playing loo], £5.10; fire irons etc.

On 17 September, he bought a wash stand, dressing table etc, and on 19 September two pedestals for busts.[6]

In the following week, Baines continued his purchases, buying at a quantity of plate and linen for £23 6s 6d at an auction in Pulteney Street and later a reading screen for 28s. October saw him attending a sale in Bathwick and ordering a bust case from a Mrs Whittaker; and December attending an auction at old Bond Street and buying a tea urn, tea pot, bread basket and plate. Just before Christmas, he was buying a warming pan and enquiring about a brass plate for his front door.[7] The priest liked the background of his life to be both comfortable and civilized, reflecting his interest in the arts.

Unfortunately Baines did not have a private income to indulge his tastes, and had to look for funds from other sources. He approached the Benedictines for financial help in furnishing his house, claiming that there was little left in the old presbytery suitable for his needs. Help was given, but at the cost of a growing resentment, which was to have unfortunate results. In September 1818, when Baines asked for further funds for furnishing the Bath chapel, Prior Barber wrote: 'When the account of this Province was read in Chapter, some remarks were made and rather severe ones upon Mr Barr for having allowed you to take up money for furnishing your house. The result was a determination to obviate the recurrence of the same thing on a future occasion.'[8]

Although he was one of their own, the Benedictine hierarchy seemed to have had doubts about Baines from the beginning. Dr Brewer, the President, wrote to Fr Lorymer on 8 July 1817: 'Mr Calderbank will return with me to Wootton and be succeeded by Baines. I am afraid with you that such changes will be attended with dangerous consequences.'[9] And when early rumours were circulating about Baines's prospects of becoming Bishop Collingridge's coadjutor, Prior Lawson sought to quash them, writing to Fr Lorymer on 6 September 1817: 'Mr Baines's character is not yet formed nor known.'[10]

The Priest in the mission

No criticism could be levied against Baines's early work in the Bath mission, in spite of the amount of time he spent in furnishing his house. During September 1817 he recorded making numbers of calls on the sick, including attending two sick men in Walcot workhouse on 11 September, and on Saturday, 20 September, telling 'Mrs Ferrars of her son's death; got insert in the papers ... went to see Mrs Westall (sick and heard her confession).' And on Wednesday, 24 September, 'Saw two poor men at Walcot Poor House.'[11]

He spent an enormous amount of time hearing confessions in the chapel and in private houses. On Saturday, 4 October, for example, he recorded the following record of confessions heard on one day in 1818.

Conf 8–9
Conf 12.30–2
Do at chapel 2–4.30
Conf from 6–10.[12]

Confessions were not confined to weekends, but took place regularly during the week. On Thursday, 6 November, he recorded in his diary: 'Conf Mr & Mrs Day – followed by breakfast with Miss Cary. Conf at 3; again at 6 and 8.'[13] In those days there was no restriction upon the priest hearing confessions in his own house, as there was to be later under the First Statute of Westminster in 1852.

Peter Baines was punctilious in visiting the dying, no matter what hour of the night or early morning. On Tuesday morning, 28 October 1817, he called before 6 a.m. to see a Mr Phelan and 'found him dying, gave him absolution and last benediction.'[14] On the following day he returned to visit Mr Phelan's widow. And again on 31 October he recorded visiting 'a poor man, sick at 13 Avon Street.

Gave him absolution – went to Mr Regan; gave him extreme unction and last blessing.'[15]

On Sunday, 10 May 1818, he recorded: 'M. Mr Dalton. Went in Lady Fitzgerald's carriage to give him extreme unction and afterwards the viaticum. Called in the evening at Mr Dalton's and staid there all night – lay down in my cloaths. Mr Dalton very ill.'[16] The priest continued to stay at Mr Dalton's for several nights during his illness.

On Thursday, 16 June 1818, he had the unpleasant experience of visiting 'old Mrs Hussey who was found dead with her throat cut. Think she must have done it herself, but in a frenzy.'[17] This did not prevent his afterwards dining with Mr Hussey.

Visiting was not always so traumatic. He enjoyed visiting new arrivals in Bath; on 20 November 1817 he went to see a Mr and Mrs Fraser, a Scottish couple coming to Bath for the season and staying at the White Hart. And in the following year there was another new arrival, whom Baines described as 'a man of colour'.[18]

He often mentioned titled members of the congregation, such as Lady Fitzgerald, Lady Stourton and Lady Mount Earl, who was in ill health, and whom he visited regularly. And later Baines became acquainted with General Iturbi, ex-Emperor of Mexico, an exile in Bath, who asked for the priest's advice about the education of his son.[19] Baines always liked to be in the centre of events, meeting the famous, and enjoyed being able to offer advice.

The mass was the heart of the mission and Peter Baines liked High Mass to be sung on Sunday morning followed by a sermon.[20] On Sunday, 2 November 1817, he noted that a solemn Te Deum for harvest was sung in the chapel; on Wednesday, 19 November, he was singing a solemn mass for Princess Charlotte, daughter of the Prince Regent, with litanies for England and prayers for the King.[21] Baines encouraged music as an integral part of worship, following the oratorial traditions of Rome and the Embassy chapels. He recorded that on Thursday, 25 December 1817, 'there was a beautiful mass by Haydn sung in the chapel, with full band'.[22] And on Sunday, 22 March 1818, that 'the music was very fine. The band was led by Mr Loder. Miss Wood sang.'[23] The 1819 Bath directory shows that Mr J. D. Loder was director of music at the Theatre Royal.[24]

Baines took great pains in preparing his sermons and noted the topics covered; for example, on Sunday, 2 November, he preached a sermon for the poor; on 23 November a sermon on the Last Judgement and on Sunday, 28 December, one on the 'Holy . . . Innocents'.[25] He was in great demand as a preacher, not only in Bath, but in missions in other parts of the country. Cardinal Wiseman later wrote of him that 'He had a power of fascinating all who approached him . . . on every topic he had a command of language . . . But his great power was in his delivery, in voice, in tone in look, and gesture . . . notwithstanding a broadness of provincial accent.'[26] It is surprising that Baines retained his strong Lancashire accent throughout his life, using it to powerful effect in all his controversies.

His delivery was dramatic and he entered fully into the passion of the sentiments he was recording. He could move his listeners to tears, but one witness recorded that he sometimes anticipated their response by weeping copiously himself. He continued to believe in the importance of the art of preaching, writing to Burgess on 5 July 1819:

> I hope you will begin to think seriously about making all the young religious good preachers. For this purpose I would thoroughly recommend the frequent public recitation of pieces of prose and poetry, learnt by heart and studied with great care. This must give a correct enunciation and forcible delivery. Then a debating society as it formerly existed will be of great use to give a fluency of language.[27]

In this emphasis on forceful preaching, Baines seemed to be following in the Protestant tradition rather than the Catholic, though more likely he was obeying his own dramatic instincts in appreciating a good performance.

Characteristically, he was intent on making improvements to the chapel. By the spring of 1818 he was drawing up plans with an architect, a Mr Lowder, for improving the altar and other parts of the chapel. He tried to involve the congregation by having an address printed telling of his plans for improvements, but not everyone was satisfied. One of the trustees, a Mr Knapp, called to see him on 30 May and told him that he might be bound in conscience to oppose the plans, particularly if they were thought by the body of trustees to be injurious to the place.[28]

The controversy reveals the obstinate side of Baines's character and his unwillingness to brook opposition. He would have been more irritated by this episode because, like many other priests, he objected to the growth of 'Congregationalism' since the end of the eighteenth century, with the appointment of wardens, lay committees and trustees to be responsible for the government of chapels. He shared the belief that this practice was undermining the authority of priests in temporal matters.

Mr Knapp continued to irritate Baines in a further letter to the priest, regretting that 'Some insinuations which fell from your lips in our late conference appear to me to be unworthy of the high character I have ever formed of you, but acknowledge a welling up to make due allowance for an apparent opposition to a favourite scheme.'[29]

Baines was not deterred by this criticism, replying to Knapp on 3 June: 'I am fully determined, as I before told you, not to suffer any person whatever except my own superiors to interfere with me in any regulations, or alterations I may think proper to make in my own chapel.'[30]

The only impediment was money. As we have seen, Baines had already been in touch with the Benedictines about financial help for the Bath chapel, but was less successful than in the matter of his house. On 23 April 1818, the Benedictine Provincial, Dom Bernadine Barr, had granted him permission to make some alterations to the chapel and to use £400 from the funds of the Bath mission for the purpose, on the condition that he set up a sinking fund for the gradual liquidation of debts. There was no question of any further money forthcoming from the Benedictine body. In spite of this setback, Baines went on with his plans, bringing in a landscape painter, who was to paint a picture on canvas behind the altar. In July 1818 he instructed Mr Lowder to make an agreement with a builder to do the chapel for £780.[31] As with his later more grandiose plans for churches, and for the mansion of Prior Park, he would brook no opposition once he had decided that limitless expenditure was necessary for the glory of the Catholic Church. And his plans seem to have been generally popular. Ann Hippisley, a stalwart of the congregation, voiced the opinion of the majority of the congregation, when she wrote to Bishop Collingridge:

> Our chapel cannot be opened yet: great praise indeed is due to our gentleman, for by changing from room to room, we have never once been without daily mass and masses . . . The alterations, far advanced, are universally approved of – the new Tabernacle is most beautiful – of metal; like a looking-glass – very high with bunches of gilt grapes and a large wheat sheaf on top.[32]

She went on to tell the Bishop that 'the mass books and crimson velvet cushions quite superb and the new Register has above 120 gold buttons to it – Ditto the tassel to the tabernacle key, which is as large as a door key and the lock cannot be picked. The service of God is truly conducted here in a manner very edifying.'[33]

A tendency to spend beyond his limited means, whether in private or public life, was always to be a weakness in Baines. If he had money, he spent it and, if he had none, he borrowed it. At times he was so short of money at Bath that he was obliged to write to

Burgess, once a student of Baines and now prior of Ampleforth, to tell him that he could not afford to pay for the journey north: 'A discovery which I lately made respecting the actual state of my finances obliges me unwillingly to remain at home, as I positively have not the means to leave it. During the present half year particularly, I shall find it extremely difficult to pay what has to be paid.'[34]

An all-rounded man

In spite of Baines's devotion to his work and to improving the chapel, he had time for enjoying the lighter side of life. He was a gregarious man and particularly liked the company of women, noting that on 3 November 1817, in the company of Miss Ferrars and Miss Fanny Ferrars, he had seen the Queen arrive at the top of Pulteney Street, and had then gone on to the Illuminations with them.[35] On 10 December, he took tea at Mrs Fryer's, Prospect Place, and listened to Miss Fryer who was a talented performer on the harp. On 11 December, he walked with Miss Cary to dine at Mrs Hartzinch's, where he stayed the night. And on 30 March 1818 he walked with Miss Lacon to see a glass manufactory in Oxford Row, then went on to Mrs Riddell's party, where he met prominent Catholics of Bath.[36] Small parties of Catholics seemed to have been a regular feature of his life.

The priest was particular about his appearance, recording his haircuts and his fittings for clothes, such as a suit of black, a great coat and a pair of pantaloons at Mr Dennie's on 30 October 1817 and ordering a pair of half-boots etc. on 17 November. The purchase of an eyeglass and a toothpick are also recorded and the regular luxury of taking a hot bath,[37] in which he was ahead of most of his contemporaries. On the other hand Baines did not approve of 'dandy priests', writing to Prior Burgess on 10 November 1821 that:

> Of all the dandies (and dandies in my mind are the most pitiful of all things) sacerdotal dandies are surely the worst as well as the most awkward . . . my principles, however, are these – A priest is a gentleman – therefore he should be neat and clean in his person and attire and his cloaths should not be made like a clown or a butcher. But a priest and therefore his dress, while it is neat and gentlemanlike, should keep within the limits of fashion and be very sober and inostentatious – as to hair powder I consider it a piece of foppery which corresponds with the vanity of female rouging and enamelling and I wonder how the ministers of religion should ever have adapted it.[38]

Baines would also leave time from his religious duties to pursue his artistic activities. On 9 November 1817 he spent the evening in looking over 'a fine collection of drawings and prints', and on 14 March 1818 he was visiting a Mr Der . . . who was a miniature artist in glass. On 30 April 1818 he went with Mr Nichell to see an exhibition of sculptures in Union Street, and on the following day to see another sculpture exhibition, this time with his friend, Fr Brindle. He also went further afield to Bristol to visit churches, noting on 12 June 1818 that he had seen Redcliffe and the college churches of Bristol: 'The former a most beautiful edifice of the Gothic style of York Chapter House; the latter curious and rather handsome.'[39]

Music was also a great interest and he recorded that he attended numbers of concerts, including one at Bath Abbey on 5 June, where he heard *The Creation* and a Mass of Beethoven's: 'The former the most beautiful music I have heard – Braham, Signore Corre, Miss Carew and Mr Tinney the principle singers.'[40]

Unlike priests later in the nineteenth century, Baines seemed to have no qualms about attending functions at Anglican places of worship.

He tried not to neglect his reading, but had to admit that in the busy days after coming to Bath he often read nothing. Mrs Hippisley's bookshop in the same road opposite the presbytery must have been a great attraction, tempting him to browse and order books.

Baines and his family

Baines continued to keep in touch with his family in Lancashire, but was not so attentive as they wished. Thomas Baines, who had taken over the family farm at Ince Blundell, was the chief correspondent, relating news of all the family. On 7 January 1820 he wrote to tell his brother that he and his wife had recently had a baby girl, christened Alice after one of their sisters. He spoke of his son, James, who was considered a fine boy, and mentioned the opinion of the Revd Mr Brewer of Liverpool: 'He thinks you should, as you are his uncle and as you can so well afford, send him to school for a few years.'[41]

Baines would not have agreed with his brother's opinion of his financial position and there is no record whether he helped his nephew. However, James Baines went on to follow in his uncle's steps at Ampleforth and to train for the priesthood.

Thomas Baines contrasted the hard life on the farm, where most of his brothers and sisters were working, with the life of comparative ease that Peter Baines was living in Bath. 'It is very hard work as things are at present. Wheat will not fetch more than 9/ or 9/6 at most and 70ff barley and oats in proportion. Hay from from 6d to 9d or 10d per 20ff, potatoes about 18d per 20ff, which is considerably lower than can be afforded according as the present rents and other things are.'[42]

There was also criticism of Baines's too-short visits home:

> Mr Bennet told me you intend coming some time this summer, which if you do you will perhaps make a longer stay with your relatives than you did the last time you came, as you did not please some of them so well with it. I have often heard folk wonder why your stay was so short with your friends. Indeed I wonder myself and my mother was very affected at it. I did not say much about it.'[43]

Anna de Mendoza

Baines now had multitudinous interests, which had taken him away from his roots, and he had also acquired a family of his own, in the shape of a vivacious and attractive young ward, Anna de Mendoza y Rios. She was the daughter of a Spanish admiral, Don Nicodemus de Mendoza y Rios of Seville, who had come to England during the French wars and married an Irish girl from Bath. Both parents died before Anna came of age and she was left as a ward to the Vicar Apostolic of the Western District and to a Madame Chaussegros. Bishop Collingridge was by this time living in a convent at Cannington and in no position to take charge of a young ward, while Madame Chaussegros could only look after Anna for limited periods. The responsibility seems to have fallen upon Baines as Collingridge's Vicar General, and by 1821 she was installed with her companion and maid at the presbytery in Pierrepont Place.

Such an arrangement in a priest's house would not have been countenanced twenty to thirty years later, and even in the more liberal days of George IV's reign it could have been a source of scandal. The fact that no one seemed to have considered the situation at all unusual was due to the matter-of-fact way in which Baines regarded it himself. Although fond of the company of women, he had much too high an opinion of himself and his own destiny to become sexually or emotionally involved with anyone. In fact, he seemed to care little for the way in which he sometimes upset the feelings of his ward, who obviously adored him.

Her arrival must have enlivened the sombre character of the presbytery and caused a flutter in the Bath mission. All the ladies were anxious to meet Anna de Mendoza and to invite her to tea, and there was much manoeuvring among some of the gentlemen. Henry Arundell, a relative of Lord Arundell of Wardour, wrote to Baines asking for his assistance:

> having heard many things from my friend, Miss Lawson, which has given me most favourable ideas of Miss Mendoza whom she wished me much to become acquainted with, and which determined me on immediately consulting you. You know it is my ardent wish to be settled, and as I presume you are fully acquainted with my character and disposition, you will be able to judge whether they will be calculated to make Miss Mendoza happy.[44]

Baines, appearing to enjoy his new position of being able to give or withhold his ward's hand in marriage, gave Henry Arundell permission to meet Anna and her companion, but stressed: 'As many considerations are required for making a marriage a source of real happiness to the parties concerned, which are often independent of the individual merit of the parties themselves, I have often resolved that I could never take any active part in promoting such matters.'[45]

Nothing came of the meeting between Anna de Mendoza and Henry Arundell, and she continued to play the field and to delight her guardian and all who knew her for the next eight years. Her presence brought other advantages to Baines besides the pleasure of her society. She helped to develop his acquaintance with Lord and Lady Arundell of Wardour Castle. Although he had known them before, having made it his business to contact all the old-established Catholic families in the neighbourhood, his visits to Wardour Castle increased after 1821 and he escaped to the peace of 'the shrubbery, the flower garden and the picture gallery'[46] more frequently than Bishop Collingridge approved. Anna sometimes went with him and was also invited for weeks on her own, as Lady Arundell seemed to have taken a great liking to her.

Baines was in his element at Wardour, revelling in the splendour of a great house, steeped in the history of the Catholic Church. The Arundells had maintained their Catholic faith throughout the sixteenth and seventeenth centuries, and by the eighteenth century had built a fine new house in the Palladian style. The Vicar Apostolic, Bishop Walmesley, opened its magnificently ornate chapel on the feast of All Saints 1776 'with ecclesiastical ceremony not seen by Catholics in England since the Reformation'. It became the centre of Catholic worship in the area, attracting about 540 worshippers from the countryside all around.[47]

Travels in France

Baines liked a holiday in France each year, particularly after the busy Easter period. There were few mission priests who would have contemplated such a luxury, but Baines had well-to-do friends who were happy to invite him to be one of their party, and other friends who lived in Normandy, whom he could visit. On one occasion in 1822, he made his own arrangements and took his ward, Anna de Mendoza, accompanied only by her maid, on a sightseeing tour of northern France.[48]

Baines was an enthusiastic but particular traveller. There was no question of roughing it. He liked the best hotels and, if one did not come up to standard, he was quite prepared to move out and find a better one. This happened on the evening of 8 May, when he and his ward arrived at the Hotel de Nord at Cambrai, 'but finding the accommodation not comfortable, I ran to the Hotel du Grand Canard and, finding this much better, we remained there'.[49]

In Rouen they stayed at the Hotel de Normandie, 'the best it is said in the town. It was some time before the lady of the house would let us her best apartments, taking us for French and wishing to reserve the apartment for the English who would pay.' This was presumably a compliment to the fluent French of Baines and Anna de Mendoza.

Although Baines found the charges rather high, he approved of the rooms and the dinner. They dined at the table d'hote at which the maitre d'hotel presided and had soup, fish and meat of different kinds in sufficient abundance.[50]

In his tour of Normandy in 1820 with a Mr and Mrs Annandale and their daughter,[51] Baines described the scenery. He noted that on the journey between Calais and Boulogne;

> The country is naked and not very fertile, without hedges or ditches ... it rises with small eminences forming an undulating surface resembling the plains of Waterloo, or the downs of Wiltshire, if the latter were cultivated. At the distance of a few miles from each other, you see villages, to which is generally attached a small wood and a neat, old church with a spire.[52]

Baines had time, too, to sketch his fellow travellers, portraying Mrs Annandale dressed in the latest fashion of the day, asleep in the corner of the coach, and her daughter wrapped up in a cloak as a protection from the cold.

Sailing down the Seine near Rouen, Baines became lyrical about the magnificent view:

> the river clear as crystal, the numberless islands it contains – the boats and large vessels gliding to and fro; in the distance the town of Rouen, with its cathedral and churches, the former rising in the air to a finely shaped spire of about 400ft in height and two handsome towers, emblematic of the superior greatness of former ages and of the superior dignity of Him to whose glory they are erected; the spreading plain, the distant hills and ridges of rocks, skirting for miles the serpentine windings of the river, all together form one of the most enchanting views that the eyes can behold and much more than the imagination can create for the amusement of fancy.[53]

Baines's main interest, though, was to visit churches and to comment upon the religious life of France in the years immediately after the end of the Napoleonic wars. He was sometimes critical as in his reference to the cathedral church of Calais: 'After hearing mass in the Cathedral, a large but uninteresting church, in bad taste and rather dustier than most French churches, we breakfasted . . .'[54]

The front or west end of Abbeville Cathedral produced quite different sentiments. Baines described it 'as one of the richest and finest specimens of the best Gothic. Its height is immense, its ornament elegant and profuse, the great number of large and very small statues which adorn it, in a far better style of sculpture than those of the same period in England.'[55]

Amiens Cathedral he regarded as a revelation, the exterior, though inimitably beautiful giving 'but a faint idea of the magnificence, beauty and sublimity of the interior. The length and height and regularity and exquisite proportion of the part, and the uncommon skill with which every object is contrived to give dignity and importance to the sanctuary produce effects too great for expression.'[56]

Baines was so impressed by Amiens Cathedral that he went back to see it with his ward in the spring of 1822. He recorded that the cathedral lost nothing the second time around, and the visit absorbed them so much that there was no time to see the hall where the Peace of Amiens had been signed.[57]

He wrote notes on the architecture of the churches he visited and illustrated them with drawings of particular features. At the church of St Ouen at Rouen he described the principles of Gothic architecture with enthusiasm; it was very different from the antagonism he was later to show to the style when his years in Rome developed his love of classicism. Characteristically, he always had to come down vehemently on one side of an argument, and seemed incapable of seeing that both styles had their virtues. Similarly, he showed his growing interest in studying vestments, a subject he was to feel passionately about as he threw himself into the controversies of later life. He filled pages of his sketchbook with illustrations of French vestments, particularly in Samer, south of Boulogne.

Baines's views on religious life in France were varied. He admired the religious fervour of many of the French, describing how, when he went to the 6.30 a.m. mass in a church in Boulogne, he found it quite impossible to enter the great western door, because of the crowds of people kneeling within: 'From the great size of the church, about 250 ft or 300ft in length and the very crowded state in every part, I should guess there must have been at least 2,500 or 3,000 people attending divine service at that early hour'.[58]

He compared this enthusiasm with the attitude of his fellow countrymen, who sauntered into churches at the 'late and lazy hours of England'. On the other hand Baines objected at Abbeville to the numbers of 'paltry and miserable statues, some of them adorned with ribbons and French laces and having tapers burnt before them by the pious, but certainly not tasteful, vulgar, and all of them gilt and painted gold and made even worse than mere shape could make them'.[59] He found it difficult to enter into this kind of religious expression, if it upset his aesthetic taste.

The same feelings interfered with his devotions, while attending vespers at the church of St Godard at Rouen. He states contemptuously that: 'the singers did their best. This consisted in shouting rather louder (for it is impossible to shout much louder) than usual and produces a discord still more intolerable.'[60]

Baines goes on to lament the state of music in French churches in general:

> To a stranger, the yells and bellowings made for the honour and glory of God in French churches is perfectly torturing to the frequenters of these places; the sound is so delightful that the audience cannot bear that the solo parts allocated to the priest should be enjoyed by himself alone and therefore the preface, pater noster etc are actually hummed by half the congregation while the priest has the privilege only of roaring louder than the rest.[61]

Such enthusiasm was obviously not to Baines's taste, and he would not have countenanced it in his chapel in Bath.

The wider scene

Despite his very full life in the Bath mission, Baines's interests and aspirations were not limited to the local scene. Only a year after his arrival in Bath, Thomas Burgess was writing from Ampleforth to discuss the possibility of his becoming Bishop Collingridge's coadjutor: 'By the by, I have heard it doubted whether the mitre is intended for Mr Marsh or you – I suppose it would be an unfair question to ask you for any information on the subject.'[62]

Burgess was more interested, however, in trying to persuade Baines to consider returning to Ampleforth as prior.

> One more argument that may induce you to a generous sacrifice of all your comfort at Bath is the consideration that our rising generation is just of an age when your past labours are about either to be crowned with success or perhaps thrown away for want of proper conclusion. They are certainly promising young men, but much depends upon their course of philosophy and divinity for making them perfect, which you would be able to manage.[63]

There is no evidence that Baines ever contemplated such a move. His sights were set on wider horizons, but he never lost his interest in school life. He was constantly enquiring about courses at Ampleforth and giving advice, as in his letter to Thomas Burgess on 14 February 1823:

> How does your divinity school go on? Have you any regular courses of instruction on the controversial parts of Religion for the older students? Such a thing ought to be in all the Catholic colleges. I see the success of it more every day. Faith which is not founded on conviction resulting from knowledge constantly gives way when the morals are corrupted. But when a firm conviction of the truth of religion has once been caught in the mind by reason of knowledge, it seldom allows young men to apostatize.'[64]

He took a great interest in everything that was being studied at Ampleforth, writing to his friend Fr Metcalfe about the sort of books he would recommend for the students and informing him that: 'I have just printed a Benedictine Directory in English for the use of this and the other congregations under our care'.[65]

He also found time to write books on Catholic doctrine, bringing out in 1822 a 500-copy edition of *A Defence of the Christian Religion*. His main object was to refute the accusations of Dr

Moysey, an Anglican divine from Bath, and his followers, that Catholics were idolaters. He said that he felt only pity or contempt for the man who slanders his religion, often knowing no better, but indignant against a dignitary of the Church of England, 'who puts on the whole rusty armour of antiquated bigotry'.

He distinguished between worship of God and respect that Catholics show for images of the Virgin Mary and the saints. He did not believe that the second commandment 'restricts the bowing down to God ... A Catholic or even a member of the Church of England may bow to the altar or at the name of Jesus. It is an act of respect as far as it regards the altar or the Name; it is an act of divine worship as far as it regards the Deity.'

Baines referred back to the Nicene Council of 325, which decreed that 'venerable and holy images, whether formed in painted colours, of mosaic work, or any suitable materials, be set forth publicly in the church of God ... that incense and lights be employed to honour them'. He emphasized that this was 'honorary worship' not adoration. The Council of Trent of 1545 also decreed that bishops and other church leaders should be 'particularly diligent in instructing the faithful on the intercession and invocation of saints, honouring of relics and legitimate use of images, teaching that the saints offer up prayers for mankind'. It was natural for people to pray for loved ones who died and to ask for their intercessions, for 'it has always been believed amongst Christians that death does not entirely sever those dear and tender ties that bind hearts together in this state of existence – the virtuous parent looks down with affectionate solicitude on those he loved and still offers prayers'. It was a theme which Baines was to develop in sermons in Bradford and Bath.

Although there had never been any idolatry in the doctrine of the Catholic Church on the subject of saints and images, Baines admitted that there had been abuses on the Continent, although he believed that these had been more superstitious than idolatrous. He lamented rather superciliously 'that in churches where architecture, painting and sculpture combine their magic powers to produce an impressive whole, some wretched piece of sculpture painted and dressed in rich attire should excite the admiration and piety of even a few old women', yet he knew that 'these things had their origin in times when taste was not so refined and more scandal may be given to the common people by attacking their ancient customs.'

In the last part of his book, Baines refuted Dr Moysey's accusation 'that it is thought lawful for Catholics to violate the most solemn engagements when made with heretics'. He denied this and maintained that if Catholics had regarded oaths so lightly they would not have chosen to die, as Sir Thomas More had done rather than take the oath of supremacy to the Crown. He maintained, too, that the deposing power of the Pope is solemnly abjured by the whole Catholic community of England. Even in the time of Elizabeth, when the Pope denounced her as an usurper, 'the catholics of England voluntarily and ardently defended her to the last', and they were to do the same in support of the Stuart kings.

Finally, nearly fifty years before the First Vatican Council, Baines was still able to deny that the Pope was infallible and could introduce what measures he wished, as Dr Moysey claimed:

> When I say that the infallibility of the Pope is not an article of the Catholic faith, I mean that no Catholic is bound to believe it, but that each may think as he pleases ... we believe the universal church to be infallible in matters of faith and morality. On all other points, we consider private individuals, Popes and even General Councils as fallible and liable to change.[66]

He was very anxious to obtain the good opinion of the clerical world on this book, writing to Thomas Burgess on 10 April 1822:

> Let me know what the gentlemen of the long robe think of this work, for as to what the geese in this part of the world say, I have little concern. I speak of the generality of the flock; for there are some whose opinion I value. The Bishop approves of it, so did poor old Coombes – the parsons here are very silent – not a word from any of them good, bad or indifferent – except two or three who approved.[67]

Baines's writings kept him in the public eye, impressing Bishop Collingridge and others of the hierarchy. He was forthright, too, in the expression of his opinions in his letters, keeping up a voluminous correspondence with many well-known Catholics. Some of these opinions were controversial, as in his letter to the Hon. Edward Clifford, son of Lord Clifford of Chudleigh, who was considering his vocation, about the role of monks and secular priests:

> What difference can it make to any secular man or to the public at large whether you or I be a monk or a secular priest or a Jesuit? Our first character is that of a priest. I was surprised to see your father striking a nice distinction between you being a priest simply and being of a religious order. He is not I suppose aware that the English Benedictine congregation was always from the time of St

> Augustine intended chiefly for the service of the mission and that it was expressly confirmed and re-established for this purpose by Urban VIII. There is no question of your being a mere contemplative in our body if you enter for the service of the mission or for the instruction of those who are intended for it. Now really if a person has a vocation to be a secular priest, I do not see why he should not have one to be a monk or vice versa.[68]

Such views were not likely to be welcomed by provincials and priors of monastic communities, and were gradually to separate Baines from the Benedictine community in which he had been educated and served for so long. These problems were some way in the future, however, for, in these early years at the at the Bath mission, Baines generally had good relations with Downside and Ampleforth, and was gaining in the approval of his bishop. From the time of his arrival in 1817, he was continually in contact with Collingridge. In September 1817, he wrote to him asking him to approve faculties for his friend, Thomas Brindle, so that he could join him in Bath as assistant priest. He described Brindle's education at Ampleforth, when Baines himself was a tutor, and his work at a mission in Knaresborough, where 'he gave great satisfaction and edification to all ... I trust and believe, that a continuance of his excellent conduct in this mission will give your Lordship no cause to regret that he is become a subject of yours'.[69]

In personal ways Baines was trying to make himself useful to the Bishop, offering him hospitality in Bath and arranging to have his watch repaired and sent to Cannington. While this may be partly the sign of a gregarious and friendly character, Baines was an ambitious man and knew that a good relationship with his bishop was indispensable for preferment.

During the next few years Baines was making himself more and more necessary to Bishop Collingridge, at a time when the Bishop was in poor health and hoping to persuade the Holy See to allow him to appoint a coadjutor. In March 1820 he was assisting the Bishop in revising a manuscript by a Mr Postlewhite, apparently a protégé of Lady Arundell. Baines told the Bishop that it would be easier to remodel the thing than to correct the original manuscript. He also undertook to discuss the matter with Lady Arundell before Easter, a task which he would have enjoyed as demonstrating his increased influence. A month later he was telling the Bishop of his stay at Wardour Castle and his discussions with Lady Arundell. He had revised Mr Postlewhite's manuscript and 'should have liked to send it to your Lordship and obtain your approbation, but had no time as her

Ladyship is so particularly anxious to have it printed before her departure from Wardour'.[70]

This high-handed action and his anxiety to put the wishes of a member of the Catholic aristocracy before those of his bishop was not conducive to increasing Baines's popularity at Cannington. Yet at this stage Collingridge seems to have been remarkably tolerant, even of Baines's many excursions away from the mission – on preaching engagements in Lancashire, on visits to Ampleforth and trips to the Continent. Some of these engagements interfered with his work for the Bishop, as on 23 June 1822, when he wrote to Collingridge from Wardour Castle: 'I have received a very pressing request from Mr Burgess, the Prior at Ampleforth, to be at the college a few days before the approaching examinations . . . I fear it will be impossible to do this and be at Cannington on the 11th.'[71] There is no record of the Bishop's reaction to this.

In spite of such incidents, Baines's standing with the Bishop was high. Prior Barber of Downside in writing to Dr Brewer, the President of the Benedictines, on 4 April 1821 wrote: 'You have heard, I suppose, that Bishop Collingridge sent up for Baines to London to consult him on Bills which are now in progress through Parliament'.[72]

The Vicar General

In the same year, Collingridge appointed Baines as his Vicar General and delegated to him any responsibilities connected with priests in the missions, such as looking into the credentials of possible recruits, and examining the conduct of others. In the latter case Baines surely went further than his powers in suspending a priest who had admitted misconduct with a woman. He wrote to the Bishop on 12 January 1822: 'I formally suspended Mr H. from all missionary functions, as Vicar General, convinced that your Lordship would have done so and considering myself as I told Mr H. bound either to disclose the business to you or to do all you could do'.[73]

There is no explanation given as to why Baines did not refer the whole matter to the Bishop to make a decision as was his right.

Baines was active in his search for new priests for the missions of the Western District, recommending various candidates to the Bishop. On 14 July 1822, he wrote,

> I send your Lordship this letter that you may judge for yourself respecting the writer – The Superior of Ampleforth objects to receive him as a religious on account of his age and because he is

> already qualified to act as a missioner. It is a pity he should lose time in making himself a monk ... It strikes me that if your Lordship would wish to pay his expenses to Cannington, on condition that he remains with you a certain length of time, having him under your eye, you might judge how far it would be advisable to retain him in your district. In the mean time Mr Norman might go pro tempore to Shepton Mallett ... I think as you want priests so much it would be worth while to give him a trial.[74]

On 10 October 1822 there was further discussion about another missioner, a Mr Depaur, and Bishop Collingridge asked Baines to ride over to Marnhull 'and see how he goes on there, or by some means procure satisfactory information'.[75]

By November 1822 there were signs that Bishop Collingridge was becoming irritated by Baines taking too much upon himself over Mr Abrams, a possible new recruit. He wrote to the Bishop

> I must have explained myself very ill about Mr Abrams. You say you have received his faculties and will subject him to an examination before he exercises them if he does not go to the north. I beg to observe that he will in all probability have been granted them without thought of any examination – of course on me will devolve all the responsibility of Mr A's capacity and fitness for missionary work.[76]

The Revd Mr Birdsall, Baines's former head prefect at Lamspringe, who had just been appointed Benedictine Provincial, also appeared to think that the new Vicar General was presuming too much. Baines had apparently written to Bishop Collingridge informing him of the appointment and Birdsall wrote to him sarcastically on 17 February 1823:

> Thank you for having written to the Bishop to inform him, since you thought it necessary, of the office having devolved on me, but I certainly should not have written to him on that occasion, nor did I, not thinking it at all in my way to write to him unless business should render it necessary, neither have I yet had anything occur, that has induced me to address either of the Bishops.[77]

Birdsall was more concerned with keeping Baines's attention confined to the affairs of the Bath mission, writing on the same day:

> You have not yet favoured me with a copy of the obligations of

masses, such as, I think you said you received from Mr Calderbank. I doubt but that when I shall receive it, I shall be able to reconcile it with the records of the Provincial books in this respect. Be so kind as to give me the whole of the obligations incumbent on the Bath mission . . . Will you also tell me how much the house in St James's Parade and how much the old chapel in Corn Street bring in annually and whether it be paid punctually – also upon what footing financially stands the house which Mrs Hippisley inhabits, what rent is fixed for the tenants contiguous to the chapel in Orchard Street and what the tenure of your own house etc etc.'[78]

Such mundane considerations were not Baines's first priority, and his inattention to detail and concentration on broad issues were to lead him into many disagreements with the Benedictine Provincial. The precise and rigid character of Birdsall and the flamboyance of Baines were to result in bitter hostility over the years.

Hostility was not only to be found in the person of the Provincial, but in other members of the Benedictine community, who were resentful of Baines's growing influence. As early as October 1817, Prior Lawson of Downside was referring to Baines 'as one of the schemers for the welfare of St Gregory's, actually considering the removal of the Downside community to Prior Park'.[79] On 5 April 1820, when there was a further discussion about a home for the community, Prior Lawson wrote to Fr Lorymer and regretted that he had consulted Baines about a possible move to Burton, Hampshire: 'In my first conversation with Baines, I realised my error and have reason to suspect that he wishes at all events to see us out of the vicinity. In the last six years he has never ceased to speak of this house in the most intemperate manner, calling it a Doghole . . .'[80]

And again on 18 June 1820: 'It is painful to me to be requested by Dr Brewer [the President] to consult Baines, tho his reverence knew well that I shall not approve the plan'.[81]

The new bishop

In spite of animosity and criticism, Baines remained supremely confident, with high hopes of obtaining the post of coadjutor in the Western District. His friend, the Revd Edward Glover, now a priest at the Crosby mission, was concerned that the Bishop was not making vigorous efforts at Rome to obtain Baines's nomination. 'I will only mention that unless Bishop Collingridge employs other agents than Gradwell at Rome, he will not get a coadjutor in his life time'.[82]

There were signs, too, that Gradwell was not supporting Baines's candidature, for a young priest named Gillow had just arrived from Rome and 'declared to everybody that Gradwell will take care to get Williams made the future Bishop'.[83]

Glover wrote to Baines on 12 December 1822, trying to reassure him

> that the affair [Baines's appointment to be coadjutor] will take its proper course yet, unless the sudden death of Bishop Collingridge should intervene and then it is all over. I am a little anxious about it because it is impossible any other can fill the office as well as you from the knowledge of affairs of the district, which your residence in it and your enjoying the confidence of the present Bishop necessarily gives you – and for other reasons not necessarily to be mentioned![84]

The Revd Richard Marsh, who had recently succeeded to the Presidency of the Benedictines on the death of Dr Brewer, wrote from Douai, also supporting Baines's candidature, telling him that: 'If Dr Collingridge procures your nomination, you have not only my consent to accept it but my earnest request you would, for the good of religion in general in the first place, but not without view to the good of that order which first planted Christianity in England of which you and I have the honour to be members.'[85]

It is significant that at this time, Marsh had no suspicion that Baines's appointment might prove to be a disruptive force. Only a short time was to pass before he had very different ideas about Baines's influence on the future of the Benedictine order.

Glover wrote to Baines again on 20 February 1823, still concerned about the delays in Rome in appointing a coadjutor for the Western District and urging Baines to accompany Fr Marsh to Rome at Easter to put the case for the appointment of a Regular. This proved to be unnecessary, as in the following month Peter Baines was appointed as coadjutor Bishop of the Western District. On 25 February 1823, Baines wrote to Bishop Collingridge: 'As I have never used any means to obtain the dignity that is offered to me and as others, who know me, think me fit for it, I consider it the will of providence that I should accept it and I trust that the graces which are necessary will be granted me to discharge its important duties.'[86]

Baines's friends and supporters believed that he possessed all the qualities needed for such an important post, which would lead eventually to the Vicariate. Many of them wrote to rejoice with him and Thomas Burgess revealed how much they had wanted such an appointment. 'Permit me to present our united congratulations with those of our friends at Bath on the happy fulfilment of our anxious wishes. May your health and life be preserved for the increase of piety and the good of religion for many years. We are anxious to know when you will be consecrated and what place you are appointed as Bishop'.[87]

So at the early age of thirty-six, Peter Augustine Baines was consecrated Bishop of Siga as coadjutor of the Western District. With the failing health of Bishop Collingridge, it was a position of considerable power, but there were doubts about the future even at this early stage of his episcopal career – the greatest of which was the tendency to arouse controversy in whatever he undertook, and his obstinate refusal to believe that any opinions which ran counter to his own could be right. Fr Marsh expressed these doubts in a letter to Bishop Collingridge, mixing congratulations with caution: 'Thank you for having Dr Baines appointed as your coadjutor. I hope he will exercise prudence and moderation in his coadjutorship. It is thought he will try to carry things with too high a hand. Your Lordship will be the judge.'[88]

There was also a small doubt about his health, to which there had been worrying references during the years at Ampleforth and the Bath mission. As early as 1810, Baines was relating how he was spending days at Hartlepool, benefitting his health by enjoying the air and sea bathing. Throughout the years there were references to chest infections, and on 16 May 1822 he noted that: 'I have at this moment an unusually bad cold which with other ailments totally disable me'. He also noted that his leg was so inflamed that he could scarcely walk or even stand.[89]

Concern about his health was to increase during the years of his bishopric, when all the tensions and conflicts put further strain upon a frail constitution. Yet in May 1823 all these were but background worries, as Peter Baines contemplated a future full of promise both for the Catholic Church in the Western District, and for the great role which he intended to play in its development.

Notes

1 J. A. Williams, *Catholicism in Bath*, vol. 1, pp. 47ff, Catholic Record Society, (London, 1975).
2 Ibid. p. 59.
3 Ibid. p. 53.
4 Ibid. p. 92.
5 Ibid. p. 53.
6 Ibid. St John's Presbytery, Bath, Journal of Peter Augustine Baines O.S.B. 1817–1819, 11 September 1817.

7 Ibid. 9 December 1817.
8 CDA, Bishops' Letters, Barber to Baines, 2 September 1818.
9 Downside Abbey Archives, E31, Brewer to Lorymer, 8 July 1817.
10 Ibid. E55, Lawson to Lorymer, 6 September 1817.
11 Journal of Peter Baines, 11, 20, 24 September 1817.
12 Ibid. 4 October 1817.
13 Ibid. 6 November 1817.
14 Ibid. 28 October 1817.
15 Ibid. 31 October 1817.
16 Ibid. 10 May 1818.
17 Ibid. 16 June 1818.
18 Ibid. 13 June 1818.
19 CDA, Baines Box Files 1–3.
20 Baines's Journal, 19 November 1817.
21 Ibid. 21 November 1817
22 Ibid. 25 December 1817.
23 Ibid. 22 March 1818.
24 City of Bath Central Library, Bath Directory, 1818.
25 Baines's Journal, 28 December 1817.
26 Nicholas Wiseman, *Recollections of the Last Four Popes* (London, 1858), pp. 325–6.
27 Ampleforth Archives, A267, Baines to Burgess, 5 July 1819.
28 CDA, Bishops' Letters, Knapp to Baines, 2 June 1818, (referring to visit on 30 May).
29 Ibid.
30 Ibid. Baines to Knapp, 3 June 1818. See also Bossy, John, *The English Catholic Community 1570–1850* (London, 1975).
31 Baines's Journal, 5 July 1818.
32 CDA, Bishops' Letters, Hippisley to Collingridge, 26 December 1818.
33 Ibid.
34 Ampleforth Archives, A267, Baines to Burgess, 4 July 1820.
35 Baines's Journal, 3 November 1817.
36 Ibid. 30 March 1818.
37 Ibid. 12 March 1818.
38 CDA, Baines Box Files 1–3, 10 November 1821.
39 Baines's Journal, 12 June 1818.
40 Ibid. 5 June 1818.
41 CDA, Bishops' Letters, Thomas Baines to Peter Baines, 7 January 1820.
42 Ibid. Thomas Baines to Peter Baines.
43 Ibid.
44 Ibid. Arundell to Baines, 21 August 1821.
45 Ibid. Baines to Arundell.
46 Ibid. De Mendoza to Baines, 22 October 1825.
47 Philip Caraman, SJ, *Wardour, A Short History*, (Bristol, 1984) p. 15.
48 CDA, Baines's Journal of his Travels, 29 April 1822.
49 Ibid. 8 May 1822.

50 Ibid. May 1822.
51 Ibid. April 1820.
52 Ibid.
53 Ibid. 2 May 1820.
54 Ibid. 22 April 1820.
55 Ibid. 24 April 1820.
56 Ibid. 26 April 1820.
57 Ibid. 7 May 1822.
58 Ibid. 22 April 1820.
59 Ibid. 24 April 1820.
60 Ibid. 27 April 1820.
61 Ibid.
62 CDA, Baines Box files, 1–3, Burgess to Baines, 8 June 1818.
63 Ibid.
64 Ibid. Baines to Burgess, 14 February 1823.
65 Ibid. Baines to Metcalfe, August 1822.
66 Peter Baines, *A Defence of the Christian Religion* (Bath, 1822).
67 CDA, Baines Box Files, 1–3, Baines to Burgess, 10 April 1822.
68 Ibid. Baines to Clifford, 22 August 1822.
69 Ibid. Bishops' Letters, Baines to Collingridge, 25 September 1817.
70 Ibid. 20 April 1820.
71 Ibid. 23 June 1822.
72 Downside Archives, E20, Barber to Brewer, 4 April 1821.
73 CDA, Bishops' Letters, Baines to Collingridge, 12 January 1822.
74 Ibid. 14 July 1822.
75 Ibid. Collingridge to Baines, 10 October 1822.
76 Ibid. Collingridge to Baines, November 1822.
77 Ibid. Baines Box Files, 1–3, Birdsall to Baines, 17 February 1823.
78 Ibid.
79 Downside Archives, E66, Lawson to Lorymer, 11 October 1817.
80 Ibid. Barber to Lorymer, 5 April 1820.
81 Ibid. E252, 18 June 1820.
82 CDA, Baines Box Files, 1–3, Glover to Baines, 2 December 1822.
83 Ibid.
84 Ibid. 12 December 1822.
85 Ibid. Marsh to Baines, 22 December 1822.
86 Ibid. Baines to Collingridge, 25 February 1823.
87 Ibid. Burgess to Baines, 1 April 1823.
88 Ibid. Bishops' Letters, Marsh to Collingridge, 25 February 1823.
89 Ibid. Baines Box Files, 1–3, 16 May 1822.

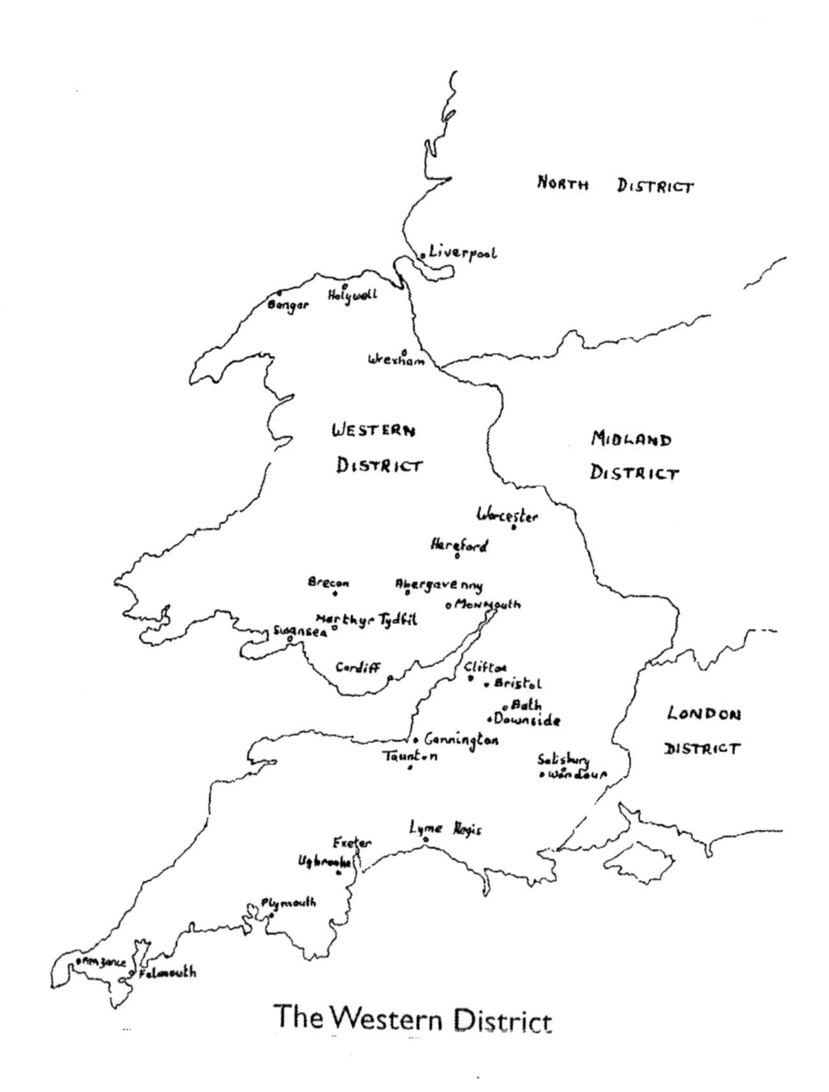

The Western District

3

The Fledgling Bishop

Consecration

Baines's appointment as coadjutor to Bishop Collingridge with the right of succession did not have an auspicious beginning. He needed to be consecrated as a bishop, a ceremony which should have been an occasion of much rejoicing among his family and friends and the members of the Bath mission. Unfortunately, however, Bishop Collingridge was not well enough to perform the ceremony and another bishop had to be found to take his place. There is a difference of opinion about the original choice of bishop to perform the ceremony. Bernard Ward in his *Eve of Catholic Emancipation*[1] implied that while Milner as senior Vicar Apostolic would have been the obvious choice, Collingridge was not prepared to allow him to conduct such an important ceremony in the Western District. Collingridge had certainly had disagreements with Milner, as did the other Vicars Apostolic, but J. B. Dockery, Collingridge's biographer, maintains that it was Collingridge who first suggested that Milner should be approached and Bishop Poynter of the London District who objected.[2] Baines also seems to have favoured the choice of Poynter, but the Vicar Apostolic had other objections, as can be seen in a letter to Baines:

> My services, which you have done me the honour to call for, in performing the sacred rite of your episcopal consecration, are at your command. I beg to say though that I much question the prudence of performing such a ceremony at Bath, in a chapel so open to the public as yours is. I should not dare to do it in a chapel in London. My opinion is, that it would be better in every respect to perform the ceremony in a more retired and quiet place than a public chapel in Bath[3]

He then suggested St Edmund's, Ware, as an alternative. Poynter's apprehensions would have echoed the feelings of many Catholics of the time, but Baines had no fears of trouble in the city where he had worked for the past six years, and still made his home. Now, as there seemed to be no prospect of being consecrated in Bath, Baines approached the Archbishop of Dublin, and was finally consecrated bishop in that city on 11 May 1823.

Collingridge's lieutenant

Collingridge hoped that Baines would be of great assistance to him in taking over many of the routine duties of the District. This was only partly the case, as Baines's pursuit of his own priorities, and concern over his growing health problems, took over; but in the first two years at least he was willing to perform numerous episcopal duties and to give advice whether required or not. In September 1823 he was advising Bishop Collingridge that there was no need to find a priest for Weymouth during the winter months:

> I do not think there are a dozen resident Catholics, and those so poor as to be able to contribute nothing to the maintenance of a priest. The visitors who are at present rather numerous and respectable, will depart with the season . . . I have however made inquiries and prepared the way for any arrangement your Lordship may think proper to adopt for next season. I have reason to believe that if it were decided to erect a chapel, some of the protestant inhabitants might contribute.[4]

Appealing to Protestants was to become characteristic of Baines in efforts to raise money for the building of churches or restoration. It is significant that Protestants appeared willing to contribute considerable sums to these causes, a practice which would have been very unlikely later in the century.

In November 1823 Baines recommended Bishop Collingridge to employ a number of Irish priests to remedy the shortage in the Western District, although Collingridge seemed to be unwilling to do this. Baines reassured him that, in Bristol at least, 'there is no impropriety in a congregation two thirds Irish being partially served by an Irish priest'.[5] At the same time, without telling Collingridge, Baines was negotiating with Prior Burgess of Ampleforth about the possibility of placing a new Benedictine priest at Bristol.

In April 1824, Baines spent a short time in Bristol conferring confirmation and helping out at the mission on Sundays. He was arranging to give confirmation in Bath at Whitsuntide and later to visit the Catholic missions at Abergavenny and Brecon.[6] He was spreading his influence by his preaching far outside Bristol and Bath. He was in demand in missions throughout the Western District, and also in the north, where people remembered his preaching from his Ampleforth days. The most highly-publicized of his sermons was made at the dedication of the Catholic chapel in Bradford on 27 July 1825.[7] As with some of his later sermons, Baines appeared to be preaching to Protestants more than Catholics, showing that he hoped to attract people from far beyond his flock. It was not unusual for Protestants to attend these occasions and for the bishops to use them to explain Catholic belief and practices.

Baines explained the most controversial doctrines of the Catholic Faith in simple language, endeavouring not to give offence to Protestants, and even trying to understand their misgivings. In this sermon he was returning to the theme of his *Defence of the Christian Religion*.

He denied that Catholics worshipped images, as many claimed; the image of the cross had been removed from many Protestant churches, but Catholics believed that it enhanced worship; 'Could a more appropriate object stand on any Christian altar?' Prayers for the dead were also condemned by many Protestants, but Catholics believed that prayers for loved ones no longer on earth found favour with God. Likewise, Baines went on, 'think of a child who has been deprived by death of a parent who through life, offered for him the most fervent supplications. Is it likely that the anxiety of a parent for the welfare of a beloved child wholly ceases in death?'

Baines went on to discuss in some detail the Catholic doctrine of Purgatory and, in particular, the false belief that the priest can liberate souls from it on payment of a fee. 'The Catholic Priest', preached Baines, 'claims no authority or jurisdiction over the dead. All he can do is to apply to the mercy of God on their behalf. He can, however, offer sacrifices for the dead.' The only remuneration the priest may claim is for legitimate expenses and additional labour in performing special services, as any Protestant minister may do.

He then went on to discuss the doctrine of transubstantiation, which had always been a stumbling block to Protestants.

> The Church teaches [he said] that by the words of consecration, a real change is wrought in the bread and wine, not in external properties, but in internal substance – that the body and blood of Christ are, in substance, truly and really present, though not perceptible to our senses. They are not present in the gross, natural state of the

mortal body, but in some supernatural and ineffable manner suited to the object of his presence.

All this was possible with God, who had 'once been presented as a baby in a stable, in the malefactor on the cross; now risen from the dead, he assumes united properties of spirit and body; he enters a room when the doors are shut and is found solid and tangible to the hands of Thomas, and appears to Mary Magdalene as a gardener.'

Baines then ended the central part of his sermon by imploring the Protestants among his congregation to show forbearance: 'If the doctrine of the Catholic Faith is incomprehensible to you, it is not on that account to be rejected, much less blasphemed.'

He then referred to a number of matters of form and ritual in the Catholic Church which were criticized by Protestants, such as the use of Latin in the mass and 'the parade of richly attired Priests'. His argument here was mainly that both gave 'dignity to the sacred mysteries', but he pointed out that translations of the mass were available in all English churches, and that the priest always preached in English. If the priests dressed in everyday garb, 'the sacrifice would be equally holy, though not equally impressive'.

Baines returned to this theme in preaching throughout his ministry, particularly in sermons to English Protestants in Rome in 1827–29, and the lectures he gave in Bath in the late eighteen-thirties. In these, he set out to explain the doctrines of Catholics to Protestants without provocation and, in his highly-criticized pastoral of 1840, to plead for reconciliation between the two.

Even at this early stage he was also concerned about wider issues, advising Collingridge not to tie down a house which he had purchased for a mission in Somerset: 'If I might venture to offer advice, it would be that you would not tie up the hand of yourself or successors to apply the purchase of a house or that of a mission – such ties appear to me to be always objectionable when too tight, and frequently render it necessary to violate the regulations with doubt and difficulty.'[8]

Could it be that Baines was already looking ahead to a time after the death of Bishop Collingridge, when he would want ready funds to put all his ambitious plans into action? Collingridge was certainly annoyed by this kind of criticism, for his financial priorities were quite different from those of Baines, preferring to build up funds which could be used to maintain priests in the missions and build new churches. Baines, on the other hand, was already dreaming of a magnificent ecclesiastical seminary for the Western District and a home for future Vicars Apostolic, the first of whom he hoped would be himself.

From this time, relations between the two bishops became more strained. In June 1824 Baines had evidently caused Collingridge extreme annoyance, although the exact issue of contention is not known. Baines, too, professed to be ignorant of the reason for Collingridge's displeasure, writing to him on 22 July:

> I cannot quit this place without once more expressing my sincere regret that I have had the misfortune to offend you. It was not my wish. God knows how sincerely I have always wished to afford you every relief and consolation. What I have ever done and said, I have done and said with the best intentions and with the fullest deliberation. You wrong me when you say I threatened you or wished you to follow my plans. I neither did one or the other.[9]

Baines was often genuinely ignorant as to why his sometimes overpowering manner gave offence, and inclined to believe that he had been hard used. He continued plaintively: 'Indeed my Lord, you have treated me very hardly, but I forgive you from my heart and I respect the assurance I have so often given you that I am ready to do everything I can to serve you or to cease from doing anything, if the latter is more agreeable to your wishes'.[10]

Doing nothing was not in Baines's nature and he continued during the autumn of 1824 and early part of 1825 to confer confirmations in Wales, and an ordination at Downside in place of Bishop Collingridge, and to make further inquiries about a priest for the Bristol mission. In January 1825 he was corresponding with Lord Arundell about the mission in Salisbury to which the latter had contributed large amounts of money. Baines hoped that Lord Arundell would continue to give the mission the honour of his patronage and the benefit of his influence. He referred to the right of presentation of priests to the mission and mentioned that Lord Arundell had agreed that this should be left in the hands of the bishop. Nevertheless Baines, ever-ready to please members of the nobility, assured Lord Arundell that: 'I need not repeat that if ever I have to discharge that duty, I shall certainly make a point to see that no person is presented who is not agreeable to yourself'.[11] Later in 1825 there was more trouble with the Bristol mission and Baines went over to restore peace between the priest, Mr Riley, and the congregation, and wrote to Bishop Collingridge that 'I was fortunate enough to satisfy both parties'. He told the Bishop that:

> Mr Riley has certainly been to blame. He has of late got into a very bad style of preaching with little or no preparation and says

> many things which would be better not said. I shall drop upon him unexpectedly some day when he preaches and hear him myself . . . You must not be surprised if you hear of a war between some of the Bristolians and me. The late affair has well nigh become a public one.[12]

There is no record of whether Baines ever followed up his threat of dropping into St Joseph's to hear the sermon, a visit which Fr Riley would have found very intimidating. Baines was becoming more and more concerned with wider issues, which would influence the whole future of the Catholic Church in England.

A seminary for the Western District

The most important of these issues was the plan to establish a seminary for Catholic priests in the Western District. Baines had been thinking and writing about the possibility for some time, even before he became Bishop Collingridge's coadjutor. This was evident in his first letter to Collingridge after his appointment: 'I shall omit no opportunity for procuring a college for the District and I look forward with infinite pleasure to Your Lordship's seeing your District provided with means for the education of priests at least equal in proportion to those enjoyed by many of the others'.[13]

Baines thought it reprehensible that the Western District should be the only one of the four without its own seminary. This placed the bishop at a disadvantage, in that he had to rely mainly upon the religious foundations, particularly the Benedictines who were established at Downside, to provide him with priests for the missions. He often had to write beseeching letters to the Provincials asking them for help in servicing particular missions, and he could never be certain that these priests might not be recalled from the missions at any time.

The main obstacle to the establishment of such a seminary was the perilous state of the District's finances, for it was quite the poorest of the Vicariates. Baines, therefore, first considered options other than building or buying a large house for conversion into a seminary, and looking naturally towards Downside with its large buildings, it teaching staff and its endowments. What more natural that the Benedictine foundation, his alma mater, should provide the teaching centre for the District? First, though, essential changes would have to be made, for the bishop must be directly responsible for priests in training and for their appointments to the missions, while the priests must owe their first allegiance to the bishop and not to their religious superiors. It is not clear whether Collingridge supported Baines's plans, or even whether he knew very much about them. Certainly he was having great difficulty in obtaining enough priests for the missions, particularly as he seemed reluctant to appoint many Irish priests; there had also been some problems with the regulars, particularly with the Jesuit, Fr Plowden, who had been forced to leave the Bristol mission in 1816. This would have made him sympathize with Baines's objectives, but his natural caution, particularly in financial matters, would have made him much more wary; he was also a much more tactful man than Baines and would have been reluctant to arouse the fears of the Benedictines.

Fr Marsh, President of the Benedictines, had given his approval in principle to the idea of founding an episcopal seminary for the Western District, but emphasized that time would be needed to bring parties together and persuade them to agree to such a plan:

> Allow me to recommend much caution and gentleness in the means of bringing this to bear. The parties concerned will probably be disposed to frustrating any attempts at harsh and compulsory measures, besides we cannot expect anyone to act so effectively as when he acts with cheerfulness and good will. This good will then we must endeavour to obtain and I think it may be obtained if proper means be employed.[14]

Caution and willingness to listen to other points of view were not characteristics of Bishop Baines, and there was no evidence that he intended to follow the President's advice. Cheerfulness and good will were still in evidence, however, when the two bishops went down to Downside for the opening of the new chapel in July 1823. A later chronicler described the great celebrations:

> The occasion marked, among other things, the adoption on the part of the monks of a semi-academic style of dress. Hitherto, since monks were prescribed by law, they had been wearing secular costume in England; it was not until 1846 that they thought it safe to wear the Benedictine habit. So what with the monks in their new choir and their new gowns, the 300 visitors in the body of the church, the Bishops and the clergy in the sanctuary, the entire school in their best clothes finding places wherever they could, and a trained team of choristers from Wells to help with the singing, the scene on that July day must have been of lively interest.
>
> The organ had been acquired from the Pavilion in Brighton, and up there in the organ loft sat the court musician, Count Mazzinghi himself, accompanying a mass which he had composed especially

> for the occasion. At the conclusion of the creed, the Count, never severe in his understanding of the liturgy, had so far spent out his score that there numbered – though in this we may be permitted to feel that he overreached himself – seventy two Amens.[15]

No one could have visualized on that joyful day, when Baines celebrated the mass, that this was to be the last time that he would be welcomed at Downside. Just over a month afterwards he wrote to Fr Bernard Barber, now Prior of Downside, asking:

> Would you be willing that the house of St Gregory should be made over to myself and successors, the Bishops of the Western District (being Regulars) as an episcopal seminary for the same on the understanding that the Bishop for the time being should be allowed to exercise the same powers over its members within his own District which is usually exercised by the President and Provincial.
>
> I am aware that this cannot be without introducing certain changes into the existing government of the said congregation. The changes I conceive to be necessary are such as should enable the Bishop to have the same control over his subjects when upon the mission as if they were secular priests, as well as in the general direction of the education they receive in the monastery ... The conditions imply certain concessions of privileges on the part of the Benedictine congregation to the Bishop of the Western District.[16]

Baines went on to list a number of advantages, which he thought would accrue to the Benedictine congregation by such an arrangement, but there was no disguising the fact that it would fundamentally change the character of the foundation: the monastic ideal was likely to be lost in the educational establishment which Baines ultimately dreamed of turning into a Catholic university. This meant little to Baines, who was first and foremost an educationalist and who claimed to see little difference between the secular and regular priest, as he had written to Edward Clifford in a letter already quoted: 'What difference can it make to any sensible man or to the public at large whether you or I be a monk or a secular priest or a Jesuit? Our first character is that of a priest.'[17]

Herbert Van Zeller describes the situation thus: 'You have Dr Baines, the enthusiast, the man with a mission, the dazzling talker, the hot-headed protagonist with the unusual good looks. You have Dom Bernard, not a man of brilliant parts, distinguished acquirements or popular manners, but provided with an eminent degree of common sense, with great firmness and remarkable prudence.'[18]

There was thus an inevitable clash of personalities between two men who both believed passionately in the justice of their cause. There is no record of Prior Barber's reply to the Bishop's letter, and it is probable that Baines destroyed it in his anger. He merely noted that the Prior had rejected his proposals '*in toto*'.

He turned then to his friend, Prior Burgess of Ampleforth, who was more sympathetic to his aims, and wanted to help him to establish a seminary in the Western District, which might also develop into the first Catholic university in England since the Reformation. The two had already corresponded about the possibility of transferring Ampleforth to the west, if the Downside authorities could be persuaded to take over the buildings of their brethren in Yorkshire. Even before he had written to Prior Barber proposing the foundation of an episcopal seminary at Downside, Baines was already telling Burgess:

> It is impossible to describe to you what a pleasure it could be to me to have Ampleforth in the west. I have not the least doubt that we should go on most prosperously and harmoniously together and be of the greatest service to each other. But alas! I fear we shall meet with great obstruction and difficulty from some of your brethren. – From its situation Downside has the first claim to my attention and it is on that account alone that I have refrained from making any overtures to Ampleforth until I had learnt what could could be done respecting Downside.[19]

After Prior Barber refused to countenance the idea of turning Downside into an episcopal seminary, Baines put his second plan into action of trying to organize an exchange of house, furniture and land between St Laurence's of Ampleforth and St Gregory's of Downside. It was a proposal that was likely to meet with an even swifter rejection than the previous one, for it was difficult to imagine that the monks of Downside would wish to leave their own surroundings, their monastery and chapel, which they had so recently established after years of moving from place to place; it was doubtful, too, whether the majority of the Ampleforth monks would have agreed to such an arrangement, although the Prior and Sub-Prior, both friends of Baines, supported the idea. Any further contemplation of the plan was ended, however, when Prior Barber wrote to Baines on 10 October 1823, leaving him in no doubt of the strong feelings of the community:

> Your last proposition which is to the following effect 'would the Prior and Council of St Gregory's consent in an exchange with the members of St Lawrence's, of house, furniture, land and arbitrators being appointed on both sides to make a reasonable allowance for differences of property?' has been discussed in Council. It is with regret that we are again reduced to the unpleasant necessity of declining a proposition which comes from so reputable a quarter.[20]

Again the main objection was that such a move would change the whole character of the Benedictine foundation. Although Baines himself could see no reason why it should do so, Prior Barber was adamant on this point: 'We conceive that any acquiescence on our parts to the proposed arrangements would tend to a fundamental and essential change in the government of the English Benedictine congregation, which may eventually end in the subversion of the society. We cannot lend our sanction to any measure which can, in the remotest degree have such a tendency . . .' He then ended with the customary gesture of politeness: 'The members of the Council send their respects'.[21]

We can imagine how Baines would have thrown aside such a letter in disgust. He was contemptuous, writing to Burgess: 'Now I think I have done with my Brethren of Downside. No one would expect me after this letter to make any further overtures. I certainly hope the Benedictine body does not contain a majority of members who see so ill their own interests.'[22]

He knew, though, that there was no hope of establishing an episcopal seminary in a Benedictine establishment, and the only possibility was to buy or rent a large house in the Western District, with the hope of persuading some of the staff from Ampleforth to come south and teach in the new college. By the end of 1823 he was considering Taunton as a good situation, and writing to Burgess: 'There is a new large and most excellent house the best in Taunton, belonging to the Bishop and adjoining the new chapel, which I believe I could have immediately.'[23]

Prior Burgess thought that the matter could be arranged more economically if Lord Arundell could be persuaded to allow a part of Wardour Castle to be used as seminary. He went on to say:

> If your Lordship is not successful with Lord Arundell, I would recommend some large abandoned gentleman's house to be got in the neighbourhood of Bristol or any part of your Lordship's diocese, where coals and provisions were not dear and where the college would be at no great distance from a river, canal or sea-port for the convenience of water carriage. I say a large gentleman's house

> because it could be bought cheaper than a smaller one, and might be large enough without being obliged to build any more.[24]

In May 1824 Baines raised with Bishop Collingridge the matter of purchasing another large house in Somerset, Monkton Court, but Collingridge was not enthusiastic and fearful of making the financial situation of the District worse. He was evidently mistrustful of Baines's plans, judging by Baines's letter of 21 May 1824. 'I hope your Lordship will not make yourself uneasy by imagining that I would speculate with the money of the District ... this would be unfair and highly blameable. But I do hope and trust that a college may be obtained without risk sooner or later to the greatest benefit of the District and of religion.'[25]

It was evident, though, that stalemate had been reached and that Baines was not going to get much further with his plans for a seminary, so long as Bishop Collingridge lived. The issue lay dormant, but relations between Baines and the Benedictines were permanently soured. Each could find little good to say about the other and appeared to be looking out for faults, as in Baines's letter to Prior Burgess in April 1824:

> I was lately at Downside and happening to peep through the refectory when the cloth was laid for dinner, it really made me sick to see the filthiness of the table cloth. Perhaps my notions have changed since the time I lived in college but I am the better able to judge of the effect which such things produce in the minds of the world. If a table cloth cannot be kept clean, it would be infinitely better not to have any.[26]

Prior Barber of Downside referred to Baines with heavy sarcasm in many of his letters to fellow-Benedictines. In July 1824 he wrote to Fr Jenkins referring to Baines's efforts to reply to a treatise of Dr Daubeny, a well-known theologian: 'His Lordship is busy answering Daubeny – he would have made a sad handle of him if he had not received some theological instruction when he was here ...'[27]

And on 5 May 1825:

> Have you heard that the L.P. [Learned Prelate] has taken a very large house 3 miles from Bath? ... the house is taken on a lease of 7 years – attached to it 10 acres of land, rent on it from 120 to 150 per annum. It is again rumoured that Bengelow is coming this quarter to be his Lordship's domestic chaplain – What shall we hear next? His Lordship sports a darling gig?[28]

Anna de Mendoza and Bathampton Manor

Some of these rumours at least were true as Baines was contemplating a move from the presbytery at Pierrepoint Place in Bath. Here he had continued to live with his ward, Anna de Mendoza, her companion, and Fr Brindle, who had taken over the Bath mission. He felt that he needed more room for his household, and his position as bishop required a larger establishment.

In Baines's many absences from home, his ward turned to other members of the clergy for companionship, since in her relationship with members of the Bath congregation, she felt obliged to keep her distance. Fr Brindle appears to have been captivated by Anna's vivacity and friendliness and wrote to her whenever he or she was away, as in his letter to her at Wardour Castle in August 1824:

> I am glad to hear that you are so comfortably rested for a time at Wardour. Do you ever take one of our walks before mass in the morning and go into the flower garden after breakfast? I wish indeed as you say, you were a witch and had a broomstick and some morning would give me a place beside you – we should ride very snugly . . . I think it would be very good fun[29] [here there is an illustration of Anna riding a broomstick with Brindle behind].

Her relationship with Brindle, though it may have caused raised eyebrows in the Bath congregation, appears to have been a lighthearted one, but in her contacts with Fr Edgeworth, the other priest who often visited Pierrepoint Place, she showed the more serious side of her nature. She was constantly concerned about his problems, financial and otherwise. His financial worries seem to have been considerable, judging by his letter to Baines in March 1825: 'I begged Miss Mendoza when she was leaving to advance me £10 which is rather less than what is due to me at this time.'[30]

Fr Edgeworth had other problems, first in the Weymouth mission, where he was unable to stay because there was not a congregation large enough to pay his salary, and then in Bristol where he had heard rumours that he was likely to be removed by Bishop Collingridge and the Jesuits restored. Anna wrote to Baines in 1825 relating his problems: 'Ever since you left us Mr Edgeworth has been something like *une âme damnée* as Madam calls it – he seems very low and well he may be.'[31]

Later, just before the move from Pierrepoint Place, she implored her guardian: 'I must beg you will tell me what I am to do about Mr Edgeworth in case he stays any time after us.'[32]

Most of Anna's letters to Baines are full of talk about the mission and the Catholic society of Bath: 'On Corpus Christi the Father [presumably Brindle] preached the grandest sermon I have ever heard him preach and I preached the grandest putting of Bathampton flowers in the vases at each side of the altar as was ever seen by mortal eye.'[33]

She related the smallest details of her social activities:

> Mrs Wyndham called upon me the day after you left and invited me to drink tea. She walked about with us some where almost every day. I am not a little amused at what she tells me. Lady Meade and others have told her that they would have called upon me but that they understood that I did not want to see anyone![34]

Domestic problems were also recounted in full, as when a housemaid let fall a bucket of slops from the top of the stairs: 'I can only say that it was a torrent of abomination and a cascade of stink.' When she and her companion returned to the house later, 'We armed our noses with bunches of syringa and new hay, but all was better than expected, and voila the end of my chapter'.[35]

She often described the antics of her little dog, Bijou, and the efforts to find homes for her puppies: 'I think you would have laughed at seeing one of them attack a great dog of Mr Knapp's. I am afraid Bee, too, will be out of favour, for she barks ferociously when she is at Bathampton [the site of Baines's new house] and is very spiteful to the rooks.'[36]

Anna often made fun of her guardian, laughing at his many and varied activities, and her letters reveal their easy relationship: 'I fancy I see you sitting under a tree rubbing your nose and chin and looking at the west side of your right ankle, revolving some new plan in your head either for refuting Daubeny, or building a pig sty or making an alb or vestments'.[37]

By July 1825 Baines had signed the contract to rent Bathampton Manor, a large house on the hills to the east of Bath. His ward contemplated the move with pleasure:

'I have reason to be grateful to Almighty God and I hope and trust that I may ever be thankful. It does not sit naturally upon me and I should be very glad to get into the house and have a few more little cares and duties. I am quite idle and dissipated.'[38]

A week later she was not so happy, writing to Baines: 'I have been in a devilish bad humour all the week and why? Why because pack and package, we had removed to Bathampton and being kept awake 2 nights by a stink and by sleeping on something stuffed with stones.'[39]

Nevertheless she assured him: 'I shall take care that your room is ready and I shall be delighted to put up your books in order and I am glad that you allow me to do it'.[40] And then she goes on to recommend an appointment, which Downside would have seized upon as further evidence of Baines's high and mighty ways: 'I wish you could meet with a good steady man by way of a footman – one who is accustomed to the country and a good Catholic'.[41]

Baines appears to have stayed away during most of July and August, while Anna sent him almost daily reports of the problems of the move: 'Here we are established on the make-shift plan. We have very few things in the drawing-room and your shelves are not done yet ... the books arrived safe – 580 volumes – besides the ones you took to Weymouth and all this I have sorted – I have never had such a job.'[42]

And a few days later:

> The carpenter is the only workman not sent to the right about – Perry and Rowe, the best painter, have mostly done and if Palmer were not ill and dilatory, he would be in the house ... And once again let me tell you that the house is not more than 2 to 3 parts furnished – these very dirty colours are to be found in many parts of the house – that some things have turned out very ill.[43]

Baines was plainly one of those men who liked everything uncomfortable to be done in his absence, and he had plenty of well-to-do friends who could make life very pleasant for him. It was not until the middle of August that there was news of his imminent arrival at Bathampton Manor. Anna then wrote to tell him how glad they all were and warning him to cross the ferry and not go through Bath, as the road on top of Hempton Hill was very dangerous. Baines would have been pleased to hear that all the household would be watching for his expected arrival and to know:

> how delighted the servants are at your coming and their alertness to do anything and everything that may please you or be for your comfort. The poor little kitchen-maid, Betty, who has never spoken to you, tho' she is one of our flock, looks important upon your approaching arrival. She told me the other day when she was taking her lesson of milking that she never thought she would live in such a grand house.[44]

Bathampton Manor was an eighteenth-century house, in the classical style which Baines favoured. For a brief time he must have found it a haven to return to after all his journeys and controversies, a place where he would be cosseted and the centre of attention. Yet Anna warned him: 'I don't think you will enjoy this place after all the fine places you have been seeing and living in. Nay I am sure you will find it like a school boy going back to school for you won't be made so much of nor feted as you have been.'[45]

Baines's relationship with his ward seems to have been one of ups and downs, judging by her letters. None of his to her have survived, although there may have been few of these, as she constantly complained. At times he delighted at her wit and vivacity and at other times it irritated him, as she was well aware. 'By the time you have got this far your patience will be fairly exhausted and you will say as you said once or twice when you were home, "What nonsense! How can you be so silly!" and sundry other like things . . .'[46]

Sometimes these differences were more fundamental, and Anna's letters on the subject reveal something of her character and his:

> And now my dear father that you are at a distance and I am pretty cool I hope I may say a little on that most painful subject. I mean all the misunderstandings we have had I think if you were to understand me thoroughly you would on some occasions be less angry and less irritated. I know I am in the wrong to give way to my impetuosity, to my little sceptical envies and little malicious imaginations and still worse to express them – all this I know I am wrong in. You on your side are very soon irritated towards me. You have become defiant and reserved. I do not say this to excuse myself because I assure you before God it does not excuse me, but I do assure you that you would help me much to get over my faults if you would condescend to my weakness – this at least first – and not only forgive as I know you do, but forget . . .[47]

Forgetting supposed wrongs was something which Baines was always to find difficulty in doing, a trait which harmed his reputation on a wider stage. It is hard to imagine, though, that he did not delight in reading such notes as the following which he received when he was staying with Lord and Lady Arundell at Wardour: 'You may be passing away the ennui of a long interval between mass and breakfast in the shrubbery, flower garden or picture gallery talking theology with one of your episcopal brethren or disputing with them about words and that stupid philosophy, the pride of which has been the ruin of many'.[48]

A winter in Rome

It was pleasant, too, to have a ward who was always concerned about his health, which was becoming a source of worry. Throughout 1824 and 1825 there were constant references in letters to Baines's ill-health, and Lady Arundell rejoiced in a letter to Anna that the Bishop had decided to move to more salubrious surroundings away from the vapours of Pierrepoint Place. In the summer of 1826, his doctor in Bath pronounced that he had an abscess on the lung and needed to spend the winter of 1826–7 in a warmer climate. Baines hesitated for some time before taking this advice, realizing that Bishop Collingridge would not be at all happy at losing the services of his coadjutor for many months. He took a second opinion, consulting his family doctor in Lancashire, and for a time considered going back home for a while to receive treatment there. Anna was given the task of writing to Bishop Collingridge to explain the situation:

> It is the Bishop's present wish and intention to go by short stages to Liverpool as soon as he shall be able, to put himself under the care of Dr McCarthy, whom he knew as a friend and in whom for the above named other reasons he places a particular confidence. He trusts also that his native air may be favourable to his restoration. He hopes that the plan will meet with your Lordship's approbation.[49]

Nothing seems to have come of this plan, and by the following month Baines was again going to his doctor in Bath for advice, and arranging to travel by slow stages to Rome to spend the winter there. In July 1826, though, he was well enough to think once more about his episcopal seminary, and even reconsidering his old plan of turning Downside into such an establishment. This arose after a confidential conversation with Bishop Collingridge. He wrote to Collingridge, asking him to confirm

> that the gentlemen of Downside did not propose to make over to the Bishop of this district the house of Downside, either absolutely or on certain conditions. If the proposal was made in writing and you have the letter by you, I should be glad to see it, if not a simple statement of the proposal and those who made it will answer the same end.[50]

Bishop Collingridge was highly annoyed by this letter, replying on 21 July 1826:

> I shall be very sorry were any use made of what I mentioned to your Lordship. I never will have imagined that names would be called, for the proposal made to you was of a confidential nature and I have done wrong in communicating it. I will not do worse in publishing names or circumstances. If any words of mine imputed or implied that it was an act of the community or done in the name of the community, I retract them – for that was not the case. The proposal was made under peculiar circumstances and these circumstances have ceased to exist.[51]

Poor Collingridge was beginning to find his coadjutor something of a trial, and relations between the two men continued to become more and more strained. He could not have been too sorry when he heard that Baines had decided to accept his doctor's advice and winter in Rome, even though he would be deprived of his services. Baines also had few regrets at leaving England at the end of August 1826. He travelled with friends, his doctor from Bath, who was accompanying him as far as Paris, Anna de Mendoza and her other guardian, Madame Chaussegros, who also intended to spend the winter in Rome. None of the party could have imagined that Baines would not return to England for three whole years.

Notes

1 Bernard Ward, *The Eve of Catholic Emancipation 1803–1809*, vol. 3 (London, 1912), pp. 97ff.
2 See J.B. Dockery, *Collingridge*, p. 308.
3 CDA, Bishops' Letters, Poynter to Baines, 10 April 1823.
4 Ibid. Baines to Collingridge, 18 September 1823.
5 Ibid. 29 November 1823.
6 Ibid. 23 April 1824.
7 Ibid. Baines, Peter Augustine, *A Sermon preached at the Dedication of the Catholic Chapel in Bradford on Wednesday, July 27th, 1825.*
8 Ibid. Bishops' Letters, Baines to Collingridge, July 1825.
9 Ibid. 22 July 1825.
10 Ibid.
11 Ibid. Baines to Arundell, 9 January 1825.
12 Ibid. Baines Box Files, 1–3, Baines to Collingridge, 16 December 1825.
13 Ibid. Baines to Collingridge, 25 February 1823.
14 Ibid. Marsh to Baines, 23 March 1823 and 6 April 1823.
15 Dom Hubert Van Zeller, *Downside By and Large* (Downside, 1954), pp. 35–6.
16 Baines Box Files, 1–3, Baines to Barber, 27 August 1823.
17 Ibid. Baines to Clifford, August 1822.
18 Dom Hubert Van Zeller, *Downside By and Large*, p. 156.

19 Baines Box Files, 1–3, Baines to Burgess, October 1823.
20 Ibid. Barber to Baines, 10 October 1823.
21 Ibid.
22 Ibid. Baines to Burgess, October 1823.
23 Ibid. 9 December 1823.
24 Ibid. Burgess to Baines, 13 December 1823.
25 Ibid. Bishops' Letters, Baines to Collingridge, 21 May 1824.
26 Ibid. Baines Box Files, 1–3, Baines to Burgess, 22 April 1824.
27 Downside Archives, F173, Barber to Jenkins, 10 July 1824.
28 Ibid. F257, Barber to Jenkins, 5 May 1825.
29 CDA, Bishops' Letters, Brindle to de Mendoza, 30 August 1824.
30 Ibid. Edgeworth to Baines, 27 March 1825.
31 Ibid. De Mendoza to Baines, n.d.
32 Ibid. n.d.
33 Ibid. 5 July 1825.
34 Ibid. n.d.
35 Ibid. 15 June 1825.
36 Ibid. 10 July 1825.
37 Ibid.
38 Ibid.
39 Ibid. July 1825.
40 Ibid.
41 Ibid.
42 Ibid. 22 July 1825.
43 Ibid. 25 July 1825.
44 Ibid. 19 August 1825.
45 Ibid. August 1825.
46 Ibid. 18 October 1825.
47 Ibid. 22 October 1825.
48 Ibid. October 1825.
49 Ibid. De Mendoza to Collingridge, 27 May 1826.
50 Ibid. Baines to Collingridge, 18 July 1826.
51 Ibid. Collingridge to Baines, 21 July 1826.

4

Roman Interlude

Journey to Italy

During the next few months Baines and his party made their way slowly across France and Italy to reach Rome by the Christmas of 1826. Prior Barber of Downside made clear the feelings of the community about Baines's departure: 'The President is really very funny about [the bishop of] Siga – he says on the occasion of a certain person leaving Bath for the continent, there will be some disposed to cry out: "*Abiit, excessit, evasit*"'.[1] (He is gone, he is off, he has escaped.)

Baines himself recorded his progress to Bishop Collingridge in a letter written from Lyons. The party had arrived there at the end of September 1826 by way of Paris, where Baines disliked 'the ceaseless and unbearable noise and confusion'.[2] He had found great relief spending a day in the gardens of Fontainebleau, 'the stillest and most silent spot I have met with'.[3]

They then journeyed on to Nevers, an old cathedral town, where Baines was laid up for several days, but by the time he reached Lyons he was feeling much better, visiting the Archbishop, 'who has been very kind to us'. Anna de Mendoza and Madame Chaussegros had asked to visit one of the convents in the area, and the Archbishop not only gave permission for this, but extended the invitation for them to visit all the convents in the district.[4]

Baines was also well enough to spend time in Lyons Cathedral, which he described as 'magnificent'[5] and to study the liturgy which he found 'very different from the Roman, particularly in high masses'[6] and to observe that: 'All the clergy wear the clerical habit (quite different from England) and the people seem more attentive in the churches'.[7]

By February 1827, Fr Ratcliffe at Downside was reporting to Fr Deday that:

> The last news I have heard of Dr Baines was that he had reached Florence. I have no doubt that it is his intention to press on to Rome, and to endeavour to needle the Pope to sanction his scheme with regard to our body. I hope our good President will be on the look out and watch his every move.[8]

Rome – a growing reputation

Fr Ratcliffe was out of date with his information as Baines and his party had been in Rome since Christmas. They had established themselves in a large apartment in the Piazza Nicosia, and Madame Chaussegros opened a salon, at which she entertained many of the nobility and other distinguished people of Rome. Anna de Mendoza must have found that this setting gave her greater scope to meet interesting people, particularly eligible men, than she had known in the limited horizons of Bath and Bathampton.

Baines himself reported to Bishop Collingridge that, although he had had a relapse at the end of the warmer weather, he was now feeling better again under the care of an Italian physician, who had prescribed ass's milk and Iceland moss for at least two or three months to come.[9] He was well enough to attend midnight mass at St Peter's on Christmas night and was carried away with the magnificence of the ocasion:

> It is impossible to convey an adequate idea of the effect of the precision, the endless variety of magnificent costumes of canons, prelates, heads of religious orders, senators, abbots, bishops, cardinals, the forest of white mitres and most of all the Pope [Leo XII] himself, borne aloft beneath a canopy distributing his benediction to prostrate thousands who fill the magnificent arcades of St Peter's. But who can conceive the effect, when in the midst of a profound silence, the Pope pronounced the words of consecration and at the same instant the cannons of the castle of St Angelo were heard in the distance and the sound of trumpets from some unseen position outside the church echoed through the vaults.[10]

A few days later Baines was delighted to be invited to attend the Pope in the Sistine chapel of New Year's Day and afterwards he and a Doctor Patterson were appointed *assistentes ad Solium* in the following year, which was considered a great honour. Following the ceremony the bishops accompanied the Pope to the sacristy to take off his cope, and Baines recorded: 'He came so near me and bowed to me with such a smiling and affectionate countenance that I could not refrain from thanking him as he passed for the honour he had done us.'[11]

Baines believed that he was making a good impression in Rome, particularly after he was granted two audiences with the Pope, 'while people of 20 times my importance have so much difficulty to obtain a single interview'.[12] In one of these audiences the Pope told him to come to him 'whenever I like – *quand vous voulez monsigneur* – and pressed me to say anything I wished respecting the affairs of my District'.[13]

This was an opportunity which Baines was unlikely to miss, but in the meanwhile he revelled in the glories of Rome. 'St Peter's', he said, 'is like another world, not earth, nor yet quite heaven, but nearer the latter than the former'. And 'The university and great religious houses are full of learned men, the libraries are magnificent and everything the world possesses worth seeing or knowing is found here.'[14] He developed a lifelong admiration for Roman architecture and Fr Brindle back in Bath was surprised to hear that he had given up Gothic architecture and even 'Grecian campaniles' to the Roman: 'The former I might have expected, but hardly the latter. Would that I was with you to explore among the churches and old ruins and especially the great church of churches in Rome.'[15]

So much was Baines impressed by it all that he talked of buying a house in Rome, which could be used by trainee priests during part of their preparation for work in the Western District. It is unknown how the Bishop proposed to finance such a scheme or provide teaching staff, and like so many of his dreams it did not materialize.

On the second Sunday in Lent the Pope came up to Baines and said: '"*Il faut que vous chantiez la messe.*" This aroused general surprise amongst the Bishops and Monsignors, and Dr Gradwell says this would have caused many of them to set them themselves down as cardinal impetto [cardinals in waiting].'[16]

Baines then described how he had sung mass at the Sistine Chapel in the presence of the Pope and the sacred college, 'with a voice as clear and as strong as ever and without any fatigue from so unusual an exertion'.[17]

Anna de Mendoza, who described the scene in a letter to Fr Rooker, showed how apprehensive she had been as to how Baines would acquit himself: 'It was daunting before so many high personages and observers, satirical as they are. I rather think that they are not quite sure that a Bishop from a barbarous country was likely to know anything about the matter.'[18]

She need not have worried, for Baines had supreme self-confidence and carried everything before him. He was growing in influence with the Pope and some of his cardinals, and Benedictines back in England were becoming alarmed. Fr Ratcliffe wrote to Fr Deday that Baines was 'in high favour with the Pope'.[19]

He was in such high favour that the Pope was concerned about his health during the hot summer of 1827 and insisted that he left Rome for several months to find cooler air. In a letter to one of the members of his former flock in Bath, Mrs Hippisley, Baines described his travels including a visit to 'your favourite Loretto' and had the happiness of saying mass in the Holy House. 'It is a most memorable building. If you continue to be good, perhaps I shall be able to present you with a little memorial when I return in the spring.'

This letter revealed that Baines had made up his mind to spend another winter in Rome, 'for the Pope would not allow me to think of returning to England this autumn, as I have wished to do'.[20]

This last remark could not have been entirely true, as Baines was enjoying his new-found fame in Rome. Many well-known clerics visited him at the Piazza Nicosia, including the Prefect of Propaganda, Cardinal Castiglioni who often called after 'Ave maria' and chatted with him and his friends over their evening tea. John Bonomi, who knew Baines well at Prior Park, later recorded the bishop's story:

> It so happened that padre Scinto, the Penitentiary for the English language at St Peter's was calling on him, when suddenly the Cardinal Castiglioni was announced. The padre remembering that it was late and that the Cardinal would be displeased at finding him from home at that hour, at once retreated into the Bishop's bedroom, through which was egress to the staircase beyond. The Cardinal was ushered at the same moment into the Bishop's salon, and the padre Scinto, who had forgotten his hat, could not return to take it . . . he was kept in the greatest dismay, fearing that the inquisitive Cardinal might ask the Bishop whose hat it was, being old and unadorned by any distinctive Prelatic band. The Bishop meanwhile had not noticed the hat and neither (fortunately for the padre) had the Cardinal. However, his Eminence only remained a short half-hour after the expiration of which, to the Bishop's surprise and the amusement of his friends, the Padre reappeared to claim his hat and to wish them a hurried 'Buona Sera'.[21]

Baines was not only moving easily in high ecclesiastical circles, but also acquiring a great reputation as a preacher at 'the English pulpit', which Leo XII had opened for English visitors to Rome. The future Cardinal Wiseman, then Rector of the English College in Rome, recorded that:

> The church, which was nearly empty when preachers of inferior mark occupied it, was crowded when Bishop Baines was announced as the orator ... He was happiest in his unwritten discourses. The flow of his words was easy and copious, his imagery was often very elegant, and his discourses were replete with thought and solid matter. But his great power was in his delivery, in voice, in tone, in look, and gesture. His whole manner was full of pathos, sometimes more even than the matter justified; there was a peculiar tremulousness of voice, which gave his words more than double effect, notwithstanding a broadness of provincial accent, and an occasional dramatic pronunciation of certain words. In spite of such defects, he was considered, by all that heard him, one of the most eloquent and earnest preachers they had ever attended.[22]

Fr Ratcliffe writing to an unknown correspondent at Downside was less complimentary: 'It seems Dr Baines is figuring away at Rome. I am told he is preaching daily to a congregation of English Protestants in some church appropriate to the purpose. Let him stay there and convert them all.'[23]

Rumours were circulating in Rome that Baines was destined to be one of the first English cardinals since the Reformation, and Wiseman confirmed that the Pope had this in mind. Leo XII wanted to raise a member of the Benedictine order to the sacred college and believed, ironically in view of Baines's relations with the community, that he would be a suitable candidate. He wished him to move from his private apartments, where he was still living with Anna de Mendoza, Madame Chaussegros and other friends, and live in the Benedictine monastery of San Callisto and to wear the episcopal habit of his order.[24]

Baines would not have liked returning to live in a monastery and giving up the social life of the Piazza Nicosia, but was obliged to do so. Despite, too, his enjoyment of all the speculation that he might be made a cardinal, it is uncertain whether Baines would have liked to have stayed in Rome indefinitely, even as a cardinal. He was still contemplating returning to England eventually, and reforming the Western District after the death of Bishop Collingridge. Whether or not he would have been able to resist such an honour if Leo XII had lived and a definite offer had been made, is pure speculation.

Concern of Bishop Collingridge

In the meanwhile, Bishop Collingridge was becoming more than concerned at Baines's long absence in Rome, and particularly by the rumours that he intended to stay there indefinitely. He was no use whatever as an assistant to the Vicar Apostolic in his day-to-day work, but was negotiating with Propaganda about the retention of a Franciscan Province in England, a matter in which Dr Collingridge as a Franciscan himself naturally took a great interest. Collingridge's biographer doubted whether Baines was the best person to be engaged in the work of preserving a religious order. His doubts are born out by a remark of Baines in a letter to Fr McDonnell, who was in charge of the Franciscan Province in England: 'My opinion always was and still is that, if the object is to serve the English mission, the keeping up of a particular name is of little moment'.[25] Yet he seemed to have had a particular regard for the branch of the Franciscan order in England and 'if it could be kept up, nothing will be better adopted to the exigences of the times'.[26]

As a result of, or despite Baines's efforts, the Franciscan order continued to survive in England.

Collingridge, however, did not appoint Baines primarily as his agent in Rome; he wanted an administrator in the Western District, and by the beginning of 1827 had decided to take steps to obtain one. Baines was reluctantly forced to agree to such an appointment, although assuring Collingridge that his return to England would not be delayed an unnecessary week. He was not to return in Collingridge's lifetime.

It was most important to Baines who the new appointee was to be. Collingridge mentioned appointing Fr Birdsall, the new President of the Benedictines, or Fr Richards, a priest from Monmouthshire. Baines notified his bishop of his preference for the latter, believing that Birdsall was already antagonistic to him.[27] It is significant that Collingridge appointed Birdsall, whom he had been consulting more and more in Baines's absence. Baines had only himself to blame, as he had prolonged his stay in Rome longer than ill health seemed to warrant, and had forfeited all claims to his bishop's consideration.

Anna in Rome

By the beginning of 1828, Baines was concerned with more domestic matters concerning the future of Anna de Mendoza. Her looks and vivacity had captured the admiration of Roman society, as they had once done in Bath, and there were at least two young men who wanted to marry her. One of them was Luigi Gentili, a well-known lawyer, linguist, and man about town, who frequented the salons of Rome. He fell very much in love with her and it seems that she gave him encouragement. Gentili applied to Baines, as Anna's guardian, for permission to marry her, but Baines refused his consent. It is likely that he thought that an Italian lawyer, however well connected, was not the aristocratic suitor he required for his ward. Gentili was so overcome by this rejection that he retired from public life and soon entered the priesthood. He was eventually to become a well-known Catholic missionary in England. Anna, in the meanwhile, was sent home to England with her other guardian, Madame Chaussegros. Her heart could not have been so greatly affected as that of Gentili, as in the following year, 1829, she married another man whom she had met in Rome, Sir Patrick Bellew, an Irish baronet, later an MP. He was more in keeping with Baines's views of a suitable husband for his ward. In any case he was to lose Anna as a companion, although she often visited him at Prior Park, showing that she felt no lasting resentment to her guardian for interfering in her romantic life. Baines himself must have felt that much of the gaiety of life had departed with her.

Baines and his episcopal seminary

In spite of all his other preoccupations in Rome, Baines did not abandon his plans for an episcopal seminary in the Western District, and was in constant correspondence with Prior Burgess of Ampleforth about the matter. Burgess, who had his own problems at Ampleforth, supported Baines's plans to form an establishment of regulars under the Bishop. He set out his ideas for such an establishment, believing that the new seminary staffed by regulars should be little different from a secular one, except for the abbey choir and the solemn vows, which after a one-year novitiate would be taken to the Bishop as President and Provincial.[28] A contemporary believed that Burgess could never have visualized that he would have to become a secular himself.[29]

From the beginning of 1827 Baines was trying to gain the support of the Pope for his plans. He mentioned the matter in each audience and told Fr Rooker, who had been a student of his at Ampleforth, that the Holy Father was prepared to listen to his plans. He then laid the whole matter before Cardinal Cappellari, with whom he was already on good terms socially, and the Cardinal directed him to put the full statement of the case down on paper.[30] This led to a further flurry of letters between Baines and Rooker and Burgess, his two allies at Ampleforth. He urged Fr Rooker to draw up a petition from the Prior and council, and as many members of St Laurence's as could be persuaded to sign it, supporting the transference of obedience of the monastery to Baines and his successors.[31] Such a petition would greatly help Baines's cause in Rome, as would the presence of an agent from Ampleforth, who would support the idea of an episcopal seminary. Baines wrote to Burgess urging him to send such an agent to Rome immediately, bringing with him documents respecting the affair and 'a moderate sized map of England to explain the limit of the District Province'. Baines also felt that copies of his own book, *A Defence of the Christian Religion*, would be helpful.[32]

Baines's friend Fr Edward Glover, now a priest in Liverpool, was supportive at this stage. Yet he was always inclined to be more cautious than Baines. He foresaw problems at home and wrote that one of the greatest difficulties to be overcome was Dr Collingridge: 'When the Principal opposes, the secondary has up-hill work'.[33] In a brutally frank letter to Baines he said: 'If we ever have a troublesome superior, we live in hope that he may be changed in four years, but if we are to have such a man as Dr Collingridge as our superior, we have no hope but in his death and no more redress . . .'[34]

Clearly, though, Glover was not fully committed to plans for a seminary. In the same week he was writing to Prior Burgess, whom he had known at Ampleforth, urging him not to throw himself into Baines's scheme without due consideration: 'Let not the impetuosity of your temperament hurry you to commit yourself'.[35]

Baines also was meeting set-backs in Rome by the middle of 1827. Although Cardinal Cappellari had first seemed supportive, he was beginning to have doubts about Baines's seminary scheme. Baines wrote to Burgess in June that the Cardinal suspected him of 'an attempt to subjugate brethren against their will to sacrifice the monastic institute to the mission'.[36] He had told Baines that any separation of Ampleforth from the congregation implied the destruction of the latter, and proposed writing first to Bishop Collingridge and then to the President of the Benedictines for their views.[37] Baines was very opposed to this, believing that writing to one or the other was the same thing, and decided to withdraw his petition for the time being. This news probably prevented Fr Birdsall, the new President of the Benedictines, from hurrying to Rome. He was adamant that he would do so if Baines attempted anything further against Benedictine liberties.[38]

Baines, the Jesuits and Bishop Collingridge

Baines remained in Rome throughout 1828 causing further dismay to Bishop Collingridge, who is said to have confided in a friend that it was worse than having no coadjutor.[39] Baines's thoughts on the subject and the continued dispute with the Benedictines can only be surmised, as most of his private letters for 1828 are missing. There is, however, some important correspondence with Collingridge surviving on the subject of the Jesuits. The Society was still not officially recognized by the Catholic Church in England, although some of its priests were accepted by the Vicars Apostolic as providing much-needed help in the missions. Collingridge himself had worked perfectly amicably with Jesuit missionaries in Bristol, a mission which they claimed as their own, until he had a prolonged dispute with Fr Robert Plowden resulting in the priest being dismissed from Bristol in 1817.

Since then the relationship had become strained and by 1828 there had been no Jesuit priest at St Joseph's in Bristol for some years. Collingridge was said to have had a change of heart about the Jesuits after a serious illness in 1827, and considered restoring them to Bristol. In January 1828 he wrote to Baines for his opinion, and Baines replied that he thought the Jesuits themselves should be left to settle the matter of their return to Bristol and, if Collingridge allowed them to do so, 'I am sure you will give no offence to the Pope'. Baines was showing off here; he wanted Collingridge to know how high Baines stood in the Pope's favour, and how familiar he was with everything going on in papal circles.

At the end of 1828 Baines was playing a prominent part in supporting Collingridge in a petition to the Pope on behalf of the English Jesuits. It is significant that at this time, Baines was looking favourably upon the society. It was not until they began to frustrate his plans in some of the missions in the Western District, particularly in Bristol and Bangor, that he became antagonistic. The signs were now more propitious for the official recognition of the Jesuits in England, as two of the Vicars Apostolic, Bishop Gibson and Bishop Poynter, who had strongly opposed it as likely to hinder the granting of Catholic Emancipation, had died, and the House of Commons, if not the Lords, was less violently anti-Catholic than it had been. In response to this petition, Pope Leo XII issued a bull of Restoration on 1 January 1829, declaring that the Vicars Apostolic could ordain members of the Society of Jesus as members of a religious community (*ad sacros ordines titulo religiosae paupertatis*) and that they could enjoy the same spiritual and canonical privilege as other religious orders in England (*quibus reliqui ordines religiosi in Anglia ipsa fruuntur*). Baines hastened to write to Bishop Collingridge, sending him, not the original, but an authenticated copy of the rescript. 'The original I shall keep as a precious relic of the wisdom, decision and kindness of his Holiness.' He went on to emphasize the prominent part he himself had played in the negotiations:

> Though I inserted your Lordship's name in the petition along with my own, I distinctly told his Holiness that I was ready to take every responsibility solely and entirely upon myself both with the Bishop and the Government as far as I could do so by openly declaring myself, if necessary, the sole author and promoter of the measure. Your Lordship may judge of his Holiness's decision in the business, when you observe that the whole rescript is written in his own hand ... not content with this he brought it with him to the capella on the day of the Epiphany and after the mass came up to me and delivered it to me with his own hands in the presence of all the attending Bishops and prelates...[40]

It was no wonder that Bishop Collingridge was becoming more and more irritated with Baines, feeling that he was already acting the part of a Vicar Apostolic even before Collingridge's own death. He must have regretted that he had ever advocated Baines's appointment as coadjutor bishop with the right of succession.

At the end of January 1829, Banies was still in Rome, and obviously worried about his financial position when he returned to England. Previously he had been allowed £50 per annum out of Collingridges's stipend, but this was now to be withdrawn:

> It appears from your Lordship's last letter that you require for your own comfortable maintenance the 50 pounds which you had made over to me and you more over intimate that it was never customary in the Western District to allow any such thing to the co-adjutor. May I then humbly be allowed to ask how you intend to support me when I return to England?[41]

Vicar Apostolic

The answer, as Collingridge's biographer intimated, was that Baines, as others before him, should have undertaken the care of a mission or the chaplaincy of a convent to earn his keep. Such unpleasant necessity was removed by the sudden death of Bishop Collingridge on 3 March 1829. Banies received the news, not from Fr Birdsall, whom he thought should have written to him, but from another: 'Upon the death of Dr Collingridge, I received, not from Mr Birdsall who has become executor of the deceased Bishop as well as Administrator and Vicar General of the District, the news of that melancholy and important event, but from Dr Bramston, who received it from Mr Birdsall.'[42]

By 18 March, however, Birdsall was writing to Baines and, after recounting the arrangements for Bishop Collingridge's burial, he goes on to describe the details of his appointment:

> Dr Collingridge had constituted me Administrator or General Vicar to govern this District after his demise *in temporale* and until one shall be appointed by the Holy See or by his coadjutor, Dr Baines, and that he communicate to me all the power which by the tenor of the faculties of the second formula he can communicate to me for the purpose of governing the Western District during the interval after his demise and the canonical appointment of some other administrator . . . He also appointed me Vicar General of the Western District, with powers relating to that office. And from the present time he may commence exercising the office *usque ad revocationem*.[43]

Such a letter must have filled the new Vicar apostolic with alarm that his authority in England was being usurped by Birdsall. In spite of this Baines did not hurry home, waiting on in Rome for the election of the new Pope. Leo XII had just died, depriving Baines of 'a valuable patron and an indulgent friend'.[44] He offered his homage and congratulations to the new Pope, Pius VIII, elected in April 1829.

Baines always maintained that Pope Pius renewed the offer of a cardinal's hat to him, but the position is unclear. He later told his friend, Bonomi, that

> Within a week of his coronation, the Pope sent Cardinal Odescalchi to me to express his continual good wishes and favour, and to offer me, if I would stay in Rome, a position at court, that the Cardinal surprisingly intimated to me his Holiness meant as a step to a higher position, which I understood to be the Cardinal's hat, for which dignity I confidently believed Leo XII had intended me.[45]

In any case Baines turned down the office of a place at the papal court, which might or might not have led to the cardinalate. He explained to Bonomi:

> My predecessor had just died; I felt in better health and spirits; I was homesick and anxious for friends and native air; I preferred just then the position of an English Vicar Apostolic, immeasurably though it was beneath the Cardinalatial dignity, and I was eager to found the seminary for the Western District and to promote, by my presence, the interests of Religion in that part of England.[46]

It must have been a terribly difficult decision for Baines to make. His explanation brings out the great contrasts in his character; his love of pomp and power vying with his longing to return 'to friends and native air'. There must also have been doubts, too, whether remaining in the papal court would really have led on to a position of power under the new pope, for Baines's influence certainly decreased after the death of Leo XII. His critics at home rejoiced at this. Fr Leavis Spain, writing to Birdsall, told him that '[Baines] appears anything but the grand Bishop at Rome and when he lost Leo XII, he lost his great friend and support'.[47]

And Fr Thomas Brown, later to be the first Bishop of the Welsh District, wrote to the Provincial, Fr Deday, that it was fortunate that, since the death of Leo XII, Baines had fallen in influence with Rome.[48]

Baines was taking a more optimistic view of the situation, writing to Prior Burgess that the new pope 'can hardly fail to be one of my friends. At all events I am sure he will be a friend of justice and Religion, which will suffice.'[49]

In the meanwhile, while waiting to see the new Pope and to lay before him the plans for the Western District, Baines also took action to counter the influence of Fr Birdsall at home. He wrote to his friend Fr Brindle at Bath, requesting him to take over the administration of the Western District, in spite of any last wish of Bishop Collingridge. He was particularly anxious that Brindle should look into the account books and papers of the late Bishop: 'I particularly wish to know what funds there are and how placed for the upkeep of the Vicar Apostolic and about the amount of the annual contribution – what the property left by Dr Collingridge and what his private instructions'.[50]

Baines was also forced to turn his attention to urgent business concerning the warring Bristol mission, which had worried Bishop Collingridge at the time of his death. Here there were two priests, one a Franciscan, Fr Edgeworth, and the other a young Jesuit, Fr Rowe, and the whole controversy was bound up with the efforts of the Jesuits to reclaim the mission which, until the dismissal of Fr Plowden, had been theirs alone: 'The congregation began to be divided and to form itself into factions, one for the bishop, another for the Jesuits'.[51]

The two priests were barely on speaking terms. Fr Rowe complained to Brindle, Baines's Vicar General, that Edgeworth neither came to breakfast at the usual hour or dined at home. The only solution was for Edgeworth to leave to bring peace to this 'ever tormenting mission . . . this long distracted place'.[52]

On Bishop Collingridge's death, Fr Edgeworth's supporters petitioned Baines, claiming that his predecessor had given approval for the Franciscan to remain at the Bristol mission and asked him to endorse this. Baines was thus forced to take some action, although he knew little or nothing about the local situation. He appears though to have been influenced by a letter written to him in Rome by Edgeworth's supporters, and claiming that the petition had been signed by 2,518 people. He tried to pass on the problem to his Vicar General and wrote to Brindle: 'If Dr C had not given his consent, do as you like, but I should choose Mr Edgeworth remain'.[53]

The two priests, therefore continued in an uneasy duo for another year, when the bishop was forced to make a more permanent decision about them. For the time being, at least, the laity in Bristol had successfully influenced the policy of the Bishop, a trend which was frowned upon by the Jesuits: 'this presbyterian spirit of interference in the appointment of pastors is, I am told, the most mischievous evil of religion in America, a greater evil even than whisky drinking, I think it cannot fail to operate perniciously if ever encouraged here'.[54]

Baines was more concerned with other things. In a letter to Prior Burgess, deploring the death of Leo XII, he wrote that: 'the death of Dr Collingridge greatly facilitates my views and fires my determination. I will not submit to the insolence of the Downside faction.'[55] He appeared to be obsessed with this issue, going so far as to question the legality of the Benedictine orders in England, which would have made all the monks seculars and subject to the authority of the Vicar Apostolic. He based this theory on the supposition that the Benedictines had not obtained permission from the Vicars Apostolic of the Northern and Western Districts to settle at Ampleforth and Downside during the Napoleonic wars, permission which he claimed to be essential. He told Burgess in a letter of 4 April that the Prefect of Propaganda, Cardinal Cappellari, agreed with him on this issue, but how far this was wishful thinking on the Bishop's part is not known. It was sufficient, though, for Baines to state categorically to Burgess in the same letter that 'the English Benedictine congregation is not canonically established in England',[56] but if Burgess was able to arrange an exchange of house, property etc with Downside, and it became a college of the District, then the Bishop would allow Burgess and the monks at Ampleforth who supported him to observe most of the rules and the constitution of the Benedictine order.

It was an extraordinary claim, which was to usher in probably the most stormy vicariate in the history of the Western District. Yet Bishop Baines finally left Rome in 1829 supremely confident in the rightness of his cause, and putting into practice the plans which had been thwarted by Bishop Collingridge and the Benedictines.

Notes

1 Downside Archives, F386, Barber to Deday, 29 August 1826.
2 CDA Bishops' Letters, Baines to Collingridge, 29 September 1826.
3 Ibid. Baines to Collingridge.
4 Ibid.
5 CDA, Baines Box Files, 1–3, Baines to Burgess, 29 September 1826.
6 Ibid.
7 Ibid.
8 Downside Archives, G26, Ratcliffe to Deday, 3 February 1827.
9 CDA Baines Box Files, 1–3, Baines to Collingridge, 3 January 1827.
10 Ibid. Baines to Collingridge, 6 January 1827.
11 Ibid.
12 Ibid. Baines to Rooker, 18 January 1827.
13 Ibid.
14 Ibid.
15 Ibid. Brindle to Baines, February 1827.
16 Ibid. Baines to Rooker, 7 April 1827.
17 Ibid.
18 Ibid. Bishops' Letters, De Mendoza to Rooker, April 1827.
19 Downside Archives, G99, Ratcliffe to Deday, 21 October 1827.
20 Ibid. G134, Baines to Mrs Hippisley, 27 October 1827.
21 Ampleforth Journal, vol. xv, 1910 (quoting from CDA; reference cannot be found).
22 Nicholas Wiseman, *Recollections of the Last Four Popes* (London, 1858), p. 326.
23 Downside Archives, G207, Ratcliffe to unknown correspondent (fragment of a letter).
24 Ampleforth Journal, vol. xv.
25 J. B. Dockery, *Collingridge, A Franciscan Contribution to Catholic Emancipation* (Newport, 1954), p. 245 ff.
26. Ibid.
27 CDA Bishops' Letters, Baines to Collingridge, 25 February 1827.
28 Ibid. Baines Box Files, 1–3, Burgess to Baines, 23 August 1827.
29 See Chapter 5.
30 CDA Baines Box Files, 1–3, Baines to Rooker, 7 April 1827.
31 Ibid. 24 April 1827.
32 Ibid. Baines to Burgess, 24 April 1827.
33 Ibid. Glover to Baines, 1 May 1827.
34 Ibid.
35 Ibid. Glover to Burgess, 7 May 1827.
36 Ibid. Baines to Burgess, 9 June 1827.
37 Ibid.
38 Ibid. 17 June 1827.
39 J. B. Dockery, *Collingridge*, pp. 245 ff.
40 CDA, Baines Box Files 3–5, Baines to Collingridge, 7 to 15 June 1827.
41 Ibid. Baines Box Files, 4, Baines to Collingridge, 12 January 1829.

42 Ibid. Baines to Burgess, March 1829.
43 CDA, Bishops' Letters, Birdsall to Baines, 18 March 1829.
44 Ibid. Baines Box Files, 4, Baines to Burgess, 28 March 1829.
45 Ampleforth Journal, vol. xv.
46 Ibid.
47 Downside Archives, G341, Leavis Spain to Birdsall, 8 June 1829.
48 Ibid. G359, Brown to Deday, 8 June 1829.
49 CDA, Baines Box Files, 4, Baines to Burgess, 28 March 1829.
50 Ibid. Baines to Brindle, 28 March 1829.
51 Ibid. Trenchard Street Chapel File, Baines to Brindle, March 1829.
52 Ibid. Rowe to Brindle, March 1829.
53 Ibid. Baines Box Files, 4, Baines to Brindle, 28 March 1829.
54 Ibid. Bishops' letters, Jesuit Provincial to Collingridge, March 1829.
55 Ibid. Baines to Burgess, 28 March 1829.
56 Ibid.

5

Vicar Apostolic: The First Turbulent Year

The homecoming

Bishop Baines arrived in London on a morning, which he described as one of 'smoke and mist and hurricane'[1] and contrasted it all unfavourably with the land from which he had come:

> My imagination is still in a country with a bright, cloudless sky and a landscape composed of vines, olives, cypresses and pines, edifices wild, luxuriant and beautiful in the vegetation productions and works of art which ravish the fancy and transport it to other worlds and other ages. Here I have not seen the sun and all that I see around me in the vegetable world seems of a character that never requires any. The neat clean houses, the wide airy streets, the well-dressed people, the splendid equipages bespeak a nation rich and comfortable – the almost total absence of everything that does not immediately contribute to bodily animal comfort and particularly of public edifices and public places for the comfort of the people bespeak, I fear, a nation selfish and unsocial.[2]

Baines went on to dismiss St Paul's Cathedral, which he toured in six minutes, as 'a pretty church or mausoleum', and compared it with the magnificence of St Peter's, 'Christianity's mighty shrine above the martyr's tomb'.[3] His three years in Rome continued to have a lasting effect on him, influencing his choice of buildings for his residence, college and churches, his views on church music and vestments, and, above all, his passionate belief in authority centralized in the bishop, a view which did not appeal to secular priests, religious, or laity.

The fourteen tumultuous years of Baines's vicariate were to see a constant struggle on the bishop's part to exert what he considered to be his legitimate authority, and on the part of others to resist encroachment of passionately-held rights. Baines's main conflict was with the Benedictines, originally because of Downside's refusal to turn itself into a seminary under the direct control of the bishop, but leading on to a dispute over the validity of their vows and their legal right to control the Bath mission. Baines was soon to become embroiled in other disputes, with the nuns of Cannington and with the Jesuits, raising similar issues concerning authority. These conflicts were to loom large in the first years of Baines's vicariate, and in London in the autumn of 1829 he was preparing to tackle them with the obstinacy, the lack of tact and stubborn courage which characterized his whole life.

Observers in different parts of the country noted Baines's arrival in London and wondered about his intentions. Fr William Dunstan Scott writing to Fr Deday, the Benedictine Provincial in the south, reported: 'I saw him for a few minutes yesterday, he looks healthy. Not a word nor a whisper passed about his late efforts with the Propaganda.'[4]

Fr Thomas Robinson, Baines's former colleague at Ampleforth and now working on the mission in Lancashire, wrote: 'Of Dr Baines's intentions I have heard something, but understand he will be stopped in the main one, namely in that of bringing the House of Downside under his obeisance.'[5]

Prior Burgess at Ampleforth was worried about his own future, which was bound up with that of Bishop Baines. He was concerned that he was so long in coming to any fixed purpose about his episcopal seminary, and the transfer of at least part of the Benedictine community at Ampleforth. He wrote to Fr Brindle at Bath:

> You are sensible how uncomfortable I feel in not daring to act in a way that will be of service to our plans. If any of the novices were to hesitate going forward or think of going to Ushaw, at present I could do nothing. Did I know for certain our future plans, I should think myself authorized in dissuading them from joining our house in the present state, to join the other where their labours were likely to do more good and where union was likely to be lasting and productive of greater happiness to themselves. At present I am at a loss what to do and know not whither to direct my thoughts.[6]

He wrote again to Brindle the following week, wondering whether Bishop Baines had any intention of coming to visit Ampleforth and picking out some boys for his new establishment. He showed his anxiety as he ended: 'You may be sure all are very anxious to hear how our fates are to be run.'[7]

Baines's seminary

Baines was in no hurry to end all these conjectures. He spent about ten days in London, before returning at the end of September to his house at Bathampton, which he had left over three years before. He must have found it very different from the days when Anna de Mendoza filled the house with life and laughter. She had married Sir Patrick Bellew and set up her own establishment in the Bath area. Baines saw her occasionally, though, and on visits away instructed Fr Brindle to ask Anna to go up to Bathampton and supervise things.[8]

After such a long absence from England, one would have expected Baines to have been immersed in the immediate problems of his vicariate. Instead, he could think only of his plans for a new seminary, which he believed to be the main means of remedying the conditions of the Western District. He sent a report to Rome giving a general outline of these conditions:

> There are about 10,000–12,000 Catholics among at least two million non-Catholics. About fifty missions served by priests of every nationality as necessity demands. The Bishop collects English, Irish, French who often do not know the language of their flock. In many places in the Western District the Catholic Religion is declining. And little wonder, when the whole of Wales with its half million inhabitants has only one priest who speaks the language. The late Vicar Apostolic who was indeed a saintly man, full of religious zeal, but frustrated in his hopes and broken up by infirmities withdrew to a convent in a remote part of the District where he was almost inaccessible to all and remained there unknown. When conscience or necessity compelled him to go forth and visit some of the missions in his vast District (for he never visited the whole of it) this venerable old man made the journey alone on the imperial of a diligence [roof of a public stagecoach for luggage and passengers paying the cheapest fares] without clerics, without servants, carrying his pontificals in a bag, a laughing stock to the infidels but a shame to the faithful.[9]

It would have been characteristic of Bishop Collingridge to have travelled as cheaply as possible and characteristic of Baines to have criticized him for doing so. This was a totally unfair estimate of the work of Bishop Collingridge, who had been a conscientious and much-loved bishop, and under his regime the problem of providing a regular supply of priests had not been an insurmountable one; some missions were served by Benedictine, Jesuit or Franciscan priests, others by priests from Ireland, where Collingridge had many contacts, and a small number by priests coming from seminaries in other Districts. Collingridge realized that financial resources were the greatest problem. Many missions were too poor to pay for the upkeep of a resident priest, and many priests were forced to supplement their meagre income and that of their church. Fr Edgeworth in Bristol, for example, was reported to have made metal crucifixes and statues for sale, and even engaged in part-time scavenging work for the city council.[10]

Baines's concentration on raising money for the new episcopal seminary deflected money from these poor missions, and later there were even reports that he used money left as endowments for particular missions. To Baines, however, the provision of a seminary for the training of priests in the District was of such overwhelming importance that it overrode all other considerations, and he was prepared to use every means, even those which some considered devious and unworthy of a bishop. Having been thwarted in his plans to turn Downside into a seminary under his control, or to persuade the Downside community to exchange with Ampleforth, he was now fastening his hopes on the idea formed in Rome that the Benedictine vows taken in England were invalid. In his view the English Benedictines were not monks but secular priests, and thus subject to the authority of the bishop. He hoped that a decree from Rome would confirm this, and any *sanatio* issued would only validate the vows of those Benedictines willing to place themselves under his direct control.

To make clear his views on the matter, Baines wrote to Prior Barber asking him and other colleagues to meet him at his house in Bathampton. He had hoped that no one at Downside knew about his efforts in Rome to have the English Benedictine vows declared invalid, but to his chagrin the news had already been spread to England by Nicholas Wiseman, the rector of the English college in Rome. Thus Prior Barber and Fr Joseph Brown, his deputy and an expert in canon law, came to Bathampton well prepared to counter all Baines's arguments and to take immediate action just as soon as Baines had declared his intentions.

Baines described the meeting in a letter to Burgess at Ampleforth, telling him of the arrival of Prior Barber and Fr Brown. In discussing the question of the bishop's authority over them, they had been prepared to concede that Baines had a right to visit Downside, but were not prepared to admit any other. Goaded on by what he regarded as this insolence, Baines launched into new demands, which he maintained were sanctioned by Rome. The Benedictines were not to send any missionaries out of the district without his permission; they were to have no secular college at all, or one restricted in numbers; they were to make an annual contribution from their funds in support of the new seminary.[11] These imperious demands brought no direct response, Prior Barber merely saying that he would have to consult his superior, President Birdsall. Baines then produced what he considered to be his trump card, saying that it was useless the Benedictines trying to oppose him, for their vows were invalid and that, as their bishop, he would not acknowledge Downside as a monastery and would claim obedience from them all as secular priests.[12] Prior Barber and Fr Brown refused to discuss the subject any further and left as quickly as possible to report the matter to President Birdsall.

Birdsall took forceful action, quite unexpected by Baines, in sending two delegates to Rome to put the Benedictine case for the validity of the vows of the English congregation. These were Fr Marsh, who had twice been Prior of Ampleforth, and the same Fr Joseph Brown who had met Baines at Bathampton.

Withdrawal of faculties

Baines was so angry at hearing the news that he took a precipitate step, regarded by some as an act of revenge. He withdrew the faculties of all the Downside monks, so that they were forbidden to exercise their priestly functions in the missions of the District. There was even some doubt whether the monks could administer the sacraments within the monastery, although they still continued to do so, and they were banned from hearing the confessions of their students. The future Bishop Ullathorne, who was training for the priesthood at Downside, described how, as a junior, he would sit on a tub in the yard outside and wait for the local mission priest to come and hear his confession.[13]

The decision aroused enormous resentment among the Benedictines and dismayed friends and former colleagues of Baines. A John Woods wrote scathingly to President Birdsall, wondering why Baines had made his profession and continued as a member of a community in which 'he now discovers so many irregularities',[14] while Andrew Ryding, another Benedictine priest, also writing to the President, stressed that it had never been necessary for founders of monasteries to ask permission of former Vicars Apostolic. These Bishops had been 'Fathers and protectors of our order. He [Baines] seeks to destroy it. I wish he would study well the character of a Bishop. Has he the power to annul our vows and to extinguish with a breath the authority and jurisdiction of our superiors? Their jurisdiction rests upon the same grounds as his own. What presumption! What arrogance!'[15]

Criticism was to be expected from such quarters. More worrying was the reaction in Rome, where Cardinal Cappellari, Prefect of Propaganda, formerly a supporter of Baines, was dismayed by Baines's withdrawal of faculties from the Benedictines at Downside, and in January 1830 wrote to the Bishop recommending that these should be restored. It was undoubtedly a factor influencing the deliberations in Rome to decide the validity of the Benedictine vows.

The disapproval of Cardinal Weld was also a blow, although he adopted a conciliatory attitude to the whole affair, trying to mediate between Baines and the Benedictines, urging the Bishop to show restraint and complimenting Downside on its patience: 'I am much edified with the temper of forbearance which has been shown by the generality of your body in the very trying circumstances in which you have been placed . . .'[16]

The Cardinal's disapproval of Baines's conduct was shared by his son-in-law, Lord Clifford, the most important member of the Catholic community in the Western District, and a patron whom the Bishop would not wish to antagonize. He tried to maintain a line of communication with him through his son, Fr Edward Clifford, a priest in Yorkshire.

It was an unnecessary dispute, which soured relationships with Baines in England and Rome, and which the bishop could not hope to win. Cardinal Weld continued to mediate between the two parties in an attempt to reach a settlement in which the Bishop would not lose face, but as late in August 1830 President Birdsall was still complaining that Fr Deday, the Benedictine Provincial, was trying to obtain renewal of his faculties from Baines.

Crisis at Ampleforth

While all this confrontation was developing in the Western District, affairs at Ampleforth were reaching a crisis. The religious novices had become so disenchanted with Burgess's regime as prior, that they sent a petition to President Birdsall during his visit to their monastery, asking for Burgess's removal from office. The petition was signed by all except Burgess's allies and fellow conspirators, Frs Metcalfe and Rooker who had always admired Baines when they studied under him at Ampleforth, and by a B. Dinmore, who concurred in the opinions expressed, but thought that the same object might be obtained by other means. Birdsall's action or lack of action on this occasion was strongly criticized by the Benedictine chronicler, Allanson. Birdsall told Burgess that, as a result of the petition, it would be impossible for him to be elected prior again at the next Chapter in the following year, thus finally persuading Burgess to throw in his lot with Bishop Baines.

At the same time Birdsall took no positive action to break up the conspiracy between Burgess, Metcalfe and Rooker, although 'sufficient evidence had come to his knowledge that the Prior was at the head of a cabal against presidential and constitutional Government of the congregation'.[17]

Birdsall could have sent Frs Metcalfe and Rooker into missions, preferably far away from Ampleforth, thus depriving Burgess of his support and making it difficult for him to carry out his plans to remove at least part of the community south to join Bishop Baines. Instead Birdsall did nothing, except alarm Burgess, and then left Ampleforth until the following spring, April 1830.

Almost immediately after Birdsall's departure, Burgess also left Ampleforth and travelled south to join Baines at Bathampton. He stayed there for eight weeks, and during this time the two discussed their plans for the next few months, in which they both hoped that Rome would declare the English Benedictine vows invalid. This would not only give the Bishop wider powers over the monks of Downside, but also convince those at Ampleforth that there was no future for them in the monastery, and persuade them to journey south to join Baines. In the first place their allegiance as secular priests would be to the Vicar Apostolic of the Northern District, Bishop Smith, but he was unlikely to stand in the way of priests wishing to leave the area.

During Burgess's stay at Bathampton, Baines was negotiating the purchase of Prior Park mansion on the hills above Bath, which he thought would be an imposing centre for his episcopal seminary. Prior Park had been on the market for some time, and Baines was hoping to buy it for about £20,000, a drop of several thousand from the original asking price, but even this was a colossal amount of money for him to raise. Burgess supported him in this decision, believing that the purchase of a large house for a seminary was now the only solution.

Burgess had not lost hope of bringing about an amicable settlement between the Bishop and the Benedictines, and saw himself in the role of peacemaker with Downside. His hopes were dashed by the refusal of Prior Barber to visit him during his long stay at Bathampton, as he later complained to his cousin, Fr Brindle.[18]

At the end of November 1829, with no final decision on the validity of the vows from Rome, and the purchase of Prior Park still not completed, Burgess decided that he would have to go back to Ampleforth. Baines then made the surprise decision to return with the Prior and remain there throughout the winter. He gave as his reasons his shortage of money and the evil effects of the Bath climate upon his health. These reasons were probably genuine, as Baines was always short of money and the dampness of the Bath air particularly affected him in winter, but there must have been other reasons for such an extraordinary decision to leave the Western District again for a long period. Once again he handed over the administration of the vicariate to Fr Brindle, his Vicar General, and also instructed Brindle to hurry on the business of purchasing Prior Park as speedily as possible.

The religious and novices of Ampleforth did not welcome Baines with any great enthusiasm, and it was not until he had been at the monastery for twenty-four hours that any sought the Bishop out to ask for his customary blessing.[19] The frosty relations did not improve, when the story spread that Prior Burgess had given Baines a new suit of clothes and a new carriage, presumably out of Ampleforth funds.[20]

Matters continued much the same until the day of a confrère's funeral when, after returning from the churchyard, the monks went into the refectory and there Bishop Baines joined them. A Fr Augustine Lowe has described how:

> Baines entered the room with a ground work plan of Prior Park in his hand and spreading it on the table began to explain it to the Religious and I think concluded by saying, 'I have purchased this for my future seminary'. Before leaving the room he asked if any of the religious would be kind enough to make him a copy of it. Mr Cockshute [the prefect] immediately offered his services to see it done by one of the boys. His Lordship became a very frequent visitor to the Religious refectory up till the time of his leaving Ampleforth. He spent at least 4 evenings in the week with the community after supper till compline, about an hour entertaining us with a recital of what he had seen and witnessed in his travels thro France and Italy, explaining how he would conduct his establishment, Prior Park, the manner in which he would bring up his young men (having as he said by travelling thro France and Italy become acquainted with many institutions and also obtained leave to send 2 or 3 students to each of them) – he would place in each of these seminaries young men to complete their education.[21]

This account demonstrates the force of Baines's personality, which was able to achieve a complete transformation in the monks' attitude towards him. He succeeded in persuading them to abandon their previous hostility, which arose from all they had heard of Baines's negotiations with their unpopular Prior and from suspicions that the two of them were plotting to overthrow Ampleforth. About three weeks before the Bishop's departure, the Religious began to seek private interviews with him, and Fr Augustine Lowe then noted that:

> Nothing was thought of but a complete break-up of this Establishment, one person contriving how the goods and chattels of this house would be removed to Prior Park . . . 2 days before my leaving for Easingwold, the novices gave up the habit, why or wherefore they took the step, I cannot positively say – they had a private conference after compline till 10 o'clock, either among themselves, with Mr Burgess or the Bishop . . . next morning they resigned the habit immediately after Prime in Mr Burgess's room, who did not seem at all surprised at the step taken. The reason appeared to me a general idea that Ampleforth was no longer to exist and that the Religious's vows were null and void.[22]

Another monk, Fr Alban Caldwell, also recorded that

> with regard to our vows, I am perfectly convinced from what I heard directly and indirectly from Dr B that they were *ipso facto* null and avoid. Baines said: 'How can that be broken which never existed.' He gave us also to understand that it was not only he who believed that our vows were null and void; Cardinal Cappellari was perfectly convinced of the same.[23]

Baines followed up his persuasive campaign within Ampleforth by inviting Fr Edward Clifford, who was working in one of the Yorkshire missions, to join him at Ampleforth. Edward Clifford, whose father, Lord Clifford of Chudleigh, had great influence in the Western District, would be an invaluable acquisition to his cause. Edward Clifford came to Ampleforth in January 1830, and it was not long before he came under Baines's spell, believing that his vows must be invalid. He was a man of unstable character, and for a short time became a staunch supporter of Baines.

Opposition to the Bishop

While Baines's cause was going well at Ampleforth, the forces of opposition were gathering elsewhere. Fr Glover was now beginning to have serious doubts about Baines, although he had always been a great friend and supporter of the Bishop. He wrote to Burgess:

> Do not identify me with all of Dr Baines's proceedings. I believe him to be possessed of great talents and resources within himself, but he is not infallible. He has warm feelings and these may occasionally lead him astray, and I do not unfortunately perhaps sacrifice my own opinion to him or anybody else, as often as I ought. There are some circumstances in Dr B's plans, which I do not know yet. He has sought an interview with me, which I have thought it prudent to avoid, on account of the official situation which I hold as one of the *Regimen*. You see therefore my situation . . .[24]

By February 1830, having heard news of Baines's activities at Ampleforth, Glover was completely disillusioned. He wrote to Burgess sorrowfully:

> I have in the first instance persuaded myself that Dr Baines would not do anything prejudicial to that order, which educated him and exalted him to his present eminence . . . [yet] as his plans became known they seem totally subversive of the Benedictine order in England . . . history will record that he gave the blow and, as he has struck Downside, he has ruined Ampleforth, at which we had been labouring these years and raised it to some degree of eminence.[25]

Baines did not seem much affected by Glover turning against him, and made no attempt to justify himself to his friend. He had a curious capacity to shake off anything he found disagreeable in the past and turn to the future. It gave him a certain strength, but also caused resentment and a sense of betrayal in those who considered themselves abandoned.

At the beginning of 1830 Baines was more worried at the rumours coming from Rome that the Benedictine delegates were gaining favour at the Vatican, and that their vows would be confirmed as valid. When Frs Marsh and Brown first reached Rome in December 1829 they were given a very hostile reception by Cardinal Cappellari, who had favoured Baines's plans, and regarded the Benedictines as uncooperative. When the two presented their case to Propaganda in a long memorial in elegant Latin, it was rejected as being too classical and the writing too small to read. Fr Brown immediately rewrote it in more everyday Latin and in a large hand, so that none could fail to read it.[26]

The delegates were given no help in finding accommodation and had great difficulty in obtaining anything suitable. Eventually they managed to find lodgings in the monastery of San Gregorio on the Coelian Hill. It was extremely cold there in the middle of winter and Fr Brown kept warm each night by skipping. News of this unusual activity reached Cardinal Cappellari, who was curious to see what was going on, and Fr Brown reported:

> Well, he came, and I shall never forget his emotion. At first I began with single strokes, and then cross strokes forwards and backwards. All these feats were duly applauded, but the furore was reserved for the double, when the old Cardinal clapped his hands and fairly shouted with delight. After that there was no more coolness at Propaganda . . . my business was expedited and everything settled to my satisfaction.[27]

Rome's decision

The appeal of Brown's personality was not the only factor which brought Cardinal Cappellari round to the Benedictine view; he was also impressed by the arguments put forward in the memorial and shaken in his faith in Baines when he heard of the latter's precipitate decision to suspend the faculties of the whole of the Downside community. By February 1830 Cappellari had already informed Baines that the vows of the English Benedictines were considered valid, and that a *sanatio* was to be issued, but not on Baines's terms. Baines had hoped that Ampleforth would receive the *sanatio* confirming the validity of vows, only if the religious agreed to transfer their allegiance to the Bishop; instead any of the religious who wished to follow the Bishop to Prior Park had to apply to Rome for secularization and cease to be Benedictines. Baines travelled south to Bathampton in February 1830 knowing what no one else knew in England, that all his plans had been overturned and that Prior Park would have to be staffed with the few from Ampleforth who would be prepared to forsake their Benedictine calling and apply for secularization. It was a bitter blow, but Baines was already planning how to react when the news of the *sanatio* would reach Ampleforth and Downside.

The effects at Ampleforth

President Birdsall took the news to Ampleforth at the beginning of April 1830. He accepted Burgess's resignation as Prior and then, before returning to his mission for Easter, asked him to remain at Ampleforth until he was able to return to receive the accounts of the House, as soon as these should be ready. Birdsall then appointed Fr Jerome Hampson as temporary superior, and departed for Cheltenham. Allanson in his Chronicles strongly criticized Birdsall for abandoning Ampleforth and leaving it for three weeks 'to the mercy of its enemies' and claimed that most of the evils which befell the community were accomplished during this interval. Fr Hampson asked Burgess to retain his authority for the time being, thus giving him *carte blanche* to do as he pleased. Burgess, Metcalfe and Rooker, together with Brindle at Bath petitioned Rome for secularization and to be placed under the jurisdiction of Dr Baines, entrusting the petition to Dr Smith, the Vicar Apostolic of the Northern District. Four of the novices also decided to leave and go to Prior Park, while Allanson claimed:

> the parents of different students were applied to by letter, petitioning to be allowed to accompany their superiors and masters to Prior Park. Even the domestic servants were tampered with, some were engaged to leave and others were hired to go to Prior Park, so that the College of Ampleforth assumed the appearance at this period of becoming nearly deserted as soon as all these arrangements were carried into execution.[28]

By the time that President Birdsall returned to Ampleforth, Allanson claimed that Burgess, Metcalfe and Rooker believed that they no longer owed any allegiance to the Benedictines and assumed a high tone. The ex-prior presented the accounts, but when these were strongly disputed by the President and Fr Glover, who accompanied him, Burgess refused to convey the property of Ryland to other names, if the accounts were not accepted. Fr Glover later claimed in his testimony that on the strength of Dr Smith's *Exequatur* to their indult of secularization, 'they bullied, they threatened they would walk off whenever they pleased and if we did not come into their terms they would advertise a sale of everything, pay the debts and go about their business'.[29]

Apparently the threat forced the President to agree to accept Burgess's accounts, and he signed a legal instrument 'agreeing to pay all the liabilities of the ex-monks, while they agreed to take their names off the title deeds of the property belonging to the Benedictines'.[30]

The dispute over the accounts and property, however, rumbled on for another five years until it was settled by arbitration in Bristol.

Burgess, although he appeared to have got the better of President Birdsall, was not happy at the course of events. He had never wanted to become a secular priest, and always hoped that Baines's episcopal seminary would be staffed by the Benedictine community. He was also irritated by Baines's lack of communication since February for, although he had known of the impending *sanatio* since then, he had not informed his allies at Ampleforth. In his letter to Baines on 3 April 1830, Burgess was critical of the Bishop for the first time, expressing surprise that the latter had made no mention of the documents that the President brought with him, documents which he had received from Propaganda in Rome. These had given Birdsall and Glover the opportunity to claim that this was a *sanatio* for the validity of the monk's vows, and Burgess had not known how to respond.[31]

Baines replied with considerable bravado that, 'My opinions respecting the original invalidity of the vows is not and cannot alter, but they must now be considered as valid and obeyed by all who receive the *sanatio* and those who do not wish to receive it must still obey, unless they apply for a personal absolution from their vows'.[32]

The Bishop was still trying to salvage something from the débâcle, writing again to Burgess with heavy underlinings: 'Tell the Religious from me that I am still as convinced as ever that the vows are invalid and that I will never recede from any promise I made to them, if they will call upon me for their fulfilment. Read this to them.'[33]

It was unlikely, however, that any of the monks of Ampleforth, except Metcalfe, Rooker and Burgess, would join Baines at Prior Park. Burgess, in spite of his irritation at some of Baines's conduct, was still intensely loyal. He wrote to Baines on 7 April: 'I beg your Lordship to consider me as a pocket handkerchief to be put in any situation you may think'.[34]

Baines clearly felt some responsibility for the ex-prior, who had sacrificed so much for him, telling him: 'You may gazette yourself as the future President, rector, or what ever we shall denominate, the person who governs the college under the Bishop, of the secular college of Prior Park . . .'.[35]

Burgess could also still be very useful to him, bringing 'to your future college all the pupils and means you can consistent with honesty, honour and good faith and without regard to what the interested and foolish may say against you'.[36] Baines continued to send instructions to Burgess throughout April, urging him to 'delay signing away your legal hold on the property till you have heard from me. They shall still have every farthing that belongs to them . . . But we must not allow them to do us more injustice than is necessary.'[37]

On 19 April Baines was discussing domestic arrangements at Prior

Park, and asking Burgess whether Mrs Davis, the Ampleforth housekeeper should come, or whether he should bring his own housekeeper from Bathampton.[38]

By May 1830, Burgess's position at Ampleforth was getting more and more difficult. He wrote to Baines that: 'Our brethren are getting virulent. Mr Metcalfe read this morning in a letter from one of them cautioning him against being led to the Devil by me and others.'[39]

And: 'The lay people are taught to believe we have acted contrary to our religious vows in what we have done ... they are trying to raise divisions ...'[40]

In spite of all this unpleasantness, Burgess was resolved to stay on for a few more weeks and, acting on the solicitor's advice, '... keep hold of the land and stock till all bills are paid or money put into our hands to discharge them'.[41]

Finally Burgess reported to Baines that a settlement had been reached with President Birdsall and Fr Glover:

> That upon the retirement of the Rev. T. Burgess, J. Rooker and E. Metcalfe, in consequence of the indult obtained by them from Rome, they recd at the time of surrender of the property into the hands of the Rev Ed Glover, the superior *pro tempore* of our establishment at that place, a sum of money as a viaticum for their journey to Prior Park, over and above the balance of accounts delivered me.[42]

It is pleasant to note that the document ended by promising the three ex-monks the offer of assistance in return for their years of service, 'when age, infirmity or necessity came upon them'.[43]

By 21 May, Burgess and Rooker were on their way to Prior Park, hearing all sorts of rumours on their way. In York they heard that many articles had been secretly sent out of Ampleforth at the midnight hour, while in Leeds that the monks were forsaking their vows in order to marry'.[44]

Burgess continued to recruit pupils for the school at Prior Park. He saw parents of Ampleforth boys, both at York and Leeds, and noted that six boys could be guaranteed from each place.[45] Rooker was to stay at Leeds for another week and then go on to see parents at Liverpool to explain the situation. These activities seem to contradict Baines's claim that no direct recruiting of boys took place.

While Burgess and Rooker were already on their way, Fr Metcalfe remained at Ampleforth for a few more weeks. Like Burgess he had a great deal to lose by going to Prior Park. He was a brilliant student of languages and appeared to be equally knowledgeable in stock management on the Ampleforth farms. By May 1830 he was already having strong doubts whether he had made the right decision. He remained loyal to Baines and intended to fulfil his promise to teach at Prior Park, but was beginning to regret leaving the Benedictine community. He had spent the past few weeks preparing his cattle for the long trek south, and on 23 May wrote to Burgess in a considerable state of depression: 'I mean to leave this place in the morning with my stock. I am tired to death with calumnies etc etc . . .'[46]

The other monk from Ampleforth, Edward Clifford, who had also applied to Rome for secularization, received news of the *sanatio* on his mission. At first he continued to support Baines but, after hearing of the 'plunder' of Ampleforth, he wrote to the Bishop on 20 May:

> I am aggrieved that such dishonourable, such ungentlemanly proceedings are going on at Ampleforth. Your Lordship is aware that you had no stronger supporter than myself, but how hurt do I feel that under cloak of religion, plunder should be the order of the day at Ampleforth and that this is the work of the hands of those who owe everything they have to a college which now they glory in having uprooted.[47]

Clifford withdrew his offer to help Baines at Prior Park and told him that he was writing to Rome to withdraw his request for secularization. To other people he was still more forceful. Fr Brown at Downside reported to the Provincial, Fr Deday: 'Clifford is now red hot with rage against Baines and co. He has gone around to the parents at Liverpool of children at Ampleforth and exposed the system of Baines and co.'[48]

The news arrives at Downside

All this was not good news to Baines, who had relied on gaining the support of Edward Clifford's father, Lord Clifford, for Prior Park. He was also disturbed by the reports from Downside, where it was rumoured that, on receiving the *sanatio* confirming the validity of the vows, the monks had celebrated well into the night. Prior Barber hastened to reassure him:

> I am sure that you will not willingly and knowingly lend yourself to a calummy of any kind and more especially against one who has never offended you. It has been reported that Mr Samuel Day and Mr Lambert were here on the day that the rescript from Rome arrived and that we remained up until 2 o'clock celebrating a

> triumph over Dr Baines. It is all a total calumny – neither one or the other or indeed any layman was in the house or with us when the rescript arrived. All the community was in bed at the usual hour of 10 o'clock – the only difference that I experienced on the occasion of the rescript was that, while none of the harsh measures pursued against me deprived me of one moment's sleep, the joy at finding that the Holy See considered me as a monk was so great that I could not sleep the whole night.[49]

It was still a humiliation which Baines felt keenly, as he did the defection of those he had thought committed to his cause. He was also angered by the criticism of one of the priests in the Bristol mission, the Jesuit Fr Rowe, who was still pursuing an uneasy ministry with the Franciscan, Fr Edgeworth; Baines wrote to the Jesuit provincial, Fr Brooke: 'He [Rowe] seems to think it incumbent on him to take part in a dispute which unhappily has taken place between me and some of the monks – and the epithets he has often applied to my motives and conduct are of the strongest and most offensive kind. He lately expressed a sort of surprise "that some of the monks did not think of killing the Bishop".'[50]

Rowe's criticisms of his Bishop were undoubtedly a factor in his sudden removal from the Bristol mission at the end of 1830. He was to be the last Jesuit priest there for seventeen years. Baines later expressed in a letter to Propaganda that, as Rowe and Edgeworth could not work together, he felt that Rowe should be the one to leave, being the younger and less experienced man, but this was not the whole story. He was irritated by Rowe's criticism and feared that he was becoming a threat to his authority in the large Bristol mission, where the young priest had many supporters. The latter's summary dismissal prejudiced the Jesuits against Baines and increased their sympathy towards the Benedictines; both came to regard themselves as defenders of the rights and privileges of the religious orders against the arbitrary conduct of the Vicar Apostolic.

Prior Park and the future

Perhaps the greatest blow to Baines at this time was the report that Lady Bellew had turned her back on him, so upset was she at his conduct. This was reported at Downside and not substantiated but, if true, would have been worse than anything he had yet had to bear. Yet, in spite of all his tribulations, mostly brought on by flaws in his own character, Baines was thinking more of the future than of the past. He moved into Prior Park on 1 May 1830, and was full of plans for his new seminary and school, and of far-off dreams of the first Catholic university on English soil since the Reformation.

Notes

1 CDA, Baines Box Files, 4, Baines to Burgess, 16 September 1829.
2 Ibid.
3 Ibid.
4 Downside Archives, G384, Scott to Deday, 16 September 1829.
5 Ibid. G385, Robinson to Kenyon, 17 September 1829.
6 CDA, Baines Box Files, 4, Burgess to Brindle, 29 May 1829.
7 Ibid. 7 September 1829.
8 Ibid. Baines to Brindle, 25 November 1829.
9 See J. B. Dockery, p. 31ff.
10 The English Province of the Society of Jesus Archives, Bristol Papers, Abbott to Grant, 18 May 1891.
11 CDA, Baines Box Files, 4, Baines to Burgess, 1 October 1829.
12 Ibid.
13 William Ullathorne, *An Autobiography* (London, 1868), p. 44.
14 Downside Archives, G399, John Woods to Birdsall, 16 October 1829.
15 Ibid. G409, Ryding to Birdsall, 7 November 1829.
16 Ibid. H149, Weld to Brown, 31 October 1829.
17 Ibid. Allanson's 'Lives of the English Benedictines', unpublished material for the English Benedictine Chapter circa 1855.
18 CDA, Baines Box File, 4, Burgess to Brindle, 1 January 1830.
19 Ampleforth Archives, A268, Lowe to Robinson: Recollections of events at Ampleforth during the winter of 1829/1830.
20 Ampleforth Journal, vol. xxiii, July 1917.
21 Ampleforth Archives, A268.
22 Ibid.
23 Ibid.
24 CDA, Baines Box File 4, Glover to Burgess, 13 December 1829.
25 Ibid. 9 February 1830.
26 Ibid. St Lawrence Papers, 11; Richard Marsh, OSB, *Reminiscences 1794–1830.*
27 H. Van Zeller, *Downside By and Large* p. 137.
28 Ampleforth and Downside Archives, Allanson's 'Lives'.
29 Ibid.
30 Ibid.
31 CDA, Baines Box Files, 4, Burgess to Baines, 3 April 1830.
32 Ibid. Baines to Burgess and Rooker, 3 April 1830.
33 Ibid. 6 April 1830.
34 Ibid. Burgess to Baines, 7 April 1830.
35 Ibid. Baines to Burgess, 10 April 1830.
36 Ibid.
37 Ibid. 19 April 1830.

38 Ibid. 7 May 1830.
39 Ibid. Burgess to Baines, May 1830.
40 Ibid.
41 Ibid.
42 Ibid. 7 May 1830.
43 Ibid.
44 Ibid. Burgess to Brindle, 21 May 1830.
45 Ibid.
46 Ibid. Metcalfe to Burgess, 23 May 1830.
47 Ibid. Bishop's Letters, Clifford to Baines, 20 May 1830.
48 Ibid. Downside Archives, H59, Brown to Deday, 27 May 1830.
49 CDA, Bishops' Letters, Barber to Baines, 19 April 1830.
50 Jesuit Province Archives, Old College of St Francis Xavier 193, Baines to Brooke, 16 December 1830.

6

Prior Park: The Years of Hope 1830–1835

Prior Park before 1830

Baines would have known Prior Park from the time he came to Bath in 1817, not only because it was the finest mansion in the area, but because of its history and literary associations. The estate had once belonged to the Prior of Bath Abbey, who built a priory to use as his summer residence. After the dissolution of the monasteries, the priory fell into decay and, apart from small farmhouses, there was no building at Prior Park until 1733, when Ralph Allen bought the whole estate.

Ralph Allen had started from humble origins to build up a substantial fortune twice over, first by reorganizing the structure of the Post Office, and secondly by opening and developing stone quarries at Coombe Down outside Bath. He was a philanthropist who used a large part of his fortune to help the people of Bath; he built the Bath Mineral Hospital to treat rheumatic diseases, and developed schemes to help the unemployed. The opening of the Bath quarries, although it brought Allen untold wealth, was mainly designed to provide work for labourers and stonemasons. In the same way he viewed the building of a house at Prior Park not only as a home for himself and his family, but as a means of providing work for hundreds of men, and as a demonstration of the durability and beauty of Bath stone.[1]

Allen employed the well-known architect, John Wood, who built the Circus and many of the terraces of Bath. Wood originally planned to erect a much more extensive building, but was not allowed by Allen to complete it as he wished.[2] He had wanted to build Doric stables, a hay house and pigeon cotes at a low level on the east side, so as not to detract from the majesty of his central mansion. Ralph Allen would have none of these, and insisted on Wood building living quarters which he and his family could occupy while the main building was slowly going up.

In his imagination, though, Wood continued to think of Prior Park as the building he had originally designed, and wrote about the Doric stables, hay loft and pigeon cotes as if they actually existed. This would confuse future historians of Prior Park such as James Shepherd, who tried to make out how Bishop Baines's extensions had risen out of these rural buildings.[3]

Wood finally fell out with his employer about the plan for the central mansion, which he had designed to look down from an eminent position towards the city of Bath. The most dramatic feature was to be a magnificent portico with six great pillars, which was to be the main entrance to the house, with a stone staircase to ascend on either side. For some reason Allen refused to have the staircase built, which meant that the entrance could not be on the north side of the house, and had to be transferred to the far plainer and less interesting south side. Wood was so angry about this that he withdrew from the work; it was taken over by Richard Jones, who finished the outside of the house to Wood's designs, except for the disputed features.

The *Bath Guide* of 1819 thought that all the majesty of the building was without.[4] And all the majesty on the north side was certainly due to Wood overcoming as he did the difficulties of building such a house in a demanding landscape. The north side has been described as 'a triumph'.[5]

The interior of the house owes little to Wood, except for the original chapel, which the same architectural historian has described as 'a place of chilling excellence. If it were in Venice, it would be celebrated as a small masterpiece – here it is little visited, overshadowed by the fine chapel of 1844 by J. J. Scoles in the west wing.'[6]

The rest of the house has been so altered by fire and subsequent rebuilding that it is difficult to visualize how it would have been in Ralph Allen's day.

Allen continued to develop the parkland and gardens of Prior Park over a period of thirty years. He planted a wilderness area of trees and shrubs on the west side, built dams across the old priory fishponds in three places, and erected across the first of these dams the third Palladian bridge to be built in England. In the 1760s he employed Capability Brown, who developed the parkland as one continuous landscape up from the fishponds to the Palladian bridge and on to the house above. On the wilderness side of the park, Allen built a grotto for his wife, receiving much encouragement from the poet, Alexander Pope, whose grotto in Twickenham had become famous; Mrs Allen spent many hours in the grotto and buried her pet Great Dane, Miss Bounce, there. The epitaph can still be seen on the floor.[7]

When established at Prior Park, Ralph Allen became the friend and patron of writers. He entertained Alexander Pope, and the novelists Samuel Richardson and Henry Fielding. Pope stayed there for long periods between 1737 and his death in 1744, establishing himself in rooms in the west wing, and spending many hours in the wilderness, in which he composed some of his poems. His opinion of Ralph Allen varied according to his mood, praising him at one moment for his generosity and humility, and at another carping at the spartan regime at Prior Park, the simplicity of the food and the single glass of wine a day. Pope was, however, well-known for imposing on his friends.

Henry Fielding was kinder in his unstinted praise of Allen, taking him as the model for the character of Squire Allworthy in *Tom Jones*: 'Neither Mr Allworthy's house nor his heart were shut against any part of mankind, but they were both more particularly open to men of merit. To say the truth, this was the only house in the kingdom where you were sure to gain a dinner by deserving it.'[8]

After Allen's death, Prior Park passed to his favourite niece, Gertrude, the wife of William Warburton, Bishop of Gloucester. Warburton, at the time an Anglican vicar in Cambridgeshire, had been introduced to Allen by Pope and appears to have spent more than half his time at Prior Park, in spite of his clerical commitments. It was through Allen's influence with William Pitt the Elder, MP for Bath, that Warburton was made Dean of Bristol in 1757 and Bishop of Gloucester only two years later.[9]

Allen also employed his builder, Richard Jones, to put the Bristol deanery and the palace at Gloucester in good repair. Jones was very critical of the Warburtons, believing that he had been ill-treated by them, and after Allen's death, he wrote a scathing report about his niece:

> in about four years after his death she strips the house of all the furniture and sold it . . . sold all the marble chimney pieces, marble tables . . . left nothing but bare walls . . . In short, I find her so arbitrary, I was glad when she ordered me off, for it would have grieved me to the Heart to have seen all things pulled down and sold for trifles . . . so that after his death he was soon forgot of them, as though he never was there.[10]

Richard Jones was very biased, and how much of this was true is not known. Gertrude Warburton was unfortunate in that she lost her only child, whom she called after Ralph Allen; after her death Prior Park passed to another of Allen's nieces, Maud, the wife of Cornwallis,

Viscount Hawarden, and was then left to their son, Ralph, who inherited in 1802. After the death of Ralph and his half-brother, Cornwallis, the mansion passed out of the Allen family and was sold first to a Mr Chandler Brown and then to a Quaker, Mr John Thomas of Bristol who, after the death of his brother, put it on the market, first in 1828, when it did not reach its asking price, and again in 1829.

Baines's great investment

It is no wonder that Baines was attracted to such a house and grounds, with its superb setting and its romantic associations with the past. He had started considering the possibilities of the estate before he left for Rome in 1826, when there were rumours that its Quaker owners would be putting it up for sale, and he instructed Fr Brindle to watch the situation for him. In 1828, he heard that the estate had been auctioned at a sale in London but withdrawn, as it did not reach its asking price, at the time said to be £25,000. It was a sum which made even Peter Baines pause to reflect.

By the time that Baines returned to England in August 1829, Prior Park was once more on the market, and Baines was hopeful that he could buy it for little more than £20,000. He negotiated with its Quaker owners until he departed for Ampleforth in November, leaving his friend Brindle to represent his interests. All through the weeks leading up to Christmas, while trying to convince the students of the invalidity of their vows and the rosy future that awaited them at Prior Park, Baines was worried that the sale of the mansion might fall through. He wrote to Brindle on 30 November:

> I get anxious about Prior Park, as we all do. I wish you would desire Mr English [his solicitor] to get with as little delay as possible an answer of yes, or nay from our Quaker friends. Let him say I neither can nor will wait any longer. I hope it may not be necessary to go beyond 20, but if it should, I still wish him to purchase and that with as little delay as possible.[11]

Baines was also concerned with the wider question of the reaction of the people of Bath to a Catholic college on their doorstep. He supported Brindle's idea of putting a notice in the *Bath and Cheltenham Gazette*, and actually drafted one himself: 'We understand that the mansion and estate of Prior Park has lately been purchased by the Rt Rev Dr Baines Catholic Bishop of the Western District, as a college of the said District and a residence for his lordship himself'.[12] Baines then worried that this was too bald a statement of the facts and wondered whether the people of Bath ought to have more details and explanation. With uncharacteristic modesty he referred the wording of the notice to his solicitor, Mr English. In the year which had seen great passions aroused by the passing of the Catholic Emancipation Act, nobody could be too careful.

In the first weeks of December, Baines was still worrying that the great prize of Prior Park might be lost, and on 10 December he wrote again to Brindle, urging him on:

> I give you clearly to understand *ab initio* that I have not limited myself to any particular sum and that should it be got for half way between 20 and 25, I should not be dissatisfied. I give you power to regulate in conjunction with Mr English whatever details should be necessary as to price, manner, time etc, I should like to get possession no later than Lady Day.[13]

Baines received the news that Prior Park was his while still in bed on the following morning, 11 December 1829. He wrote immediately to Fr Brindle to tell him that everyone rejoiced:

> We all thank you for your sensible decision not to let the place be lost. As to the price, *providebit Deus*. I fancy I see his holy hand in all these events so wonderfully combined and all tending as far as human foresight can enable us to judge, to the greater glory of religion and the so long desolate district of the west.[14]

Brindle had agreed on a price of £22,000 for the mansion, and had paid a £100 deposit on behalf of Baines. He also signed a deed of mortgage for £5,102 9s, but he, together with everyone else, had no idea where all the money was to come from to buy Prior Park and to pay for all the alterations and improvements which Baines planned. He wrote on 20 December 1829: 'The feelings on all sides about your Lordship's purchase is very great. All are glad, Catholics and Protestants, rich and poor, friends and enemies, the last mentioned, because they say it will do Bath so much good. All are surprised where your Lordship has got the money. The price is not known positively – some say extravagant things.'[15]

Baines's friend, Fr Glover, also had his doubts about the price, writing to Baines from Crosby:

> As to the material, I am of course unacquainted with your resources. But £20,000 8s is an enormous sum!, a great deal too

> much I think for the property [actually £2,000 less than Baines was to pay]. And where is it to come from? I must own I have no complete confidence in the collection which will be made thro the Kingdom for you. However I hope it may be found some where.[16]

Another correspondent, Stephen Morgan, concentrated on the likely reaction of Downside to the purchase of Prior Park: 'I am extremely glad to hear that you have purchased Prior Park. This establishment will ere long sorely annoy the Downside people, whilst it will prove of the utmost importance to your District.'[17]

In the next few years the school at Prior Park, with its proximity to Bath and the publicity attached to its foundation, was to take pupils from Downside. Yet in the long term Downside was to survive, while Baines's school did not.

It is doubtful whether Baines himself had any clearer idea as to where the money was to come from, although the bishops agreed to support him by having a collection in every Catholic chapel in the kingdom. This collection was never to bring in more than a few thousand pounds, and Baines was forced to turn to individual benefactors, well-to-do women, who were willing to risk their money on his behalf. The Hon. Miss Crewe lent him £20,000 and a Miss Bettington £5,000. Fr Brindle's uncle also agreed to lend him £1,500. So Baines soon had ready money at his disposal, but was disinclined to remember that he would have to make regular payments of interest or annuities.

By Christmas time 1830, Miss Bettington was becoming worried about sinking her money in such an uncertain investment. Brindle reported to Baines that:

> She began to ask questions whether her money would be safe or rather whether, in case of disturbance and revolution in England, she should and could be certain that it would. I told her that I would, if necessary, sign the promissory note she had from your Lordship, binding myself to the payment of it if anything should happen to your Lordship – and getting other names to the same effect if she wished it. With this she seemed satisfied, but I think it would be as well to obtain the money at once. She will only expect the first half year's annuity at Michaelmas next, but she hopes the masses for her sister may commence immediately.[18]

Miss Bettington must have been convinced by all this and lent the £5,000 for Prior Park, but the following year Baines was apparently trying to borrow another £1,000. Again she was very agitated by the request, particularly as it would mean selling some of her shares at a loss. Fr Burgess, who seemed as little concerned about her fears as Baines, wrote to the Bishop: 'If you could persuade her that the reduced capital will be of more advantage than the whole afterwards, and how much you esteem her charity for the good of the Church and your needy district, you will undoubtedly get it'.[19]

The whole episode throws an unpleasant light on Baines and his supporters, particularly when Burgess went on to say: 'You are in high favour with the good lady; if you strike the iron when it is hot you may succeed, but more fear may be had by delay'.[20]

Miss Bettington does not seem to have been put off by her experiences with Baines and Burgess. In 1833, Fr Brown of Downside was reporting that she had lately purchased a house in Bath for herself and had appointed Fr Burgess as her chaplain at a salary of £200 a year. There were also rumours that Miss Bettington intended to leave the Bath house to Baines for use as a chapel, together with a much larger sum of money.

Baines's other main benfactor, the Hon. Miss Crewe, was a far wealthier woman than Miss Bettington, and lent large sums of money. Like Miss Bettington, she was never to see her capital again, but there is no record of her showing any mistrust of Baines's financial activities, or less devotion to him. Her nephew, though, witnessing her sinking the bulk of her fortune into Prior Park, later showed an antagonism to the Catholic Church, which was probably influenced by the way in which Baines had treated his aunt.

The move to Prior Park

By February 1830, Baines was back at Bathampton and waiting impatiently to gain possession of Prior Park. He spent some time composing a prospectus for the new lay college to be built by H. E. Goodridge in the east wing. He hoped that it would soon bring in the necessary funds to maintain the whole establishment, and to make possible the opening of an ecclesiastical seminary in the west wing. He wrote to Burgess that: 'This establishment is intended to supply to a limited number of Catholic young gentlemen the benefit of a university education, which the existing laws do not allow them to receive at home, as well as to supersede the necessity of lavishing an expenditure in a course of travels, dangerous, often ill-directed, and generally ineffectual'.[21]

He listed a wide range of subjects, similar to those which had been offered at Ampleforth, but also included 'A study of Rome and other antiquities sacred and profane under the celebrated Sgr Nibby'. This was to include a visit to Rome, as early as the summer of 1830, for those students whose parents were willing to pay an additional amount above the basic £100 pension. While the plans were very imaginative, Burgess believed that they were not practicable. He wrote to Baines, wishing that he would postpone such a detailed programme for another year, 'till we have got things on a good footing at Prior Park'.[22]

By April, Baines was able to take possession of the east wing of Prior Park. He wrote to Burgess that: 'It wants nothing but a little furniture, which I shall send'. On the other hand, he was also saying that there would be a great deal of work to be done, involving at least six men, 'in the mending of pavements, walls, buttresses etc.'[23]

Baines planned to move into the east wing himself on 1 May, although the main mansion and west wing would not be available for a further two weeks. He took it as a good omen that 1 May was the anniversary of his consecration and 'we shall have a pretext for keeping May Day annually as a day of Jubilee'.[24]

He was concerned with more mundane matters, urging Burgess not to send any students for at least a month, for he had only fourteen or fifteen beds in the place. 'What must I do about bedsteads and bedding?' he wrote. And later: 'Where are beds, bed linen and blankets to be had? I wish you would let me have white coverlets instead of the dun-coloured ones you have, which are evidently made to hide the dirt.'[25] Presumably Burgess had a source of supply in York, where he had had contacts for many years, and was able to buy goods for Baines at reduced prices.

Baines's arrival at Prior Park aroused enormous interest, both in Catholic and Protestant circles. President Birdsall wrote to Prior Barber of Downside giving him the news followed by two exclamation marks, and Baines, writing to Burgess on 8 May, reported gleefully that a Protestant Bishop, Dr Moysey, had held a visitation at Bath Abbey and expressed his terror at the immense establishment which was rising up before them, exhorting his clergy to double their zeal. He observed: 'Our flock are falling away from us day by day'.[26] (Dr Moysey was Archdeacon of Bath, not a bishop. Baines must have known this, and may have been exaggerating in order to make his book seem of more importance.)

Benjamin Thomas, one of the Quaker brothers who had sold Prior Park to Baines, also thought the sale sufficiently noteworthy to rush across Park Street in Bristol to speak to a well-known Catholic, Mr Husenbeth: 'Dost thou know Peter Baines? I have just sold him Prior Park.' This made such an impression on Husenbeth's son that he repeated the story forty years later, with the concluding words: 'You may be sure that my father duly resented his disrespectful manner of speaking of the good Bishop'.[27]

Burgess and Rooker arrived to assist Baines at the end of May, and Metcalfe, driving his herd of cattle, at the beginning of July. They formed the nucleus of the distinguished staff which Baines hoped to build up at Prior Park, supplemented by part-time tutors in music and the arts whom he hoped to obtain from Bath. It is evident, though, that he had doubts whether Burgess, at least, would be able to fill the role of an academic professor if the new Catholic university came into being.

By August the first students were starting to arrive. James Shepherd, who came down from Ampleforth, reported that there were about twenty lay students; nine ecclesiastical students, including James Baines, the Bishop's nephew; John Bonomi, later to become Vicar General in the new diocese of Clifton; Shepherd himself; and three novices from Ampleforth, Leonard Calderbank, Moses Furlong and Peter Hutton.[28] The lay students were to occupy the west wing, and the ecclesiastical students were to live and study in the central mansion, as the east wing was unlikely to be ready for several years.

The first term seems to have been chaotic, as workmen were still busy converting and improving the property. An article in the *Morning Herald* gives some idea of the disruption:

> The beautifully situated mansion was heretofore well known as a possible residence for Charles X, or of Latel, the ex-Archbishop of Reims.
>
> It has an immense number of spacious rooms and a chapel forming one wing of it and numerous out-buildings. Beyond these they are now building a refectory, a dormitory, studies etc, in a style to correspond with the plain solid character of the other parts – up to 100 workmen are on it.
>
> The chapel is already converted into a R.C. chapel with rows of new wainscot seats for scholars, a new organ, furnished by Loder. The old pulpit has been removed and in its place a throne for Bishop Baines, which has a rich canopy, cushions etc. The old altar piece has disappeared, and a new marble one surmounted by a tabernacle erected on its site – marble, said to have been brought from Italy, exquisitely and richly wrought. In the centre of the building a new library is forming.[29]

The writer was also impressed by the number of scholars, up to forty in number, he says, consisting 'of sons of baronets and wealthy R.C. families and of those, who to quote the language of a visitor, were not exactly R.Cs, but all of whom attend the chapel service, mass etc.'[30]

To those in the know, the administration of the new establishment left much to be desired. Burgess was nominally in charge, but had to refer everything to Baines, who had no time to involve himself in the details of administration. Within a few weeks the three from Ampleforth, particularly Burgess and Metcalfe, were regretting that they had given up everything to follow Baines to Prior Park. On 29 November 1830 they went to the Bishop, impressing upon him the necessity of drawing up regulations to run the college: 'We have to hear from others, not from your Lordship, the orders of the day. We think this shows very little consideration for the sake of those who have forsaken everything to promote the interests of the Establishment'.[31]

They also expressed alarm at the amount of money being spent, deeming it vital 'to impress upon your Lordship's mind the necessity of laying out no more money than is absolutely necessary to complete the first intended alterations'.[32]

Curbing Baines's expenditure was never likely, and nothing improved in the organization of the college, so both Burgess and Metcalfe had resigned by Christmas 1830, Burgess becoming chaplain at Cannington, and Metcalfe a chaplain to the Mostyn family at Talacre. Baines did nothing to dissuade them, giving the impression that he did not consider them of high enough academic calibre for the staff of the new university which he dreamed would rise up at Prior Park. His lack of concern confirmed the impression that he was inclined to use people for his own ends, and then drop them when they were no longer useful. Against this, he did appoint Burgess to the convent at Cannington, which the ex-prior had always dreamed of as a haven for his old age. Unfortunately for Burgess, it was to prove another bed of thorns.

The resignations brought Baines immediate problems of staffing. 'What will Baines do if all his teachers leave him?' wrote Fr Ratcliffe at Downside to Fr Deday. 'Good idea if he has to become a teacher himself and take him away from further mischief.'[33] Baines, though, turned to his old friend, Fr Brindle from Bath, made him President of the college, and promoted Rooker as his deputy. About this time he was fortunate in securing the services of Dr Logan, an eminent mathematician, and also of Canon Shattock, formerly chaplain and tutor at the court of Charles X, who had been forced to leave France at the 1830 Revolution. He also appointed more part-time tutors from Bath.

Lay staff, however, had to be paid salaries, and Baines was

looking around for further funds to cover expenses and to finance all the improvements, including the gradual transformation of the east wing into an ecclesiastical seminary. Birdsall wrote to accuse the Bishop of purloining funds that were not his:

> Having been informed that you are about to lay your hands on that portion of the property of the late Dr Collingridge, which consists of ground rent on certain houses at Taunton belonging to Mr Manley, I hereby give you notice that the property is not the property of the Western District and cannot be used by your Lordship, its use and destination being specified in Dr Collingridge's will.[34]

The dispute rumbled on for several years, and there were also accusations that Baines was using endowments for missions to finance Prior Park, but nothing was proved. Burgess, now distant from the problems of Prior Park, wrote to Metcalfe to express his concern:

> There is no end of building and alterations ... Mr Brindle is much behindhand in the payment of bills ... the Bishop is incomprehensible on the question of expense ... he goes on as if money and stones came from the same quarry.[35]
>
> ... To add to the Bishop's worries he is up to his ears in mortar ... It looks very well, and will be useful if he can bear the expense. I suppose he can, he has still greater works in hand ... Poor Mr Brindle is out of his element. The Bishop trusts to Providence without being sensible of the awful risks he is running. I hardly like to dwell on the subject.[36]

Growing reputation of Prior Park

Outwardly, however, everything appeared to be going well and greatly impressed the people of Bath, as well as the Catholic press. In 1831 the first annual exhibition was started, run on the same lines as Baines had developed at Ampleforth, in which students were examined orally in front of an audience of parents and distinguished guests. Prizes were given for a wide range of subjects, including Religion, Mathematics, English, Rhetoric, Humanities, Classics, Modern Languages, Music and Drawing. The evening display ended with productions of *Julius Caesar* and *Le Bourgeois Gentilhomme*.

In that same summer the first of the famous outdoor processions were held at Prior Park, possibly the first to take place in England since the Reformation. In 1834 these became still more impressive, when Baines had had two magnificent flights of steps designed by Goodridge to lead up to the portico. The north front of the house became as John Wood had planned it nearly a hundred years before.

The *Catholic Magazine* described the ceremony as: 'transcendentally impressive ... it could not fail to strike the mind with the sublime power of the external worship of religion and the sublime grandeur of the service of the Catholic Church'.[37]

Baines had brought the Catholic Church out into the open by acquiring such a magnificent mansion for his seminary, and still more so by inaugurating such impressive ceremonies in surroundings which brought crowds of people flocking up the hill to Prior Park. The Bristol press was also taken with the reports of great social gatherings at Prior Park:

> A splendid entertainment was given at Prior Park on Thursday last by the Rev Dr Baines. The Duchess of Berry and suite with several respectable residents of Bath were among the guests. Every delicacy of the season with exquisite wines were served in abundance. The evening's entertainments were vocal and instrumental, dancing etc; The company did not disperse until a late hour, after partaking of a magnificent supper.[38]

Downside reported that Anna de Mendoza, now Lady Bellew, with her new husband, Sir Patrick, were often seen at these splendid ceremonies at Prior Park, revealing that any rift between her and Bishop Baines had been speedily mended.

While all this may have been good for public relations, such an extravagant outlay must have been a sore point with priests trying to make a meagre living in the missions, desperate to raise funds to maintain their churches and help their poverty-stricken congregations. Baines would have insisted that it was all for the glory of God and the Catholic Church, but others less charitable would have ascribed it to the Bishop's love of pomp and ceremony, in which he was always the centre of the stage.

Some observers noted that they thought the press were making too much of all this. Admittedly the establishment was magnificent and supported in splendid episcopal style, but it was not extravagant. A Joseph Tempest considered that they should be concentrating more on the behaviour of the boys, 'the most gentlemanly he had ever witnessed in a school', the boys were 'well acquainted with their authors and their dancing, playing, public speaking were equally satisfactory'.[39]

Tempest also said that he had read an article in the *Taunton Courier*, which in the usual way of journalists had concentrated on the gaiety and splendour of an evening party at Prior Park, and had not mentioned 'the Literary Department, the studies, the proficiency of the boys, the system of education, the distribution of premiums . . . and similar subjects which may lead the public to appreciate the really valuable and substantial role of the College and cause the benefactors to consider that their money is well disposed of, when contributing towards its support'.[40]

Prior Park and Rome

In the midst of all this drama, Baines was forced to leave England to spend most of 1834 in Rome, defending himself over continuing allegations from the Benedictines. On his arrival he was taken ill and confined to his bed for some days, complaining to Fr Brindle that 'it was great mortification to me not to be able to preach last Sunday when the King and two Queens of Naples were to attend and when I had, at the Pope's own personal request, to explain to the English the concern of Cardinal Weld and induce them to be a little more orderly than usual'.[41]

When he was up and about again, Baines seized the opportunity to further the future of Prior Park, first by interesting the Pope, Gregory XVI, in his plans for a Catholic university. It is characteristic of Baines's tenacity that, in spite of all his difficulties of staffing and finance, he kept this goal constantly before him. Lord Clifford was also in Rome, and Baines told him a great deal about Prior Park and talked of his plans for a university. In another letter to Fr Brindle, Baines told him that Lord Clifford 'had caught at the idea warmly and said that it would be the greatest possible advantage to religion in England. He concluded by paying me a number of flaming compliments, observing that it was improbable that a person who had done so much for religion . . . should be received otherwise than most kindly in Rome.'[42]

In an audience with the Pope, Lord Clifford had already talked about the advantages of having a Catholic university in England, and told Baines that the Pope had actually asked him '*Why cannot you have one at Prior Park?!!*'[43] By May 1834 Baines had seen the Pope himself and, fearing opposition, had talked about the establishment of a university at Prior Park as a settled thing, and asked only for the Pope's approbation. Gregory XVI appeared to be somewhat alarmed by being rushed into a decision, and the possibility that the British Government might become concerned, and Baines then hastened to reassure him. He promised 'to draw up a memorial stating the objects and plans and requesting a Brief of Establishment'.[44]

Baines had to wait some months for the Pope's approval of his plans for a university, as he did for an agreement about the arbitration dispute with the Benedictines.[45] With little to do, he thought nostalgically of home and his lady admirers, who wrote regularly to him. He sent a request, via Fr Brindle, to a Miss Harriet Fairfax, who had described to him 'a beautiful little spot in her botanical garden': 'I shall beg to have a seat that is not occupied by herself with the privilege of now and then culling a flower of her rearing. Make her the request with my kindest and most affectionate regards.'[46]

And Baines's ward, Anna, now Lady Bellew, was not forgotten. 'Tell Madam', he wrote to Fr Brindle, 'that she is a goose, a mere "dindonneau" [young turkey]. To pretend to compare the tapering towers of Paris, fit only for her own petticoat, with the splendid and elegant embroidery of Rome!!'[47]

In June 1834 Baines was diverted from these dalliances by the sudden death of Lord Arundell, who had also been staying in Rome. Baines had always counted him as one of his closest supporters, and wrote to Fr Brindle about the severity of such a loss. He had ministered to Lord Arundell on his deathbed, and was particularly pleased to be asked to sing the funeral mass. A postscript added at the end of this letter to Fr Brindle comes as rather a let down. 'It is said', wrote Baines, 'that Lord Arundell has left all his library to Stonyhurst. Never mind, say a number of masses for him just the same.'[48]

At last, on 26 August 1834, Baines had a favourable reply from the Pope about his plans for a university.

> We have been informed, Dear Brother, [the Pope wrote to Baines] of the course of studies you propose for a university to be established at Prior Park. It is a commendable venture, which clearly shows your foresight and ardent wish to spread the Catholic faith; which in these calamitous times there can be no better undertaking than to educate the minds of young men in the ways of true judgement and honourable conduct.[49]

The Pope, having already experienced Baines's tendency to act on his own without consultation, urged him to discuss the scheme with other English Vicars Apostolic 'and consider seriously with those what might be achieved, so that this endeavour which will be attended with much effort and expense, might be brought to a successful and fruitful conclusion'.[50] He then asked Baines to send him the full details of his completed plans, after full consultation.

This was enough inducement to Baines to continue dreaming and planning, but he had tried to assure Bishop Briggs, the Vicar

Apostolic of the Northern District, that he was not undermining the influence of the other bishops:

> You know my plans. I have explained them to his Holiness just as I explained them to Dr Penswick, and I think to yourself, and it appears that [his Holiness] had previously made a proposal of such a thing, to prevent the Catholic youth from going to protestant universities in case of these being thrown open to Catholics. But I have not asked his Holiness for any grant or privilege that could give you offence ... the Jesuits are the persons who are already in the field of higher education. If the Bishops will assist me or remain mute, I shall not fear even this powerful body.[51]

In a further letter to Bishop Briggs, Baines continued to plead his cause, pointing out that the foundation of a Catholic university at Prior Park might become 'a measure of the greatest practical utility to all, as giving to the Episcopal Body a peculiar share in the education of the Catholic youth, which has heretofore been assumed almost exclusively by the regulars and which has been the chief source of their overwhelming influence'.[52]

Baines could not help showing his strong feelings against the Benedictines and the Jesuits even in his campaign for a Catholic university. More to the point were the practicalities of funding such a secular institution and attracting scholars of European renown to teach. The most likely candidate appeared to be Dr Nicholas Wiseman, head of the English College in Rome. He had a great reputation as an inspiring lecturer and a scholar of ancient languages; like Baines he was not a good administrator and like Baines, too, he was inclined to be vain and carried away by his own enthusiasms. He was enthusiastic about all he heard of Prior Park, writing many years later: 'I saw in Prior Park the beginning of a new era for Catholic affairs; in education, in literature, in public position, and in many things which now are realities, and then were hopes'.[53]

Baines had the idea of making Wiseman his coadjutor with special responsibility for Prior Park, but the Pope was not in favour. He believed that Baines was too young to need a coadjutor and Wiseman too young to be a bishop. He did support the idea, however, that Wiseman should be rector of Prior Park under Baines, with the aim of building it up to become the first Catholic university in England since the Reformation. It was, therefore, agreed that Wiseman should visit Prior Park in the following summer of 1835.

Baines then turned his attention to a less exalted matter, the task of obtaining teachers for Prior Park at a minimum expense, and this could only be achieved by attracting members of one of the religious orders. He had followed the career of Luigi Gentili since the time he rejected him as a husband for his ward, Anna de Mendoza; while Baines was not prepared to accept the wealthy young Roman lawyer as a suitor for Anna, he was perfectly prepared to employ Gentili the dedicated priest, as a teacher and spiritual director at Prior Park. Since 1829 the changes in Gentili's life had been dramatic. He had not only given up his old, flamboyant style of living and become a priest, but had joined the strict order of the Institute of Charity, vowing complete obedience to his superior, Fr Rosmini, and dedicating himself to a life of prayer and fasting.

After some correspondence with Rosmini, Baines travelled north to Domodossola, where he found Gentili in charge while Rosmini was away, and having complete authority to finalize arrangement about a move to Prior Park. Gentili was to take two other priests with him and between them they were to teach French, Italian, Philosophy and Theology. They would receive no salary, only expenses, but would be given a house at Prior Park in which they would hold retreats as members of the community. Rosmini had insisted that, while Gentili and the other priests should do all they could to follow Baines's wishes, they should do nothing contrary to the essential rule of the Institute.[54]

After concluding all this business to his great satisfaction, Baines returned to England and to Prior Park to a great welcome from his staff and students, and to await the arrival of Dr Wiseman and members of the Institute of Charity, whom he hoped would stabilize his staff and bring the prospects of a Catholic university nearer. It was his supreme moment of hope and confidence in the future.

Notes

1 See Benjamin Boyce, *The Benevolent Man: A Life of Ralph Allen of Bath* (Harvard University Press, 1967).
2 Tim Mowl and Brian Earnshaw, *John Wood, Architect of Obsession* (Millstream Books, 1988) pp. 101–18.
3 Ibid.
4 City of Bath Central Library, Guide to Bath, 1819. See also Tim Mowl and Brian Earnshaw, *John Wood*, p. 116.
5 Mowl and Earnshaw, pp. 101–18.
6 Ibid.
7 *Prior Park, Landscape Garden*, National Trust, (London, 1996).
8 Henry Fielding, *A Life of Tom Jones, Foundling*, paperback edition, (Ware, 1992), pp. 8–9.
9 Edith Sitwell, *Bath* (London, 1932), pp. 196–200.
10 Ibid.

11 CDA, Baines Box Files, 5–7, Baines to Brindle, 30 November 1829.
12 Ibid.
13 Ibid. 10 December 1829.
14 Ibid. 11 December 1829.
15 Ibid. Brindle to Baines, 20 December 1829.
16 Ibid. Glover to Baines, 6 December 1829.
17 Ibid. Morgan to Baines, 24 December 1829.
18 Ibid. Brindle to Baines, December 1829.
19 Ibid. Cannington File, 68, Burgess to Baines, 31 October 1831.
20 Ibid.
21 Ibid. Baines Box Files, 5–7, Baines to Burgess, 14 April 1830.
22 Ibid. Burgess to Baines, 17 April 1830.
23 Ibid. Baines to Burgess, April 1830.
24 Ibid. 30 April 1830.
25 Ibid. 8 May 1830.
26 Ibid.
27 Ibid. Baines Box Files, 9–11, Husenbeth to unknown, 24 May 1871.
28 James Shepherd, *Reminiscences of Prior Park* (Bath, 1886), pp. 5–6.
29 *Morning Herald*, 6 October 1830.
30 Ibid.
31 CDA, Baines Box Files, 5–7, Burgess to Baines, 29 November 1830.
32 Ibid.
33 Downside Archives, H192, Ratcliffe to Deday, 20 January 1831.
34 CDA, Bishops' Letters, Birdsall to Baines, 12 March 1831.
35 J. S. Roche, *A History of Prior Park College* (London, 1931), pp. 140–50.
36 Ibid.
37 *Catholic Magazine and Review*, July 1834.
38 *Bristol Mercury*, 26 April 1831.
39 CDA, Cannington File, Larkins to Baines, 2 August 1834.
40 Ibid.
41 Ibid. Miscellaneous Letters recently received from the City of Bristol Record Office, Baines to Brindle, 29 March 1834.
42 Ibid. 17 April 1834.
43 Ibid.
44 Ibid. 31 May 1834.
45 See below, chapter 10.
46 CDA, Miscellaneous Files, Baines to Brindle, 31 May 1834.
47 Ibid.
48 Ibid. 21 June 1834.
49 Ibid. Prior Park Files, Pope Gregory XVI to Baines, 26 August 1834.
50 Ibid.
51 Ibid. Baines Box Files, 5–7, Baines to Briggs, 22 May 1834.
52 Ibid. June 1834.
53 Ampleforth Journal, vol. xv, May 1810, Wiseman to Bonomi (quoting from Letters in CDA, but these cannot be found).
54 Denis Gwynn, *Father Luigi and his Mission* (Dublin, 1951), pp. 84ff.

7

Baines and the Nuns of Cannington: 'A Set of Ignorant, Uneducated Women'

How Baines, immersed in all the problems of Prior Park and continuing strife with the Benedictine monks, could have involved himself in another dispute is difficult to comprehend. Like some of Baines's other conflicts, this one started with a local disagreement, this time between the Bishop and the Prioress of the Cannington convent, and spread until it became a subject of argument throughout the Catholic Church in England and of furious discussion in Rome.

The Ladies of Paris

Up to 1829, when Baines became Vicar Apostolic, these Benedictine nuns, the Ladies of Hope in Paris, had lived peacefully at Cannington for many years. They were a branch of the English Benedictine nuns of Cambrai, who moved to Paris about 1623. Their constitution was agreed upon by the Archbishop of Paris, and they were also granted certain privileges, such as the right to free election of their superior and the freedom to choose their own confessor. The latter privilege was to prove important in the dispute with Bishop Baines.[1]

The nuns escaped from France during the French Revolution and, after a temporary resting place at Marnhull in Dorset, Lord Clifford granted them a permanent home at the Court House at Cannington in Somerset. Since the seventeenth century, this house and extensive grounds had belonged to the Cliffords, one of the foremost Catholic families in England; by the time of the French Revolution, the family had moved to their other estate at Chudleigh in Devon. For the past thirteen years, Mary Clare Knight had been Prioress of the convent. She was a member of a well known local Catholic family, and had been on such good terms with the former Bishop, Peter Collingridge, that she offered him a home at Cannington. He remained there for many years until his death in 1829, and was mourned by the nuns as a gentle pastor and a benefactor to the community.

The Bishop and the Prioress

Their reaction to the appointment of the new Vicar Apostolic was very different; they feared that Bishop Baines's reputation, as a man of decided views who would not brook opposition, augured ill for the community. In the early days, though, relationships seemed surprisingly good. In September 1829, Baines and the then Prior Burgess of Ampleforth, who was staying at Bathampton, went down to Cannington to look at Bishop Collingridge's papers. Baines was at his most charming, and greatly impressed the Prioress; she was also flattered by Prior Burgess's declaration that when the time came for his retirement, Cannington was the place which he would choose above all others.

Baines then returned to Ampleforth with Burgess, and the Prioress saw no more of him for several months. In February 1830 she was writing to him at Ampleforth: 'We are longing to know when we shall see you again and when we will be able to talk over the plans for our new chapel'.[2]

Several months later Baines had still not returned to Cannington, and the Prioress wrote again to remind him that he had promised to make regular visits to the convent. Plans for the opening of the new chapel had to be postponed, but the Prioress was grateful to Baines for providing the community with a new missioner, Fr James Lyons, an Irish Dominican. Their present missioner, Fr James Dullard, who had also been confessor to the community, was in poor health, and there were other, undisclosed, reasons why the Prioress wanted him removed. The Prioress looked forward to the arrival of Fr Lyons, but told Baines: 'We cannot feel the advantage of our excellent acquisition while the present incumbent remains at Cannington'.[3]

In spite of this hint, Baines did nothing to remove Fr Dullard from Cannington, and there were the first signs that relations between the Bishop and the Prioress were becoming strained. The Prioress wrote to Baines that she had received a letter from the Abbé Prémord, who had been confessor to the community for many years, until he was appointed as chaplain to King Charles X of France in 1823; with the revolution of 1830, he was forced to flee from France again, and had agreed to resume his charge as confessor to the community. The Prioress pointed out that, owing to his age and infirmity, he would not be able to combine the duties of confessor and missioner. Mr

Lyons' arrival would, therefore, be most opportune, and she stressed that 'Mr Lyons understands that he is to direct his attention to the care of the congregation'.[4]

The continued presence of Fr Dullard at Cannington was the only cloud on the Prioress's horizon and, thinking that Baines might have difficulty in placing him, she made suggestions of her own: 'I hear Mr and Mrs Honnington are in need of a chaplain – Likewise the Lanherne nuns, we understand, are poorly situated from the ill health of their chaplain.'[5]

Baines was the last person to take advice about how he should place his missioners, particularly from a woman, and he made this very clear to the Prioress. He continued, too, to be irritated by her letters pressing for the immediate removal of Fr Dullard: 'I again presume to approach Your Lordship on the subject of Fr Dullard's removal from Cannington ... He has informed me that he fears to leave Cannington, without receiving a command from Your Lordship to leave and adds that I may state this to Your Lordship. I most willingly do so, knowing how extremely uncomfortable his remaining here makes Mr Lyons ...'[6]

And again, nine days later. 'Knowing how precious every moment is to Your Lordship, I am sorry to be under the necessity of troubling you with another letter ... I am persuaded Your Lordship would not have so long delayed Mr Dullard's removal, had you known how extremely uncomfortable Rev Mr Lyons is situated ... I am anxiously looking for every post.'[7]

Baines eventually took notice of these continual requests and offered Fr Dullard the choice of two other missions in his district. The priest, however, turned down both offers, pleading ill-health, and accepted a temporary home in the village of Cannington, cared for by a Mrs Arundell. The Prioress was not too pleased at having him installed so close to the convent, but there was nothing she could do about it, and she rejoiced that peace had now been restored to Cannington. The Abbé and Fr Lyons got on well together, and the relationship between the Prioress and the Bishop was still reasonably good. If only Baines had left well alone, these harmonious relations might have continued indefinitely, but in December 1830 came the news that he was transferring Fr Burgess from Prior Park to Cannington.

Fr Burgess at Cannington

Ideally Baines would not have wished to do this, but he was in a quandary about what to do with Burgess. The latter had asked to be relieved of his post at Prior Park, realizing that he could no longer work with the Bishop. Baines was not sorry to see him go, but felt under an obligation to the man who had given up so much for him in leaving Ampleforth.[8] He remembered that the ex-prior had once expressed a wish to end his days at Cannington, and resolved to appoint him as chaplain to the congregation in place of Fr Lyons. The Prioress professed to be delighted by the arrangement: 'How favoured and fortunate we consider ourselves in your appointment of the Rev Mr Burgess ... my brother, too, is delighted and will raise his salary to £60 a year – we will willingly forego any payment for Mr Burgess's keep.'[9]

Privately, the Prioress had doubts about the removal of Fr Lyons, who had only been at Cannington a short time, and got on so well with the Abbé Prémord. Baines, however, pressed on with the appointment, which he must have considered unwise if he had looked back on Burgess's career at Ampleforth. Burgess, a tactless man, had aroused antagonisms and factional strife at the monastery, which he could not control. It was doubtful whether he was the right choice for a community in which he had to maintain good relations with a confessor of long standing, and with a Prioress who believed very strongly that she was the best person to make decisions for her nuns.

Early in 1831 there were growing signs of conflict. Fr Burgess could not work with the Abbé as Fr Lyons had done before him. Their uneasy relationship was further soured by a dispute concerning two nuns who wished to go to Fr Burgess to make their confessions, instead of the Abbé. These nuns, Sisters Mary Placida and Mary Peter performed duties in the chapel, where Burgess was in charge and likely to have influenced them. The Abbé appeared deeply hurt by their decision to leave him, their appointed confessor, and prefer the spiritual direction of another priest; the Prioress felt bound to support him, particularly as she believed that the nuns' actions were an attack upon her own authority. It was a trivial dispute, which should have been settled by the parties concerned, but it developed into a major confrontation, between the Bishop and Fr Burgess on the one hand, and the Prioress on the other. Both parties took their stand on a matter of principle, the right of each to make decisions relating to the convent, and there was also another element underlying the dispute, which today would be called sexism. Both Baines and Burgess were more indignant at the stand taken by the Prioress and some of the other nuns because they were women, dismissing them as 'ignorant and uneducated'.

In April 1831 the Prioress wrote to Baines to tell him the details of the controversy, which he had already heard about from Fr Burgess:

> Though I have the highest opinion of Mr Burgess, I cannot help feeling convinced that the arrangement [the two nuns going to him for confession] will produce a division in the community. It is a mere whim, which from their character, I think should not be indulged. Both are in offices which give them daily opportunities of being more with Mr Burgess than any of the other nuns.[10]

At the same time Burgess was urging his Bishop to write to the Prioress about the dispute, although from his knowledge of Baines he must have realized that this was more likely to prolong it. He told him that the Bishop's authority was not received with enough deference in the convent, a remark which would have only served to put Baines on his mettle. Then a few weeks later Burgess was writing again to Baines, giving him graphic details of events at the convent and his own opinion of the Prioress:

> I feel some of the nuns will go mad if the direction of conscience is not entirely taken out of the hands of Mother Prioress or any woman! Some nuns go to the Prioress to rehearse their state of conscience before going to confession. Can it be right to subject the divine authority with which we are invested to the wisdom or whim or ignorance of a woman? There can be no cure until the Prioress ceases directing the consciences of the nuns.[11]

Later he continued the attack: 'Many nuns seem to think the Prioress above priest or Bishop. They read and make things out to their own convenience; as protestants read the Bible.'[12]

Burgess influenced Baines to consider all this as an attack on his own authority, instead of an internal matter which could have been settled in the convent. Admittedly, the Prioress appears to have been a strong-minded woman too quick to stamp out dissent, but many of her nuns were prepared to speak highly of her, as a Sr Mary Angela told Baines: 'You cannot be so well aware as those who observe her daily how much nature and divine grace have combined to form a character comprising more eminent qualities than those already found centred in an individual'.[13]

In the meanwhile the Abbé Prémord also wrote to Baines, offering to resign his post as confessor if this would ease the conflict at the convent. At the same time, he was circulating a paper to all the nuns, asking them if they wished him to continue as their confessor. All but two of the nuns answered 'yes': Sr Mary Placida replied 'no', and Sr Mary Peter appears to have abstained. The Abbé accepted this as a vindication of his own position, and was prepared to show the paper to Baines, who was soon to make another visit to Cannington.

Baines's visitation to Cannington and its aftermath

The date had been fixed for the dedication of the nuns' chapel on 7 July 1831, and Baines decided that it would be advisable to combine this event with a formal visitation to the convent. He stayed at Cannington for several days and, after performing the ceremony, saw a number of people: Abbé Prémord presented him with a long account of all he had done for the convent in the past, and the trials he had suffered in escaping from France; a number of nuns asked to see him, as was their right, most supporting the position of the Prioress, but Srs Mary Placida and Mary Peter complained that the Prioress had forbidden them to go to Fr Burgess for confession. Baines then saw the Prioress and left instructions with her concerning the future treatments of her nuns. At this time he also discovered that the Prioress had invested convent money in Spanish securities, an investment which he thought most unwise, and advised her to remove it. There were rumours that Baines wished her to invest the money in Prior Park, but both parties denied this.

Baines then returned to Prior Park, but was disturbed to receive two letters, which showed him that his instructions had been ignored. The Prioress wrote to thank him for his visit and his advice, but showed that she had no intention of following it with regard to the Spanish investments. She had contacted her financial adviser only to be assured that the funds were perfectly safe, and that she would lose a great deal of interest if she withdrew them at that stage. If it had been proved to be otherwise, 'I would have felt great pleasure in obeying Your Lordship . . .'[14]

Baines was not mollified and was even less so when he received a letter from Sr Mary Peter telling him that the restrictions placed upon them had not been lifted, and in fact were becoming worse:

> Shortly after you left us, we were forbidden to go to the parlour to speak to Mr Burgess . . . without special leave from Mother Prioress. Even if he sent for us, we were not to go until her leave was procured . . . On Friday last, in Chapter, we were forbidden to attend on Sundays or Holy Days at the sermon or the evening instruction . . . I fear this command arises from Mother Prioress's constant fear of her nuns getting to prefer Mr Burgess's spiritual direction to Abbé Prémord's . . . [15]

Baines then wrote to the Prioress showing considerable anger:

> I shall not tell you what I have felt and thought of your conduct

respecting the money in the Spanish funds and the advice which caused you to adopt that conduct. Henceforward you will not be troubled with much advice from me. You will therefore consider the following regulation as coming, not from a counsellor who throws away his advice, but from a superior who expects to be obeyed.[16]

Baines went on to order the Prioress to withdraw all the money from the Spanish Funds and to put up in a prominent position a copy of his *Acta*, given to her at the end of the visitation, so that all the nuns could see it. The main points of these *Acta* were to make clear that, in the Bishop's absence, the Prioress could rule on any doubts of interpretation concerning the constitution, but the Bishop reserved the right to correct her; all the nuns had the right to send letters direct to the Bishop, or to ask to see him when he visited the convent; the nuns also had a right to go to whichever confessor they chose; and no major funds were to be paid out or invested by the convent without the Bishop's permission.

After this letter had been received, the Abbé complained that Baines's Directives were then displayed in such a prominent position that all the servants could read them, as well as the nuns. It was as if the Prioress was pointing out to everyone how badly she had been treated by the Bishop. She felt it as a direct attack upon her authority, but was prepared to be conciliatory for the time being, writing to the Bishop immediately: 'Your Lordship's ordinances have been posted up in a conspicuous part of the Chapter room, together with the *Acta* of your last visit, for the public inspection of choir nuns, lay sisters, novices and servants ...'

Yet she made it clear to Baines that she was submitting under protest: 'I accept with entire submission this humiliation and public reprimand. I leave to Almighty God the justification of my conduct ...'[17]

The Prioress was also writing to Cardinal Weld in Rome and to the president of the Benedictines, John Birdsall, relating the problems which confronted her and asking for advice. Fr Burgess, hearing rumours of this correspondence, wrote to tell the Bishop. Baines was particularly incensed by the news that the Prioress was writing to Birdsall, whom he regarded as his foremost opponent. He wrote again to reprove her and also told her of his concern that she was ordering her nuns to leave the chapel before Fr Burgess preached. The excuse given was that the constitution forbade the nuns attending sermons. This was quite untrue, claimed Baines, and in any case, 'How was it then that the nuns only leave the chapel when Mr

Burgess is preaching?' He was so concerned about the whole situation at Cannington that he authorized Fr Burgess to investigate and make a full report on the problems at the convent. As Burgess himself was one of the main sources of conflict, this seems a curious decision, but Baines maintained: 'I have no other person I can employ and no time nor health to do it myself.'

Delay in a novice's profession

Both the Prioress and Abbé Prémord accepted the need for an investigation, and at the end of October the Prioress wrote a more friendly letter to Baines, sending him £15 in expenses for his visit to the convent, and asking that arrangements should be made for a novice, Miss Sidgreaves, to be professed. All the disturbances at Cannington had delayed the ceremony, and Miss Sidgreaves was becoming anxious. The Abbé also wrote, assuring the Bishop of his loyalty and defending the Prioress, whom he claimed that Baines had misunderstood. Baines replied that he was prepared to believe that her intentions were good, but went on scathingly: 'It is a great pity that a person of such excellent disposition, but of such limited abilities and education should have acquired such confidence in her own judgment – [can you not] induce her to show by act as well as in words the obedience she owes to the Bishop?'[18]

Baines showed his bias here because, although the Prioress may have had limited academic education, she was acknowledged by many to be a woman of intelligence and plenty of common sense. She had decided views and was prepared to stand up for them, which Baines did not like. He would have resented it in a man, but still more so in a woman, as his ward, Anna de Mendoza, had experienced to her cost. He did not reply to the Prioress's letters for some time and, in what may have been deliberate policy, did nothing about arranging for Miss Sidgreaves's examination before her profession. The Prioress wrote again in December 1831, expressing sorrow at the Bishop's continuing silence, and telling him: 'The novice feels the delay in her profession, as you have withdrawn permission for her examination'.[19]

Baines then decided that he had better take action about the matter and gave directions to Fr Burgess to perform the examination. He then wrote to Miss Sidgreaves, particularly telling her to answer the questions and listen to Fr Burgess's instructions on the subject of obedience. He wanted to make clear to the novice that the attitude adopted by the Prioress was not the norm in convent life, for 'The right of judging of Doctrines relating to duties of catholics belongs exclusively to the bishops and those whom they appoint . . . Religious Superiors, particularly women, are not authorised by their office to interfere.'[20]

Baines then went on to warn Miss Sidgreaves, in case she decided to support the Prioress: 'If they ever presume to do so, they are not to be followed in opposition to the lawful pastors of the church'.[21]

A disputed document

A strange, undated document is to be found in the Cannington files, which must have been written about this time. It is in Fr Burgess's handwriting, but was probably produced on the orders of Baines. The prioress was asked to sign a declaration that:

> I declare that the Rev Thomas Burgess was sent to Cannington at my request, and that I thanked the Rt Rev Dr Baines, Vicar Apostolic of the Western District, for sending him in the warmest terms, and that it is utterly false that the Bishop ever asked me to fund our money in Prior Park, or to obtain over it any control whatever.[22]

The Prioress wrote underneath: 'It is impossible for Mother Prioress to sign the first part of the above declaration as the following will prove.'[23]

She then quoted from a letter written by Bishop Baines in December 1830, in which he had only spoken of Burgess's great wish to return to Cannington, when he could relinquish some of his responsibilities; there was no mention of the Prioress's wish to have him. She acknowledged, however, that when Burgess was appointed she probably thanked the Bishop for providing the convent with such a worthy missioner. With regard to funds being invested in Prior Park, a reference which Baines had probably included because of all the rumours going around, the Prioress confirmed that she had never been asked to invest money in the project.

The Prioress was backed up in her statement by a Sr Mary Benedict Clifford, a relative of Lord Clifford of Ugbrook, who added a footnote and also wrote to Baines separately. She told him that she supported the Prioress's testimony unreservedly, insisting that 'any deviation from the truth is so odious to me that when called upon by any just cause to declare it, as in the present, I do it without reserve'.[24]

Baines was incensed by this letter coming from such a lowly source. He believed that nuns had no business to stand up for themselves and refute the statements of their religious superiors. It is noteworthy that such a nun at this period in the history of the Catholic Church should have the strength to stand up for her opinion and dare to write to the Bishop, particularly one of such a reputation as Bishop Baines. In his reply, after castigating Sr Mary Benedict for asserting what she could not know, Baines claimed that the Prioress had requested the appointment of Fr Burgess on his original visit to Cannington in the autumn of 1830. This was something which could not be proved; in any case it was a point which it was completely unnecessary to bring up at this juncture, and it could only have exacerbated the situation.

A new declaration

This unpleasant dispute, in which both parties virtually accused one another of lying, adding to the continuing obstacles put in the way of Miss Sidgreaves's profession, brought an unpromising start to the New Year of 1832. Baines decided the time had come to exert his authority anew, although a period of calm would have been more appropriate. He sent Fr Burgess a declaration for the Prioress to sign, in which she was to acknowledge that it was incorrect to say that 'the professions of the nuns are made to the Prioress, the Bishop being the head superior of the convent, whom both subject and superior are bound by their professions to obey'.[25]

The Prioress refused to sign this declaration, replying pertinently to Baines: 'I have always understood that the nuns made their vows to God'.[26]

She did acknowledge, however, that all religious by reason of their vow of obedience engage to obey the Pope, the Bishop and the local superior. In this case, though, she explained in a later letter, she could not sign such a declaration; it had never been required before of her or any of her predecessors and 'I will not acknowledge that my actions do not agree with the Bishop's and confess to my religious sisters that their superior does not deserve their confidence as they cannot rely on her word'.[27]

After the Prioress refused to sign the document, Fr Burgess increased the tension by writing to Baines to tell him of a new plot being hatched at Cannington. Lord Clifford, who was visiting the Prioress, had met her with her council and Dr Coombes, the missioner from Shepton Mallet in the Abbé Prémord's room: 'There was a great deal of chuckling about what a happiness it was that Lord Clifford had come, that his Lordship promised to support Mother Prioress and that Cardinal Weld in Rome knew them all'.[28]

Burgess also told Baines that the Prioress was again writing to Rome and to her Benedictine supporters at home, and there were rumours in the village, where all the locals must have been enthralled at all that was going on at the convent, that he (Burgess) was about to be removed. Baines himself, who was also beginning to come round to the fact that such a solution might be forced upon him, wrote angrily to the Prioress: 'I am far from being satisfied with your explanation; and still less with the conduct you have pursued in spreading far and wide your complaints against me, to the great scandal of the pious and the serious injury of your Superior. May God forgive you and your indiscreet advisers.'[29]

He then took a rather injudicious swipe at Cardinal Weld:

> As you have thought proper to carry this affair before the authorities at Rome, I must claim the right of self-defence, which will not be denied to me. I cannot bring myself to believe that Cardinal Weld has so forgotten the rule of ordinary prudence, and the deference due to the office I hold, as to give decisions on this case without hearing from me. I have great respect for his character and dignity, but I flatter myself that I am as well acquainted with the duties of my office as either his Eminence or any of your advisers, and you deceive yourself if you expect to intimidate me by such means as you have adopted.[30]

Baines ended his letter by refusing to allow either the profession of the novice at the convent or the admission of a postulant, until he had taken further advice on 'the insubordination now existing in your house'. A few days later he went on to write to Cardinal Weld defending his own conduct, and deploring that he had not been given a chance to put his own case to Rome; he also defended the actions of Fr Burgess, whom Cardinal Weld appeared to believe had shaken the stability 'of that edifying and holy community' at Cannington. For the sake of peace, however, he had decided to move Fr Burgess from Cannington, but this could not in all justice be done without removing the Abbé Prémord as well. In Baines's judgement, the whole dispute had arisen 'As such disputes in convents often do, in certain silly partialities and jealousies relating to the two priests, who are both excellent men, tho' the poor Abbé appears not to be what he was, either in mind or temper.'[31]

The withdrawal of Burgess and the Abbé

Baines then announced, at the end of February 1832, that he would shortly be transferring Fr Burgess to his new chapel in Bath and withdrawing the Abbé's faculties to minister at the convent, although he would allow him to remain at Cannington. This news spread quickly among Benedictines. Fr Cooper of the Bath mission wrote to Fr Deday, his provincial, telling him that the Abbé 'is forbidden to exercise his faculties at the convent and Mr Burgess is required to leave, as soon as his place can be filled by another priest'.[32]

Fr Cooper went on to relate how the nuns had applied to Rome, who had defined the Bishop's powers and come down in favour of the nuns, adding with some drama, 'Thus one war follows another'.

Fr Brown from Downside also wrote to Fr Deday drawing a comparison between Baines's dispute with the nuns and the long drawn-out conflict with his monastery, for 'he wished to regulate according to his views the internal concerns of the convent.'[33]

The Abbé then wrote to Baines denying all the allegations that the bishop had made and defending the nuns, who were, if the Bishop only realized it, 'one of the most regular, edifying and submissive religious houses in the Western District, even in the three kingdoms'.[34]

Baines was sceptical: 'Alas I am sorry to say', he wrote, 'that I do know them, only too well. What is worst of all, I know them by their fruits.'[35]

He was then faced with the difficult task of replacing the Abbé and Fr Burgess with a priest who would combine both offices. It was more difficult because the problems of Cannington were now widely known, and priests were reluctant to undertake such a thankless task. Fr Edgeworth from the Bristol mission, who would have been acceptable to the nuns, told Baines that he considered his duty lay with the much more important Bristol mission, and the Bishop could not help but agree with him. Eventually Baines appointed an Irish priest, Dr John Tuomy, who had studied in America. He had been a missioner at Cannington for a time under Bishop Collingridge, but had not been popular with the nuns. Baines told Cardinal Weld that Dr Tuomy was a man of great learning and piety and of very mild and conciliatory disposition, but the latter characteristic was far from evident. His appointment turned out to be even more disastrous than that of Fr Burgess.

Dr Tuomy at Cannington

Instead of trying to bring about reconciliation between the parties, particularly the Prioress and the Bishop, Fr Tuomy only aggravated the situation. During the months following his appointment in April 1832, he sent a series of rambling letters to Baines describing in the minutest details events at the convent which he imagined were slights upon himself or the Bishop. He related that Dr Coombes, the missoner from Shepton Mallet, had on several occasions visited the convent and remained closeted for some time with the Prioress and the Abbé, without ever consulting him. In this he made no allowance for the fact that Dr Coombes had been for many years a friend of both of them. It also served no useful purpose to annoy the Bishop more by telling him that the Prioress was again writing to her 'Roman Cardinals'.

Like Burgess before him, he became a confidant of the two nuns, Srs Mary Placida and Mary Peter, who had refused to go to the Abbé for confession. He told Baines that the Prioress had placed them in public disgrace because of the stand they had taken, and related in some detail the penance placed on Sr Mary Placida, which had been continuing for over a month:

> The Prioress called her from the fire in the infirmary, and gave her a penance to work in the cold, while she was sick. The Prioress said that it was but for a short while, and that the sun was shining through the window. The penance is that Placida is obliged to go last to all the public duties, her natural place being high among the senior nuns . . . here is a public penance for a private fault, if it is a fault . . .

He told the Bishop, too, that the Prioress had reported the case of the two nuns to Rome, in spite of his objections: 'No, I said, you cannot do this; the affair is in the Bishop's hands, and you must wait for a fair investigation; the witnesses who heard the proposition must be examined and the truth ascertained. But behold! Immediately after, they tell me that they had sent the matter to Rome'.'[36]

The Prioress was undoubtedly an imperious woman who liked to exert her authority, but there were rights and wrongs on both sides, and Fr Tuomy did not help matters by making so much drama out of the situation. Baines was constantly stirred up by these regular letters from Fr Tuomy, and allowed himself to become too much involved in all the details. He wrote to the priest on 29 May 1832, telling him to refuse communion 'to those who you think may justify it', a fatal piece of advice, as it turned out. He also told him to forbid the Prioress and some other nuns to go to communion daily, a practice which he himself intensely disliked, although it was becoming more common.

Baines even went into details about the nuns' reading matter, betraying a cynical attitude towards their intelligence and judgement:

'[You] must not only prohibit books of false or dangerous doctrines, but also books not suited to the nuns, eg; Aquinas is deserving of the respect of theologians, but is not suitable for nuns. Certain French works preaching perfection are not suitable. We want the duties of justice, truth, charity and meekness, *not* rapture and extremism.'[37]

Sr T. J. Knight, the Cellarine, and the sister of the Prioress, wrote about this time complaining to Baines that Fr Tuomy had forbidden her the sacraments, giving as his reason that she had tried to go to confession and communion with Dr Coombes instead of himself and had treated Srs Placida and Peter as outcasts.[38]

Baines and Cardinal Weld

Baines, in the meanwhile, was becoming more worried about the reaction at Rome to the Prioress's complaints. In April and May 1832 he wrote several letters to Cardinal Weld, in which he stressed that the Prioress was usurping her authority, and implied that the Cardinal was aiding and abetting her:

> The Prioress read the first of your letters to her religious as a proof that she was right and the Bishop wrong in the dispute about religious obedience. She even carried your letter to the kitchen and read it to the cook to prove that she was a better divine than your humble servant ... thus the Bishop of the District is placed in a position too ridiculous to excite compassion and too ruinous of his authority to be submitted to ...[39]

Baines tried to convince Cardinal Weld that the Abbé Prémord had been the cause of all the trouble at Cannington, and expressed the vain hope that the new director, Fr Tuomy, 'will be able to allay the storm raised in the pious and well-meaning, though not very theological ladies of Cannington'.[40]

A few weeks later he was writing again, telling the Cardinal that he had sent a message to the Prioress, informing her that he would agree to the acceptance of the postulant and the novice, delayed for so long, if she would sign an amended declaration acknowledging his authority. The Prioress had refused and 'Now', Baines exclaimed, 'I have nothing to do but to go on my knees to the ladies, or refuse to comply with your Eminence's request [to receive the postulant and novice as soon as possible]'.

He had been mortified to hear, presumably from Dr Tuomy, that the Prioress had told one of her nuns: 'We are only waiting to see if the Bishop will come round to our opinions which are so strongly sanctioned by the Cardinal; if not, we will be taken from his authority'.

He was inclined to treat this idea as a joke, not realizing that it was beginning to be seriously contemplated in Rome. He believed that he was in the right in the stand that he had taken, and was highly indignant that: 'a set of ignorant and uneducated women set me at defiance and maintain their silly and dangerous dogma in spite of me . . . You cannot but be aware of the sad effects such things have on ecclesiastical discipline.'[41]

Cardinal Weld was not in the least sympathetic. He rejected the idea that the Abbé Prémord was the cause of all the trouble and advised Baines to restore his faculties and to appoint a missioner acceptable to the community; this would be the only way of bringing back peace at Cannington. He supported the Prioress's objection to signing the amended declaration, which Baines had sent her, 'the vows are made to God in the presence of the Prioress and the Bishop'.[42]

For the first time Cardinal Weld mentioned the serious possibility that, if the dispute could not be solved amicably, the community might be withdrawn from the Bishop's authority and put under his own, until the controversy could be settled. This could, he told Baines, 'prevent the Bishop from being judge in his own case and the other party from saying anything in their own defence'.[43]

In a later letter, Cardinal Weld was more urgent, deploring the bad publicity that the affair was giving to the Catholic Church in the area: 'It must be notorious to every inhabitant of Cannington that a misunderstanding exists between you and the house – that the inmates have been forbidden to say anything in their defence and are suffering extremely from the state of restraint in which they are kept, deprived of the advice of their friends and their old confessor'.

He ended with a passionate appeal to Baines: 'I beg you for God's sake to take the only certain means of putting an end to a state of things which is such an affliction to so many'.[44]

Baines expressed surprise and grief at the Cardinal's advice that he should reinstate the Abbé and protested at the great injustice to himself which would be occasioned if Cannington was taken from his control. He maintained that the act, 'will be attended with great public scandal', and claimed that at least 'there should be an independent investigation at which he could be allowed to defend himself'.[45]

Dr Tuomy increases the tension

Dr Tuomy continued to bombard Baines, and occasionally Burgess, now installed in Bath, with detailed accounts of 'goings on' at the convent. He reported to Burgess that the lay sister, Benedict, was coming repeatedly into the garden to water the plants. She was about his door and window and Tuomy suspected that this was a pretence and she was really trying to contact the Abbé. Mother Dubuin, the French nun, also came into the garden to bring refreshments to the Abbé, and Tuomy wanted Burgess to use his influence with Baines to prevent this. He then wrote to the Bishop urging him to come to Cannington as soon as he could, as the situation was becoming impossible.

Baines did not reply to this and Fr Tuomy wrote again: 'Sister Cellarine has told me that I am not fit to be their confessor . . . Sister Benedict Austin is more like a fury than a nun . . . the others have rancour, bitterness and indignation boiling from their hearts, faces and tongues.'[46]

Tuomy saw nothing for it but to suspend the sacraments from the Prioress, the Sr Cellarine and all the nuns who supported their Superior and opposed him. This last stupidity meant that the priest had lost any hope of obtaining the confidence of the nuns, and his position was impossible. The Prioress asked Dr Coombes to administer the sacraments to them, when he made occasional visits to the convent, but Tuomy prevented this. The Prioress wrote to Baines to protest: 'Dr Tuomy refuses us the sacraments from misinformation he receives from others. He will not hear our protestations and uses the most horrifying language. He compares our conduct to "hell" and the nuns to "devils".'[42]

She suggested to the Bishop that, if he disapproved of Dr Coombes administering the sacraments, he could arrange for Frs Edgeworth or Wheatman to do so. Baines does not appear to have answered this letter and, bombarded by letters from all sides, he probably did not know which way to turn. Dr Tuomy wrote again, regretting that the Bishop had not yet come to Cannington to investigate. He had heard that Baines feared to be insulted by the nuns, but 'Is the episcopal authority to be trampled in the dust by half a dozen impudent and arrogant women?'[48]

Burgess also urged Baines to go to Cannington, where he thought he could cause 'a wonderful revolt against the Prioress' and 'represent things to Rome in your own way'.[49]

Sr Mary Peter, one of the nuns who had caused the original dispute by going to Fr Burgess for confession, wrote that, if Baines did not come himself, it would be useless to send Burgess as his representative. The nuns simply would not accept him. She herself wished to be removed from Cannington as soon as possible.

The Bishop's second visitation

Finally on 10 July 1832, Baines decided that he would have to go to Cannington to investigate the situation, particularly all the complaints against Dr Tuomy. In the meanwhile, he told the Prioress, he would suspend the missioner and 'in order to restore to you the comfort of the sacraments', an extraordinary confessor would be appointed.[50]

On 17 July, the Bishop went down to Cannington, accompanied by Frs Edgeworth and Lyons, who both had the confidence of the nuns, and Fr Burgess, who had not. In a letter to Cardinal Weld, Baines described something of the proceedings, in which he said that he and the other three priests had 'laboured incessantly to restore harmony and peace to the community'. He blamed the whole dispute on 'An entire misconception on the part of the nuns of the nature of religious obedience, on which we found them extremely ill-informed, particularly the Mother Prioress and her council'.[51]

Showing his irritation at the attitude adopted by Cardinal Weld, Baines later went on to regret that the cardinal had listened to unsubstantiated complaints against him by the nuns. If only he had made clear to the nuns that he would not listen to such complaints against their lawful superior, 'tranquillity might easily have been restored'.[52]

Before leaving Cannington, Baines told Cardinal Weld, the four of them had succeeded in restoring the sacraments to the majority of nuns; nothing could be done about the case of the Prioress and her deputy, Sr Mary Benedict, who refused to go to Dr Tuomy for confession. No action was taken against Dr Tuomy himself, who was the real source of the conflict. He was restored to his faculties and the Prioress informed that 'nothing has been elicited which would induce the Bishop to interfere with Dr Tuomy in the administration of the Holy Sacraments', and the Bishop did not think 'he need appoint any other to the office of ordinary Confessor of this convent'.

Fr Edgeworth's recommendation

Fr Edgeworth, who stayed on at Cannington for a few days, had strong reservations about Dr Tuomy, who had been questioning individual nuns about what had happened at the enquiry, and making the extraordinary statement that he needed the details 'to guide him in the confessional'. Fr Edgeworth had rebuked him, telling him that it was up to the Bishop alone to remedy whatever abuses may be found to exist.[53]

He was becoming convinced that no peaceful solution could be reached at Cannington while Dr Tuomy remained there, and in a further letter to Baines he asked:

> Would it not be better to replace Dr Tuomy after a week or two by one in possession of the whole case and of sufficient firmness to do what is right but with the tact to avoid the appearance of what is wrong? ... [this] suggestion has proceeded as much from apprehension that Dr Tuomy's manner will be injurious to Your Lordship as from any other cause ... I am concerned, too, about the very good and timid portion of the community who are driven by Dr T's manner to seek comfort from the Prioress or some other ...[54]

Baines himself must have realized the inadequacies of Dr Tuomy as he continued to receive long, rambling letters from him recounting his grievances. He had been picking grapes in the garden, when the Abbé rushed up, saying, 'They are not ripe. This is my garden ...' And he had been reviled by the Prioress and some of the nuns as not fit to celebrate the sacraments – 'Am I, My Lord, to be insulted in the performance of my most sacred duty?'[55]

He told, too, the extraordinary story of miracles being performed in Baines's favour. At the beginning of the Creed one Sunday morning, Sr Veronica saw black and white spectres descending on all the nuns, the black ones on the heads of the Prioress and her party and the white, bright ones on those of Baines's supporters. 'The ten who came to me for confession were still all bright, all the rest were black.'[56]

More seriously, this letter revealed that the majority of the nuns were now refusing to go to Dr Tuomy to receive the sacraments. Even Sr Mary Bird, who was sympathetic towards Baines, wrote to him: 'It is impossible to go on without more help than Dr T. can give us – he is very hot and imprudent. What we go through on confession days in going to Dr T., I cannot describe.'[57]

At last, after all the damage had been done, Baines resolved to remove Dr Tuomy from Cannington. He and Fr Edgeworth went out to Westbury-on-Trym near Bristol, and persuaded Fr Larkin, the priest there, to move temporarily to Cannington until a permanent replacement could be found. He was received frostily by the Prioress and her council who made it clear that he was not the confessor of their choice. They had come to resent any priest appointed by Baines.

Fr Larkin was not given the usual missioner's room, but was eventually allowed to stay in the guest room.

At Baines's request, poor Fr Edgeworth returned to Cannington to try to resolve outstanding difficulties. He told the Prioress that Dr Tuomy's faculties were being withdrawn; the nuns would be allowed to submit three names to the Bishop, from whom their new confessor would be chosen. He listened to various other requests of the nuns, including that they should be allowed to exercise all the privileges and rights of their constitution, as they had done formerly; they believed that these had been undermined in the controversy with the Bishop. Fr Edgeworth felt that this request was too vague and needed more discussion, as did the request that Sr Mary Peter should be removed from the convent. Two other minor requests were granted.

The Prioress wrote Dr Wiseman, who was visiting England, telling him that she was reasonably pleased with the arrangements made by Fr Edgeworth.'Much though', she told him, 'is still wanting before perfect tranquillity can be restored - pray that God will send us a director who will promote this'.[58]

The search for a new confessor

Such a director was to be some time in coming, as all three of the priests whose names were submitted by the nuns refused to accept the appointment. The Abbé Prémord, their first choice, said that he could not take on such a responsibility again, while both Dr Coombes, the missioner from Shepton Mallet, and Fr Jenkins from the Bath mission, also declined, the latter writing to tell his Provincial, Fr Deday:

> Mr Edgeworth called upon our house . . . and told me that he had just come from Cannington and he wanted to know if I would want to be director there. I told him that I could not . . . for my superiors must order me. I know not whether you are acquainted with the very strange goings on at Cannington by the Bishop, led into the mess by that paragon of obstinacy, Fr Burgess . . . Mr Barber can edify you by a long and true account of the fantastic tricks played before High Heaven that make the angels of peace weep bitterly.[59]

After consulting Baines, Fr Edgeworth asked the nuns to put forward three more names. By this time they believed that things were moving in their favour at Rome, and that they could demand any terms from the Bishop, so they proposed one name only. This was a Fr Rollings, a Benedictine monk from the Northern District, whom neither Baines nor Edgeworth knew at all. It seems that the Prioress knew little about him either, but to the nuns he had the great advantage of coming from outside the Western District, so that he had never come under the influence of the Bishop. Fr Edgeworth found that the Prioress had already written to Fr Rollings and to the Benedictine President, Fr Birdsall.

Baines regarded the development as a deliberate slight and refused to countenance the appointment. It seems unlikely that he could have known anything against Fr Rollings personally, but the fact that he was a Benedictine monk would have weighed heavily against him in Baines's eyes. He wrote to Dr Wiseman, the English representative in Rome, asking him to put his case to Propaganda, as 'I fear that whatever step I take, it will be made a subject of accusation against me'. Although he maintained to Dr Wiseman that his predecessor, Dr Collingridge, had never given the nuns any choice in the appointment of a confessor, he had allowed them to submit three names, all of whom had declined to be considered. Now the nuns were insisting that they would only accept a Fr Rollings, a Benedictine monk from the Northern District, and Baines was not prepared to agree to this. He explained to Wiseman that: 'the appointment of any monk at present would cause Cannington to become another centre of dissension'.[60]

This was already the case, as Fr Edgeworth reported to Baines: 'Peace', he said, 'has certainly not returned to the community'.[61]

Fr Larkin was still finding himself unwelcome at Cannington and many of the nuns were refusing to go to him for the sacraments. Dr Coombes from Shepton Mallet and Fr Wheatman from Taunton continued to visit the convent and administer the sacraments to those who wished. Baines wrote a polite letter to Dr Coombes, but his exasperation came through. If Dr Coombes still thought it necessary to visit the convent each week, 'It will be useless to detain Mr Larkin any longer from his own flock, and I will then request you to take up residence at Cannington till my instructions arrive from Rome or some permanent settlement is made'.[62]

Dr Coombes plainly had no intention of doing this and, because of his long-held and highly respected position in the District, Baines dared take no further action. He wrote again to Dr Wiseman, urging him to push his case in Rome, since he had done all he could to reach a compromise with the nuns, depriving another mission of a priest to accommodate them: 'For the love of God I implore you, do what you can for my unhappy flock, who are suffering for the silly whims of those misguided nuns'.[63]

End of Baines's jurisdiction

Baines was clearly worried that the nuns were putting their own case at Rome, claiming that they were being denied a confessor of their own choice. At this stage they probably were being unreasonable, but past events had led them to lose all confidence in the Bishop and the priests he had appointed to minister to them. Baines's appeal to Wiseman was almost certainly too late to help him at this stage. When Fr Edgeworth visited the convent at the end of February 1833, the Prioress's abrupt manner showed that she had triumphed at Rome and considered that the community would soon be taken from the Bishop's authority. Fr Edgeworth asked her why she had not been able to accommodate Fr Larkin in the priest's rooms, where all his predecessors had lived, and the Prioress replied that she would accommodate the priest in whatever rooms she chose. She would not have used such forthright terms at an earlier date and her additional remark that she had received 'positive instructions from the authorities in Rome not to admit Fr Larkin to the priest's room' confirms that she believed a decision in Rome was imminent.[64]

The momentous Papal Brief was issued on 20 June 1833, signed by Pope Gregory XVI. It suspended Baines's jurisdiction of the community from 16 July, and appointed the '*Dilectum Filium Cardinalem Weld*' the Pope's vicar in charge of restoring peace to Cannington, with the power of delegating authority to a vicar in England. Cardinal Weld immediately appointed the Abbé Prémord as his vicar, and the Abbé confirmed the appointment of Fr Rollings as confessor to the convent. Fr Larkin was to be allowed to stay on as a missioner.

There was no immediate reaction by Baines, who must have felt completely humiliated by the decision. He was not at all mollified by a letter from Fr Larkin, who seemed to be happily settled at Cannington. He told the Bishop that, 'The nuns will feel greatly comforted and delighted if I could inform them that your Lordship is reconciled to the arrangements'.[65]

If he could have read the letter that his longtime opponent, Fr Birdsall, wrote to the Prioress, Baines would have been even less pleased: 'Among the many congratulations which your present good news will call forth, I beg to offer also mine, for indeed I, too, will know what a painful anxiety must have accompanied your long protracted uncertainty, not to understand with what joyful heart the Roman news was received by your family!!!'[66]

With a far from joyful heart, Baines wrote to Wiseman on 4 September 1833:

> I have waited in anxious expectation that a letter from you might explain the inexplicable ... that a formal brief should be issued bearing the name and authority of the head of the Church asserting that the contentions and discordance at Cannington arose not from the nuns themselves but from others, and in consequence suspending my jurisdiction and transferring the nuns to Cardinal Weld, no reasons being assigned for this act of unexampled severity towards me ... is what I cannot explain, even after the treatment I have received and continue to receive on the score of the monks ...[67]

Baines went on to describe 'the dreadful suffering this sad affair has caused me', and 'what a position it places me in'. He had been too distressed to do anything, had not communicated directly with any of the other bishops, and had deferred a visit to Devon and Cornwall 'till I can dare to show my face'. He had remained silent for some time, hoping that that this would appear to be justification of his conduct against the ridiculous application of the nuns 'to be removed from my *tyranny* and obliging these refractory ladies to return to obedience'.

Instead the Holy See had made a decision which

> not only confirms in the public mind the false accusations that have been made against me, but coupled with the former accusations of the monks, the truth of which was in like manner confirmed by decisions of the apostolic see, render me an object of general pity or contempt, and reduces my authority over my subjects ... The affair is already known all over the Kingdom and I am daily called upon by friends for an explanation.[68]

Baines beseeched Dr Wiseman to give him an explanation of what had happened. He went through step by step all the measures he had taken in the dispute, and required to know exactly where he had gone wrong. He felt completely humiliated, especially by Cardinal Weld's first act of appointing the Abbé as his vice-regent and superior of the convent: 'Thus their triumph and my defeat are complete'.[69]

Attempts to undermine the settlement

No explanations came from Rome, and there were indications that Baines was determined not to allow the Cannington affair to rest. A letter came from Fr Larkin in which, after telling the Bishop how happily he was settled as a missioner at Cannington with a cottage and garden, he says:

> It will give great pleasure to hear that Your Lordship considers it finally settled. The prospect of attempting to continue the contest is truly unpleasant and may end in consequences I fear. I am aware of what precautious have been taken to prevent all communications between the nuns and their former ecclesiastical superiors. I think that any attempt must prove ineffectual.[70]

A few days later there was news that Fr Burgess, whether acting on his own authority or that of Baines is not clear, had written to Miss Bettington, who was living at Cannington, and commissioned her to tell the nuns that: 'His Lordship does not consider the question settled, that it was not the decision of Propaganda, that they were not to sign any documents, make any arrangements etc.'[71]

The Prioress obtained knowledge of this letter, and Fr Larkin told Baines: 'Though before there was reconciliation, now there are symptoms of disunity, disaffection and discontent. Fr Burgess is so identified with Your Lordship that what comes from one is said to originate from the other . . .'[72]

The move from Cannington

This was very true, and if Burgess had acted on his own initiative, he had done no service to the Bishop. The matter was bound to be reported to Rome, and was likely to increase the antagonism felt by many towards Baines. About this time Cardinal Weld advised the Prioress to look for a new house out of the Western District. By 1835, she had found a suitable place in the village of Colwich near Stafford, and the nuns began to move out; by April 1836, they had left the convent where they had lived for thirty years and established themselves happily in the Midland District under Bishop Walsh.

Baines must have been pleased to see the nuns depart, for they were an ever-present reminder of the way in which his authority had been flouted. Both parties must take some blame for the prolongation of such a dispute, which surely could have been settled long before if there had been a spirit of compromise. But the Bishop and the Prioress were strong-minded characters, who were inclined to stand on their dignity and defend their cause to the end. Baines believed that he was championing the position of Vicars Apostolic to be the ultimate authority over a convent, and to appoint the confessor and the missioner; the Prioress claimed that she was defending the order's constitutions, which had been granted to them two hundred years before. There must also have been some element of sexism in the dispute, as Baines, Burgess and Tuomy were constantly making disparaging remarks about the nuns as 'women', while they resented the fact that the Prioress was taking such a 'masculine' stand against them. Baines was not well served by these two priests, Burgess and Tuomy, and showed poor judgement in sending them to Cannington, Burgess, in particular being one of the main causes of the original controversy. It is curious that Baines and others seemed to place so much confidence in Burgess, who had shown considerable lack of tact since his Ampleforth days; the lack of judgement was to be compounded by Rome, when they appointed Burgess as the third Bishop of Clifton in 1851.

The Cannington dispute was unfortunate for Baines's reputation, both in England and in Rome, where he had once been a favourite son of Leo XII, but was now coming to be regarded as a source of disruption. It was to prejudice Propaganda and Pope Gregory XVI against him in the greater battles that were to come.

Notes

1 CDA, printed from old manuscript of St Benedict's Priory of Colwich (no date or publisher).
2 Ibid. Cannington File, 17, Prioress to Baines, 26 February 1830.
3 Ibid. August 1830.
4 Ibid. 23, Prioress to Baines, 7 October 1830.
5 Ibid.
6 Ibid. 25, Prioress to Baines, Sunday morning, 1830.
7 Ibid. 26, Prioress to Baines, 26 November 1830.
8 See above, chapter 6.
9 CDA, Cannington File, 27, Prioress to Baines, 7 December 1830.
10 Ibid. 28, Prioress to Baines, 9 April 1831.
11 Ibid. 60, Burgess to Baines, 2 May 1831.
12 Ibid. 61, Burgess to Baines, June 1831.
13 Ibid. 2, Sr Mary Angela to Baines, 1831.
14 Ibid. Bishops' Letters, Prioress to Baines, 16 August 1831.
15 Ibid. Cannington File, Sr Mary Peter to Baines, 4 September 1831.
16 Ibid. 164, Baines to Prioress, 18 September 1831.
17 Ibid. 162, Prioress to Baines, 18 September 1831.
18 Ibid. 140, Baines to Abbé Prémord, 22 December 1831.
19 Ibid. 32, Prioress to Baines, 19 September 1831.
20 Ibid. 139, Baines to Sidgreaves, 22 December 1831.
21 Ibid.
22 bid. Declaration for Prioress to sign.
23 Ibid.
24 Ibid. 5, Sr Mary Benedict to Baines, 18 January 1832.
25 Ibid. 6, Baines to Burgess, 7 January 1832.
26 Ibid. Bishops' Letters, Prioress to Baines, 17 January 1832.

27 Ibid.
28 Ibid. Cannington file, Burgess to Baines, 13 January 1832.
29 Ibid. 142, Baines to Prioress, 16 February 1832.
30 Ibid.
31 Ibid. 143, Baines to Weld, 20 February 1832.
32 Downside Archives, H420, Cooper to Deday, 7 March 1832.
33 Ibid. H421, Brown to Deday, 18 March 1832.
34 CDA, Cannington File, Prémord to Baines, 30 March 1832.
35 Ibid. Baines to Prémord, April 1832.
36 Ibid. 94, Tuomy to Baines, 4 May 1832.
37 Ibid. 140, Baines to Tuomy, 29 May 1832.
38 Ibid. 13, Sr Knight to Baines, no date.
39 Ibid. Bishop's Letters, Baines to Weld, 2 April 1832.
40 Ibid. 5 June 1832.
41 Ibid. 21 June 1832.
42 Ibid. Weld to Baines, June 1832.
43 Ibid.
44 Ibid.
45 Ibid. Cannington File, 148, Baines to Weld, 30 July 1832.
46 Ibid. 97, Tuomy to Baines, 23 June 1832.
47 Ibid. 34, Prioress to Baines, July 1832.
48 Ibid. 101, Tuomy to Baines, 9 July 1832.
49 Ibid. 78, Burgess to Baines, 9 July 1832.
50 Ibid. 135, Baines to Prioress, 10 July 1832.
51 Ibid. 148, Baines to Weld, 30 July 1832.
52 CDA, Cannington File, 42, Baines to Weld, August 1832.
53 Ibid. 128, Edgeworth to Baines, 30 July 1832.
54 Ibid.
55 Ibid. 102, Tuomy to Baines, 11 September 1832.
56 Ibid. Tuomy to Baines, 2 November 1832.
57 Ibid. Sr Mary Bird to Baines, 1 November 1832.
58 Ibid. Bishops' Letters, Prioress to Wiseman, 26 November 1832.
59 Downside Archives, H499, Jenkins to Deday, 15 November 1832.
60 CDA, Cannington File, 149, Baines to Wiseman, 29 December 1832.
61 Ibid. 48, Edgeworth to Baines, 28 February 1833.
62 Ibid. 152 Baines to Coombes, 18 January 1833.
63 Ibid. 123, Baines to Wiseman, 6 January 1833.
64 Ibid. 50, Edgeworth to Baines, 28 February 1833.
65 Ibid. 16, Larkins to Baines, 10 August 1833.
66 Downside Archives, H379, Birdsall to Prioress, 10 August 1833.
67 CDA, Bishops' Letters, Baines to Wiseman, 4 September 1833.
68 Ibid.
69 Ibid.
70 Ibid. Cannington File, 117, Larkin to Baines, 12 September 1833.
71 Ibid. 118, Larkin to Baines, 15 September 1833 (reporting on letter of Fr Burgess to Miss Bettington).
72 Ibid.

8

A Cry from the Missions

While Baines was submerged in the problems of Prior Park and conflicts with the Benedictines, his priests were coping as best as they could with the day-to-day concerns of the missions. If asked, they would probably have replied with one voice that the great priority was to provide financial resources for the missions, rather than to invest every spare shilling in the expensive enterprise of Prior Park, laudable as this may have been.

Somerset and Devon

In the rural areas the prosperity of the Catholic missions depended on whether they were fortunate enough to be supported by a wealthy patron. There was only one Catholic member of the nobility in the south-west counties of Cornwall, Devon and Somerset; this was Lord Clifford, who had large estates around Ugbrooke in Devon, and owned other land in Somerset. His chapel at Ugbrooke was available for local Catholics to attend mass and he also gave financial support to members of local missions. Downside in Somerset also sent out some of its monks to administer the sacrament in the surrounding countryside, so the Catholics in these areas were reasonably served.

There were also a number of missions in these counties, where smaller Catholic landlords lived who were generous to the Church and left legacies. The priest retiring from the Shortwood mission in Somerset reported to Baines that a new priest would have a regular small income from a trust fund of £800 and this would be increased by a future legacy of an old lady of about £300 a year. In addition he would have a house to live in, furniture, plate and books.[1] This would insure him a reasonably comfortable life, quite unknown by many priests.

Yet Catholic landlords moved or died, and could be replaced by men who had no sympathy with the Catholic faith. In one case a Devon mission near Barnstaple had been dependent on the goodwill of a Catholic landlord, but he died in 1837 and the estate was inherited by a Protestant, Mr Chichester, who would do nothing for the mission. The priest was left with no means of support, as the Catholic population was too small and too poor to make a reasonable contribution.[2] He appealed to Baines for support, but there is no record of whether he received any. New financial demands of this kind must have brought increasing worry to the Bishop, already beset with debts.

The Taunton mission in Somerset had never been fortunate in securing a patron and, although the congregation had a chapel, described as 'neat and commodious', there was no house for the priest and no fund for his support. The congregation was very poor and the small amount they gave in collections was quite inadequate to provide a reasonable salary. The Catholic *Directory* appealed for funds for the mission, for 'unless assisted by distant friends, the congregation is in danger of being left destitute'.[3]

Cornwall

Baines occasionally visited the Somerset and north Devon missions, and at least once went to Cornwall, but the Falmouth, Truro and Penzance missions were so remote that this involved a very difficult and hazardous journey. He could not have understood the extent of their problems, or he would have realized that sending an appeal for Prior Park to the priest at Falmouth was scarcely tactful. The Revd Robert Platt replied that the great poverty of the congregation prevented him from raising a subscription for Prior Park, and then went on to inform the Bishop of all the problems that confronted him in south Cornwall. Although there was a chapel in Falmouth, there was still a large debt on it, which there was little prospect of paying off. 'In this congregation, there is but one respectable family, that of Mrs Carpenter, whose husband is a protestant, from whom I once received the sum of 12s – the rest with one or two exceptions are pedlars, sailors and soldiers, among whom a subscription is made on Sundays, after mass, which frequently does not amount to more than eight pence.'[4]

Other small groups of Catholics lived in Truro and Penzance, where there was no chapel, the former 12 miles and the other 25 miles from Falmouth. The priest travelled to both places about once a month to celebrate mass, usually on foot, unless he could get a lift by horse and cart. As it was not possible to return in the same day, he had to spend money on food and lodgings, for which expenses the meagre collections were quite inadequate.[5] The priest appealed to

Baines for help for the mission and also for himself: 'As my finances are at present low it would greatly oblige me if you would remit what is due of my salary up to the 11th inst of this month, which amounts to 27 pounds, 3 shillings and fourpence'.[6]

Baines sent him most of the money asked and must have registered the need for another priest in Penzance, although it was some years later, after receiving a petition from the congregation there, that he took action. He then sent them a priest from Ireland. This poor young man, straight from the seminary, wrote to Baines to describe the extraordinary situation he found on his arrival:

> I found the room, 5ft long, which they promised to have as a temporary chapel, occupied, so that from the difficulty of finding a proper place, there was no mass on Sunday. In the course of the week I took a room about 30ft long, I should think. This being a school room, we can only occupy it on Sundays. Having got it cleaned and sanded I said my first mass on Sunday week.[7]

There was another problem, as the priest, the Revd William Priny, had left his missal behind in Ireland, and there was not another in the whole area. He was forced to walk over to Falmouth to borrow one from the Revd Robert Platt, and then return it, for the priest had to borrow one himself.[8]

He was appalled by the state of the congregation: 'I cannot give you an idea, my lord, of the poverty of the poor Catholics who signed the petition [to have a priest]: with the exception of half a dozen water guards . . . they are all objects of commiseration and all put together cannot raise more than 20 pounds a year.'[9]

It was enough to make any young priest despair and William Priny went on to say that 'nothing but the goodness and providence of God can make a mission take here unless a clergyman has more for his support . . . I am willing to live on sea-weed rather than to give a victory to the protestant and dissenting swarm':[10] (the area was particularly strong in Methodism).

They desperately wanted a chapel and William Priny wondered whether he could obtain the address of wealthy Catholic noblemen to appeal for subscriptions for such a building; otherwise he did not know what they could do, for 'we are now in a deplorable state'.[11]

There is no record of any reply from Baines to this appeal, but in any case there was probably little he could do about it. All available money was tied up in Prior Park: he had already appealed several times to the Catholic noblemen of England for additional funds, and the response had been disappointing. The small number of wealthy

Catholic families had so many appeals that they must have been suffering from charity fatigue.

The southern and central counties

In the southern and central counties of Baines's vicariate, Wiltshire, Dorset and Oxfordshire, some missions fared better. Lord Arundell, who lived near Salisbury, and the Weld family at Lulworth Castle in Dorset, contributed a great deal to the Catholic Church in the area. The chapel at Wardour Castle attracted large numbers of Catholics over a wide radius; Lord Arundell also supported the Salisbury mission and gave money to others. Some Catholic missions were also in holiday resorts or on the tourist route to the coast, thus attracting money from outside the area. In the village of Bonham House near Mere, for example, a chapel had been built and on Sunday the congregation was able to attend High Mass celebrated at 11 a.m. and vespers at 3 p.m., whereas many other communities had to be content to attend mass once a month. In the *Catholic Directory* of 1837 its attractions were listed in these words: 'The chapel is near the Stourton Inn, adjoining the beautiful gardens of Stourhead and being in direct line for tourists from Bath, Weymouth or Salisbury in visiting Longleat, Fonthill and Stourhead'.[12]

Priests at Weymouth had been struggling for many years to raise enough money to build a chapel there. Fr Edgeworth, who later went to Bristol, had attempted it in the early 1820s and despaired of ever raising enough money to pay an adequate salary for a priest or funds for building. As has been seen, he was often in financial difficulties, having to obtain an advance from Anna de Mendoza.

The difficulty was that, although Weymouth had a number of well-to-do Catholics during the summer season, during most of the year the congregation was very poor indeed. In 1830 the priest, the Revd P. A. Hartley, reported to Baines: 'To give your Lordship a better idea whether this mission should be given up altogether, I will state the census of my people as near as I can, including children of various ages and adults; it is about 53. In this number I don't reckon Irish clothmen, nor servants of protestant visitors, nor strangers of any kind.'[13]

The priest obviously wanted to build a chapel, thinking that 'a public chapel might be better attended than a private room in an inferior situation ... I am inclined to think that a decent public chapel would induce them to become punctual in their attendance.'[14]

There was further correspondence with Baines about whether the priest should embark on the project, and Hartley wanted the Bishop to authorize him to draw his half-year's salary, if it was decided that the priest should stay in Weymouth. No priest ever seemed to be certain when or if the next payment would materialize. In spite of the problems and his obvious wish to go ahead with the project, Hartley tried to be conciliatory: 'Should your Lordship consider the expense of building a chapel here too considerable, or should there be no funds for this purpose or otherwise wanted for the more important object of Prior Park, I am willing to abandon the undertaking'.[15]

Baines, who had spent many holidays in Weymouth, must have listened to this plea, as the 1836 *Catholic Directory* announced that: 'Through the liberality and charity of many, the chapel and dwelling house attached to the mission are completed without any debt being left'.

Two years later more money was also raised to build a school, 'in which poor children can have a moral and religious education gratis. Before this it was distressing to parents of poor children obliged either to endanger their faith by sending them to anti-Catholic schools, or to abandon their morality to the contagion of the streets. A great struggle is required to maintain this school and donations are sought.'[16]

By this time the Revd P. A. Hartley, worn out with his labours, had retired to the more peaceful mission of Chepstow in Monmouthshire. He was one of the valiant Catholic priests of the early nineteenth century, who had to take on the work of fund-raising and all the details of planning a new building as well as the duties of a parish priest; all this he did for a pittance, which he could never be sure of receiving.

Poole was more fortunate in having a well-to-do Catholic, Edward Doughty, living at Upton House nearby. He offered to build a chapel at the resort at his own expense and wrote to Baines in July 1838:

> The chapel at Poole is getting on, the tiles will be ready in a week and we shall have it completely roofed in in a short while and I hope it will be finished by the month of October. I have been in treaty for the purchase of a house next door to the chapel which I believe, when completed, will be a good residence for the priest . . . I therefore think that it is highly desirable and it will meet your Lordship's convenience to come to us in the autumn to open the new chapel.[17]

Baines had been a friend of the Doughty family for many years and a regular visitor to Upton House, so that his liking for socializing with the great Catholic families in the land, strongly criticized in some circles, did in this case produce lasting benefit to the Catholic Church. He finally dedicated the church in Poole on 16 August 1840, and it was described as: 'a very handsome and convenient church in the Gothic style of architecture'. This was a feature which Baines would not have approved of, as he was to lambast Pugin's medievalism and favour the Classical style, 'Roman', as he preferred to call it. Wealthy benefactors, however, must be allowed to build churches in the style they pleased, particularly as, in Edward Doughty's case, he provided a salary for the regular priest; and with the help of regular contributions from the poor congregation, and more from summer visitors, it was hoped that this appointment would be a permanent one.

At the other Dorset resort of Lyme Regis, there was more difficulty in financing a church for the small number of Catholic residents and the more numerous holiday visitors. There were no wealthy patrons in the area, but better-off members of the congregation were prepared to take the responsibility of raising a subscription for building. There was a Mr Henry Farnall and a Mr and Mrs Bellingham, the latter another admirer of Bishop Baines, sending good wishes to him via visiting priests. Baines himself took a particular interest in the building of this church, agreeing to become a trustee and drawing up his own plans for features of the interior. Some of his Gothic sketches for the High Altar and the Bishop's throne still survive.

The subscription raised enough to buy the land and to pay out £325 on the building, the full cost of which would be £1,090, with the addition of £325 to be paid out on other work. The trustees, therefore, decided to mortgage the property and to finish the building of the church by H. E. Goodridge only so far as to allow it to be used, leaving other desirable but not essential features to be added later. At first the congregation could not afford to maintain a priest, and Mr Farnall wrote to Baines putting the proposition, 'of one priest doing the duties of the parish of Lyme and Axminster. When we have the means of supporting a priest, we will solicit your Lordship again to establish a separate mission in this town.'[18]

By August 1836 the builders were demanding more money than had already been paid out on the Lyme Regis church, and were calling upon the unfortunate Mr Farnall. He immediately wrote to Dr Brindle, Baines's Vicar General, as Baines was away: 'The Builders are anxious to know whether the Bishop or yourself are at present the contracting party, as the chapel will be entirely finished within three weeks. Some arrangement must of course be made in order to prevent unpleasant consequences to either party. I shall be much obliged to you to speak to the Bishop . . .'[19]

A compromise must have been reached with the builders, as Baines dedicated the chapel later in the same year, and in 1837 was corresponding with Mr Bellingham about the possibility of Lyme supporting a permanent priest, such as Mr Larkin. Mr Bellingham replied: 'We should do our best to make him happy and comfortable, but we cannot promise him £60 a year ... There are, however, in the summer always some Catholic visitors to Lyme. Their contributions will in all probability increase the priest's income to about £80.'[20]

Some debts were still owing, however, and Baines was worried that these might fall upon him, as revealed in another letter from Bellingham:

> Your Lordship says that you cannot become responsible for any debts. We should indeed be extremely sorry if you were responsible for any of the debts of the church ... but I must assure your Lordship that I never for one moment imagined that the responsibility was to fall on me ... I would gladly have given the money, but I do assure Your Lordship that it is *quite out of my power* to do so ... the only way is to make collections which I do on every occasion.[21]

Baines never appointed Mr Larkin to Lyme, for some reason, and Mr Bellingham started looking around for himself. He wrote to the Bishop at the end of 1837 to tell him that he thought that he had been successful: 'I have the pleasure to inform you that, if it meets with your approbation, I can now obtain a clergyman from Kildare'.

Such independent action angered Baines, who wrote to tell Bellingham that he himself would provide a suitable priest for the Lyme mission in the following spring. Bellingham replied with tact, but also demonstrated a considerable independence of spirit:

> It is with much pleasure that I am informed by your letter, that your Lordship had nominated a priest for our poor little mission. It is much more gratifying to us than being obliged to have recourse to Ireland, but I hope your Lordship has not forgotten that when we were very distressed for a priest, you recommended us to try our interest with our friends in that country. We are at the same time much disappointed that this mission has to wait until after Easter to obtain the services of a clergyman.

He then went on to recount all the reasons why the Lyme mission should not have to wait so long, particularly the state of the fifteen Catholic children in the congregation, who were attending a school run 'upon the British and Foreign system and one of the regulations of the committee requires that all the children coming to the school shall receive religious instruction at least once a week from their respective clergymen'.[22]

The Lyme mission, with its doubts about the money it could raise to supply a regular income, still had to wait until the summer of 1838 for the arrival of its first priest.

Catholic patrons did not always fulfil their promises and Baines believed in keeping them up to the mark, as shown by his letters to a Lord de Manley at Heythrop in Oxfordshire, which combined a deference to the nobility with a veiled threat of what might happen if Lord de Manley did not fulfil his obligations:

> I am very sorry to inform your Lordship that I receive continual complaints and lamentations from the catholics of Heythrop on the state of religious destitution in which they are left ... Your Lordship promised that they should at no distant period be provided with a chapel ... I feel confident that in the midst of your many weightier affairs this trifling matter may have escaped your Lordship's recollection and I humbly hope that you will give it your kind and early attention ...

Lord de Manley had promised to provide a priest with an income of £40 a year, but Baines did not consider this enough. As he had maintained over the Lyme mission, £60 was the minimum amount necessary to support a priest without additional support from other funds, which were not available. Unless Lord de Manley should increase that amount, Baines could only send occasional assistance in the person of Revd J. Michael of Chipping Norton. Baines ended by the somewhat bald statement: 'If you would have the goodness to order whatever you consider due to be paid to my account at Wright and Co, London, I will apportion the amounts'.[23]

The English border counties

In the western counties of Herefordshire and Gloucestershire, Baines encouraged sponsors of Catholic missions, whether they were grand or low. He welcomed the Jesuits giving of a magnificent Catholic church to Hereford, the church of St Francis Xavier, which opened on 8 August 1839. Although he had had disputes with the Society of Jesus, particularly over one of the priests in the Bristol mission at the beginning of his vicariate, this did not prevent him rejoicing at the fine acquisition. At the same time Baines was encouraging a Mrs Neve from Gloucestershire, who had promised that she would provide a lowly establishment for Catholic worship at Horton near Chipping Sodbury, where 'there was a wreck of a congregation that had been abandoned for want of clergy and money'.

Baines must have been pleasantly surprised to receive a letter which, instead of the usual request for money to provide a chapel and the income for a priest, announced that:

> Having heard your Lordship so frequently express your wishes that a decent place should be provided for dispensing the august mysteries, I did not attempt formally to announce it to your Lordship until I was in so forward a state as to be ready for the reception of a Pastor. The distressing and universal complaints of trouble and vexations from the delays of workmen, I have not been spared from, so that it will take some time before the plans will be ready to receive your Lordship. At present there is scarce a chair in the house, as is there a room in which to place one in. . . . Great pleasure shall I have in receiving your information as to when you will do me the favour of inspecting my humble concern, but it is a beginning, and Heaven grant that the congregation may in a few years require a larger and more respectable accommodation.[24]

A few months later the 1840 *Catholic Directory* announced that Bishop Baines had opened the new church at Horton, a mission which had been founded by the liberality of Mrs Neve. Baines was dependent on the liberality of similar benefactors throughout the west and south of England, and it is extraordinary how he seemed to raise contributions from the most unlikely sources.

Wales

In Wales, which remained part of the Western Vicariate until 1840, the possibility of obtaining Catholic patrons of missions was most unlikely. There were only small isolated pockets of Catholics left in the country, which in the 1830s were being augmented in the south by an influx of Irish settlers, many of them labourers from the poorer western regions of Ireland who settled in the run-down areas of Swansea and Cardiff, adding to the poverty and degradation already there.

The oldest Catholic mission was in Brecon, where the stable population of about 100 had continued to survive since the Reformation. Until the end of the eighteenth century they had no chapel and were served only by visiting priests. In 1788, however, Bishop Walmesley was able to appoint a resident priest, a Franciscan, Fr John Williams. He was a hard-working and dedicated man, who raised enough money to buy the old inn at Brecon, the Three Cocks, as a chapel, a residence for the priest and a further source of revenue by letting part of it to a pastry cook. This unsuitable accommodation was still used in Bishop Baines's day, and the hope of building the first Catholic church was still a dream. Baines himself had little contact with Brecon, apart from approving the transfer of Fr Lewis Havard, a Welsh priest, who was anxious to return home to Brecon from the London District.

Swansea, until the middle of the nineteenth century the largest town in South Wales, was quite different in character. It also had an old Catholic mission, originally much smaller than Brecon, and until the early nineteenth century had no regular priest. A succession of Jesuit priests made the long and often perilous journey from Bristol every few months to provide mass for the Swansea congregation, which was augmented by others coming from Llanelly and Carmarthen to the west, the Swansea Valley villages to the north, and Neath to the east. The most well known of these Jesuit priests was Fr Plowden, who took a seven-year lease of a room in an old church formally belonging to the Knights Templar, and then drew up plans to build a chapel in Nelson Place, in a run-down part of the town near the docks. He saw the possibility of developing the good work in Swansea, for the town was 'a large trading centre and most frequented by the Irish, and there was the great probability of the establishment increasing, so as to be a good and permanent mission'.[25]

By the time of Baines's vicariate his prediction had been realized; the number of Irish settlers had increased dramatically, there had been a permanent priest in Swansea for many years, and the congregation had been attending services in their own chapel since 1814. Fr Plowden's plans to build never seemed to have materialized and it was in 1813, nearly the end of the Napoleonic Wars before a French priest, Fr Séjan, succeeded in raising enough money to build the first Catholic chapel in Swansea since the Reformation. By Bishop Baines's time, however, it was getting too small for the increased number of Catholics and the work of the priest was becoming more and more demanding, as he ministered to a number of very poor Catholics with some rough elements; he often needed protection when visiting some of his flock in the tenement buildings of the Swansea slums.

During the eighteen-thirties, there appears to have been some trouble in the Swansea mission; whether the priest, Fr Bonde, was acting contrary to the instructions of the Bishop is unclear, but Baines dismissed him and sent in Fr Charles Kavanagh from Newport to take the services. This displeased a number of the congregation, who sent a petition to the Bishop to have Fr Bonde reinstated, which Baines ignored. Fr Kavanagh reported to him that: 'It is not necessary for me to inform your Lordship that some of the people of Swansea did not like to see a successor to Fr Bonde and indeed some of the expressions uttered in my presence highly displeased me'.[26]

Despite this, Fr Kavanagh's tact and pleasant personality seem to have won him friends. As he told Baines:

> I have received great marks of kindness from the most respectable Catholics here. Mr Staunton (one of the persons who presented the petition to your Lordship requesting the return of Mr Bonde) has absolutely insisted on my considering his house as my own. He is a very nice man and in his manner more like a priest than a secular person.[27]

Baines had apparently gained an unfavourable impression of the Swansea Catholics, and Fr Kavanagh tired to convince him that this was an erroneous impression. Many of them were very poor and were quite incapable of supporting a priest or raising funds for a new chapel which was urgently needed. The existing one built by Fr Séjan was in a ruinous state, much too small and the lease soon due to expire. The number of Irish coming over to work in the iron and copper mines was growing all the time, making the building of a new chapel even more imperative. The holiday trade in Swansea was also increasing and Fr Kavanagh believed that the building of a new church would encourage 'more respectable catholics to frequent the beautiful watering place'. As had been found in other sea-side resorts, the visitors would bring much needed funds to the poverty stricken community.[28]

Baines made Fr Kavanagh's position permanent, and this was one of the most perceptive and successful of his appointments. Fr Kavanagh was a dedicated and enterprising priest who, after Wales had been removed from the Western District in 1840, raised enough money to build a much larger church. He toiled among the poor and deprived members of his congregation, particularly the Irish settlement in east Swansea, and in the cholera epidemic of the late 1840s was an heroic figure, ministering to the dying, regardless of whether they were Catholic or Protestant. He died much loved and lamented at the early age of 47.[29]

Cardiff, unlike Swansea, did not have an indigenous Catholic population, and there were no Catholics at all until the late 1820s. Then there was an influx of poor Irish settlers who had come over to work in the Welsh coal mines and iron industry. Within a few years the numbers had risen to about 2,000 and Fr Metcalfe, visiting the Newport area, reported to Baines:

> There certainly is a large congregation at Cardiff and another as great if not greater at Pontypool – and they seemed disposed at each place to try to support a priest. It is certainly an advantage for a priest to know

> Irish, as some cannot speak English, but if they are in health and wish to see only an Irish priest, you know we have one in Merthyr.[30]

Baines took his advice and appointed a permanent priest, Fr Millea, to Cardiff and the surrounding area, but there was still no church until some years after Wales was taken out of the Western Vicariate. The new priest had to hire a couple of rooms, in one of which the altar was erected, and the other held the congregation, which spilled into a shed. Numerous appeals were made for funds to build a chapel.[31]

The Irish priest, Fr Carroll, at Merthyr Tydfil, mentioned by Fr Metcalfe, had under his care 700 poor Irish Catholics employed mainly in the iron and coal works. The 1840 Catholic *Directory* described him as 'a very talented and zealous pastor'. Although he had no chapel, he said mass twice every Sunday, once at Merthyr Tydfil in a granary over a slaughterhouse and another six miles away in a wash-house, and he had to travel between the two places on foot. He had also succeeded in starting a school for about 50 children in a one-horse stable about 8ft by 16ft.

The priest lived in a workman's cottage, without a single article of decent furniture, and often had insufficient food. Baines, who had appointed him, offered to move him to a more comfortable mission after a few years, but he had declined.[32] He wrote to Baines in 1838, in reply to a letter from the Bishop asking whether he had any children for confirmation, telling him that:

> I could not conscientiously recommend any of my flock for confirmation . . . Although I have encouraged many of them [the parents] to get their children to quit the Methodists and come to mass on Sundays, I have been obliged to purchase cloth to induce the wretched parents to send their children to catechism on Sundays and devise schemes to make them repeat even the short version of Fleming's catechism.[33]

Fr Carroll was worried that his Irish flock would suffer from the intolerance of bigoted Baptists, Wesleyans or Independents – or worse, Unitarians. He warned Baines, who was talking of visiting Merthyr Tydfil, to preserve the strictest incognito: 'For if once the parsons or the dissenters perceive anything like an approach to a Catholic establishment here, this will be the signal for the dispersal of my poor flock which entirely consists of labourers not initiated into the works, who would soon be replaced by English Protestants'.[34]

Baines would not have liked travelling incognito, but he took the lesson to heart in his later attacks on the campaign for the conversion of England to Catholicism. Yet he would have approved of the priest's robust language and his hopes for the future of Catholicism, although he would not have entirely shared his optimism. Fr Carroll told him that: 'We must not steal into the enemy's camp, or the Irish will be banished and there are no English Catholics here. And if we give no alarm here, the children of the Irish born will in a few generations make this a Catholic country.'[35]

Other Catholic outposts in Wales were at the opposite end of the country, at Bangor, Wrexham, Talacre and Holywell. The latter, as its name implies, was the site of St Winefrede's Well, the only shrine in the country to survive the Reformation. It was particularly sacred to Catholics, and the maintenance of a mission here was considered vital. Well-to-do women in the eighteenth century had endowed it, and the Mostyn family from Talacre contributed generously, so that by the beginning of the nineteenth century it was supporting both a secular and a Jesuit priest, and a small chapel was built in 1808. During Baines's vicariate this was superseded by a large church, built in the classical style by the architect, J. J. Scoles in 1833.

Bangor and Wrexham also had chapels and the small mission at Talacre was maintained as a family concern by the Mostyn family, but there were always financial problems. Bangor's already impoverished state had been made worse by the dispute between Baines and the Jesuits, which had rumbled on since the Bishop removed the last of the Jesuit priests, Fr Rowe, from the Bristol mission soon after becoming Vicar Apostolic. For many years the Jesuits at Stonyhurst had bestowed an annual grant of £50 on the Bangor mission, a not inconsiderable sum in those days. In 1838, however, the new Provincial, Fr Bird, announced that this would be withdrawn, giving as his reason that the Vicar Apostolic of the Western District was hostile to the Society and had deprived it of the Bristol mission. This was hard on the Bangor mission, which had nothing to do with the dispute, and Baines wrote immediately to Fr Norris at Stonyhurst protesting at the move. He stressed the great poverty of the Bangor mission and then went on to say: 'Whatever I may individually be, I cannot think that the Society would wish to punish me by inflicting privation on my poor flock'.[36]

Baines was deep in debt and had a variety of other problems at the time, but he still found the time to plead the cause of one of his furthest-flung missions. Nothing came of the appeal, however, and Baines was forced to withdraw the resident priest from Bangor for a time. The mission still soldiered on with visiting priests until, by the time Wales became a separate vicariate, it was once more served by a resident priest and had both Sunday and week-day masses. It is possible that the Jesuits at Stonyhurst restored its grant when Baines was no longer Vicar Apostolic of Wales.

The northern Welsh missions, as well as those in the west of Wales, were so far from the centre of the District at Prior Park that maintaining any kind of contact was difficult. It was becoming obvious by 1840 that Wales needed its own ecclesiastical jurisdiction, and Baines was not altogether sorry when it was removed from his District to form the separate Vicariate of Wales and Menevia.

The Bath and Bristol missions

Most of the Western District in Baines's time was rural, but he also had on his doorstep two cities with growing Catholic populations. Bath had few of the problems of most missions. It had little poverty, as it was supported by the contributions of wealthy Catholic visitors coming to take the waters at the spa, and was supplied with priests by the Benedictines of Downside, who also made considerable financial contributions to Catholic life in Bath; nor had it any great influx of Irish settlers to bring increased tensions to the community. It had different problems, however, arising out of the antagonism between the president of the Benedictines, Fr Birdsall, and Bishop Baines, which led to a conflict as to who should control the Bath mission. This conflict will be discussed in the next chapter.

The Bristol mission, on the other hand, had all the problems of the rural missions writ large. It had an indigenous Catholic population of about a thousand, but this had been supplemented by a large influx of Irish immigrants who arrived in Bristol in the 1820s and 1830s. Most of them came from the poorer western parts of Ireland and were looking for general labouring work; they settled in the poorest parts of the inner city near the docks and fairly close to the small Catholic church of St Joseph's. There were no wealthy members of the Catholic gentry living in the area and, particularly after the Jesuits temporarily severed their connection with Bristol in 1827, the mission depended a great deal on the generosity of a number of well-to-do Catholic tradesmen and professional men who attended St Joseph's. Their contribution was not enough to provide a reasonable salary to the two priests, Frs Edgeworth and O'Farrell, or to maintain the church, let alone to provide a new building, which was urgently needed for the growing population. Fr Edgeworth calculated that, by the time of Catholic Emancipation in 1829, the numbers had expanded to about 6,000.[37]

Fr Edgeworth was a man of forceful personality and great enterprise, determined to overcome all obstacles. We have already met him as a priest at Weymouth, when he visited Anna de Mendoza at Bathampton Manor and confided in her about all his financial and other problems in the mission. He had gained a high reputation in Bristol, not only among Catholics, but also among some Protestants, who had admired his conduct during the Bristol Riots in 1831. At great risk to himself, he had gone out into the thick of the fray to persuade some of his Irish flock to refrain from joining in the looting and return home. One observer described how

> From 8 p.m. on the Sunday night until 3.30 a.m. on Monday morning, he was engaged in endeavouring to check the progress of depredation, in prevailing on all who he knew to desist from taking that which they pleaded would otherwise be destroyed. When he thought that the Custom House would otherwise be attacked, he obtained admission from the King Street side, and told one of the officials that his presence would prevent any of the poorer Irish from assaulting the premises.[38]

Baines clearly thought highly of Fr Edgeworth and had shown his regard for him as early as 1829, when he had resisted the Jesuit Provincial's attempt to have him removed from Bristol and replaced by a Jesuit. So when the priest came to him in the early 1830s full of plans for a large new church in Bristol, Baines greeted them with enthusiasm. It is likely that he had much to do with the choice of the imposing building planned, as the grandiose conception was in keeping with his views of what a Catholic church should always be, built in the Neo-Classical or grand 'Roman' style. The plan showed a building larger and more ornate than even a greatly increased Bristol congregation required, so it is possible that Baines was already dreaming of it as a future cathedral for the Western District. Such a concept would have been in keeping with his vision of the future of the Catholic Church in the west.

As usual, though, the Bishop could provide no money towards achieving such a magnificent building, and he left Fr Edgeworth to raise the funds entirely through his own efforts. This he appears to have done, raising funds to buy two acres of pasture land described as 'Lower Stoney Fields', Peace Hill, for £1,500, and another piece of land adjoining, consisting of a disused quarry, for which the price was not known. Fr Edgeworth appointed a John Tilladen to act for him, as he was afraid that there might be opposition if it became known that the land was wanted for a Catholic chapel.[39]

By August 1834 *Felix Farley's Bristol Journal* noted that: 'Labourers are now excavating the foundations of a catholic chapel in

Portrait of Bishop Baines, Ampleforth Abbey. By courtesy of Ampleforth Abbey Archives.

Lamspringe Abbey, Hanover. Architect's drawing circa 1730. By courtesy of Ampleforth Abbey Archives.

The organ at Lamspringe (1691). By courtesy of Ampleforth Abbey Archives.

The nave of the Abbey Church, Lamspringe (1691). View from the monks' choir. By courtesy of Ampleforth Abbey Archives.

The original house at Ampleforth to which the Benedictines moved in 1802 – from a painting at Ampleforth. By courtesy of Ampleforth Abbey Archives.

Ampleforth Abbey in 1852. The trees are where Baines says he planted them in 1814 (Diary). By courtesy of Ampleforth Abbey Archives.

Exterior of Downside Priory Chapel in 1823. The Chapel (centre right) was dedicated by Bishop Collingridge at a service during which Bishop Baines preached the sermon. From 'Downside Abbey and School, 1814–1914' Exeter 1914.

Interior of Downside Priory Chapel, dedicated in 1823. From ‘Downside Abbey and School, 1814–1914’ Exeter 1914.

An aerial view of Wardour Castle in 1934, the chapel hidden in the right-hand wing. By courtesy of the English Catholic History Association.

The interior of the chapel of Wardour Castle. By courtesy of Wardour Chapel Trust.

Particulars

OF

The Valuable Leasehold Estate,

(TITHE FREE,)

HELD FOR

A TERM OF ABOUT EIGHT HUNDRED YEARS,

WITH PART

FREEHOLD,

PRIOR PARK,

IN THE PARISH OF LYNCOMB AND WIDCOMB,

About One Mile from the City of BATH,

COMPRISING

A CAPITAL MANSION,

SEATED ON AN EMINENCE,

Erected, in the most substantial manner, about the Year 1738, by RALPH ALLEN, Esq.

PLANNED FOR THE ACCOMMODATION OF

A NOBLEMAN, OR FAMILY OF DISTINCTION;

A PORTER'S LODGE AT THE ENTRANCE, with WOOD and PIGEON HOUSES; AVIARY;

Carriage Drive to the House;

A SPACIOUS LOFTY ENTRANCE HALL,

Paved;

A DOOR, OPENING TO

A MAGNIFICENT PORTICO,

SUPPORTED BY MASSIVE COLUMNS, SURMOUNTED BY CORINTHIAN CAPITALS;

An Inner Hall,

LEADING TO

AN EXCELLENT DINING PARLOUR,

Walls Coloured, finished with Black Mouldings;

AN ELEGANT LOFTY DRAWING ROOM,

Walls Papered and Bordered, beautiful Statuary Marble Chimneypiece, with Sienna Columns and Ionic Capitals, Windows commanding beautiful Prospects of a fine Sheet of Water, fed by Cascades, and the Palladian Bridge;

BED CHAMBER,

Vaulted Roof, handsome Cornice, Recess for Bed, with Screen of Columns, Composite Capitals, Turkish Marble Chimneypiece, Closets, &c.

DRESSING ROOM, ADJOINING;

A BREAKFAST PARLOUR,

Wainscotted and Panelled, Dome Roof, Dove Marble Chimneypiece, and Closets;

Gentleman's Morning Room;

The sale notice of Prior Park Mansion in 1828. By courtesy of the Clifton Diocesan Archives.

Prior Park Mansion in the eighteenth century. By courtesy of the Clifton Diocesan Archives.

Prior Park Mansion. By courtesy of G. Hatfield.

Prior Park Lake. By courtesy of G. Hatfield.

Prior Park Mansion today, view from the north west, showing Baines' steps and the College of St Peter and St Paul. By courtesy of the Head Teacher, Prior Park College, Bath.

View of Bath from Bishop Baines' steps. By courtesy of the Head Teacher, Prior Park College, Bath.

The church of S.S. Michael and George, Lyme Regis, Dorset, (early C19 print). Bishop Baines had a great deal to do with the negotiations for the building of the church. By courtesy of the Plymouth Diocesan Archives.

The entrance to the church of S.S. Michael and George, Lyme Regis, Dorset, circa 1900. By courtesy of the Plymouth Diocesan Archives.

Cannington Court, now the Somerset College of Agriculture – from a sepia wash drawing by W.W. Wheatley, 1845. By courtesy of the Somerset County Archives.

An undated photograph of Cannington Court, taken by Robert Gilo of Bridgwater circa 1860–1870. By courtesy of the Somerset County Archives.

The Church of St Francis Xavier, Hereford, dedicated in 1839.
Exterior in 1910.

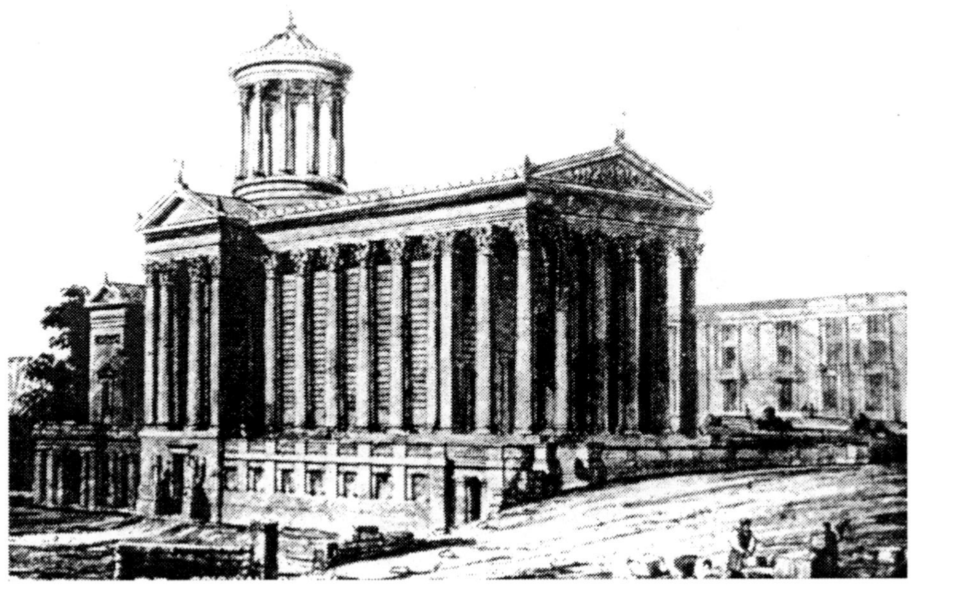

The original design for the Church of the Holy Apostles, Clifton (1831). Never completed to the original scheme, it opened as a pro-cathedral in 1848. By courtesy of the Clifton Diocesan Archives.

Baines's tomb at Downside Abbey, – from 'Downside Abbey and School 1814–1914' Exeter 1914.

the field opposite Meridian Place'.[40] By October of the same year, Fr Edgeworth and his assistant, Fr O'Farrell, laid the foundation stone of what would eventually be the new cathedral for Clifton. They did so with little ceremony, choosing an early morning hour so as to avoid Protestant antagonism. The great work was entrusted to the Bath architect, Henry Edmund Goodridge 1797–1864, who envisaged a massive structure large enough to hold 2,000 people, of temple-like form with a portico. It seems extraordinary, however, that an experienced architect could have planned such an immense building on land once used as a quarry; the dire consequences were to be seen as soon as the work on the walls and massive pillars began to progress: the face of the old quarry started to slip and to carry part of the foundations with it. All work on the new building had to stop, leaving six partially-completed columns, which could not support the roof as they were originally intended to do.[41]

The disappointment of the Catholic congregation and Fr Edgeworth can only be imagined, but the priest persevered. He raised enough money to build a small chapel and presbytery further down the slope from the original building, and came to live there to minister to Catholics in Clifton, leaving Fr O'Farrell at St Joseph's. His other task was to find enough money to repair the damaged foundations of the new church and to recommence building. By November 1842, a year before Baines's death, the priest had succeeded in securing a mortgage of £3,500 on the site so that rebuilding could start. The project was never viable as the foundations immediately collapsed again: Fr Edgeworth was declared bankrupt, and forced to leave Clifton.

For several years he returned to his chapel every Sunday to say mass, as civil debtors could not be arrested on the Sabbath; but at midnight he had to leave.[42]

Eventually Fr Edgeworth was forced to flee to the Continent to avoid imprisonment, and he died at Antwerp at a comparatively early age. An example of the total self-denial of some nineteenth-century Catholic priests, he willingly suffered bankruptcy and exile for the great cause he believed in – the expansion of the Catholic faith. By the time of the priest's bankruptcy, Baines was already dead, but it is unclear whether he gave Edgeworth much support during the priest's last tragic years in Bristol. There is a large correspondence between Baines and Edgeworth during the early eighteen-thirties, but nothing in the later years. The Bishop may have seen the priest at Prior Park or Bristol, but there is no evidence of this. Financially he could have done little anyway, owing to his own mounting debts, but there is an unpleasant feeling that he abandoned Fr Edgeworth to his creditors and to his fate. He was always full of enthusiasm and support for men who brought him the promise of great achievements, but did not like losers. And the cathedral they had both envisaged remained as a desolate shell, described by *Felix Farley's Bristol Journal* as 'an eyesore to the inhabitants of that part of Clifton'[43] until the arrival of Bishop Ullathorne as Vicar Apostolic in 1846.

A pastoral bishop

In spite of the defects in his character, which he exhibited in some of his relations with individuals, one cannot help being impressed by Baines's enormous correspondence with his priests during the years of his vicariate. Obviously most of the surviving letters were written to him, but constant references to previous correspondence show that he wrote a great many himself, in spite of being submerged by other problems and having to write them all in his own hand. He visited the missions, too, mainly in the southern counties, Somerset and Gloucestershire and the border counties of east Wales. He knew a great deal of what was going on, although it is doubtful if he fully understood the extent of the poverty existing in such far-flung missions as Swansea, Bangor and Falmouth, where he offended the priest by his lack of tact in asking for contributions for Prior Park. He made some perceptive appointments to the missions, too, appointing the right men to the job in such places as Swansea and Merthyr Tydfil and refusing to allow Fr Edgeworth to be removed from Bristol.

He could seldom help his priests financially, partly because of the huge commitments he was making at Prior Park. He ran down the mission funds, which Bishop Collingridge had built up to provide a bulwark in hard times or to help in church building, and he made it clear to priests that they were on their own in raising funds for expansion. On the other hand, Baines had a great many influential contacts, and did not hesitate to use them to persuade wealthy men and women to contribute large sums to help their local missions. Thus, in one way or another, numbers of churches were built and mission rooms dedicated during his vicariate. And most of his priests must have found Baines approachable as they continued to write copious letters, showing that they regarded him as a pastoral Bishop rather than a lordly figure living in the pomp of Prior Park.

Notes

1 CDA, Bishops' Letters, Hunt to Baines, 24 August 1837.
2 Ibid.

3 *The Laity's Directory*, 1840.
4 CDA, Bishops' Letters, Platt to Baines, 2 November 1830.
5 Ibid.
6 Ibid.
7 Ibid. Priny to Baines, 18 April 1832.
8 Ibid.
9 Ibid.
10 Ibid.
11 Ibid.
12 *The Laity's Directory*, 1837.
13 CDA, Bishops' Letters, Hartley to Baines, 1 December 1830.
14 Ibid.
15 Ibid.
16 *The Laity's Directory*, 1836.
17 CDA, Bishops' Letters, Doughty to Baines, 7 July 1838.
18 Ibid. Farnall to Baines, 30 January 1836.
19 Ibid. Farnall to Baines, 19 August 1836.
20 Ibid. Bellingham to Baines, 8 August 1837.
21 Ibid. Bellingham to Baines, December 1837.
22 Ibid. Bellingham to Baines, 25 December 1837.
23 Ibid. Baines to Manley, 4 June 1839.
24 Ibid. Neve to Baines, no date.
25 Ibid. Trenchard Street File, 1787–1845, Plowden to Sharrock, 25 November 1803 and 28 January 1807.
26 Ibid. Bishops' Letters, Kavanagh to Baines, November 1839.
27 Ibid.
28 Ibid.
29 R. T. Price, *Little Ireland; Aspects of the Irish and Greenhill, Swansea* (Swansea, 1992), pp. 23–5.
30 CDA, Bishops' Letters, Metcalfe to Baines, 21 June 1827.
31 *Laity's Directory*, 1837–1840.
32 CDA, Bishops' Letters, Carroll to Baines, no date, but circa 1838.
33 Ibid.
34 Ibid.
35 Ibid.
36 Ibid. Baines to Norris, 25 July 1838.
37 Ibid. Trenchard Street File, Edgeworth to Collingridge, 11 August 1828.
38 City of Bristol Reference Library, The Report of the Bristol Rioters, 1831.
39 CDA, John Cashman, typewritten notes on Bristol Pro-Cathedral based on recollections of Monsignor Russell, V.G.
40 Felix Farley, *Bristol Journal*.
41 CDA, John Cashman, typewritten notes on Bristol Pro-Cathedral.
42 Ibid.
43 Felix Farley, *Bristol Journal*.

9
A Question of Authority: Baines and the Bath Mission

Bishop Baines was not only concerned with pastoral care in the missions, but with his authority as a bishop. On his appointment as Vicar Apostolic in 1829, he wrote to every mission in the District:

> Being now returned [from Rome] and having taken upon myself the administration of the Western District, I deem it right and comformable to custom to address a few words to you my beloved flock, on our common concerns ... If there is one point of revealed religion clearer than another, it is this, that every moral and religious duty may be reduced to obedience, and thus consequently religion and obedience are almost synonymous terms ... The obedience which religion commands varies according to the authority to be obeyed. In temporal matters, she commands obedience to temporal rules, in spiritual matters to the Pastors of the Church.[1]

It was a hard teaching, which Baines himself had sometimes been reluctant to abide by in the monastery and which some missioners also found difficult to accept. Soon Baines was complaining to Cardinal Weld of the limited control he could exercise over his priests. He acknowledged ruefully: '... The authority of an English Vicar Apostolic is little at best and is wholly dependent upon the persuasion in the minds of his subjects ... when a contrary opinion prevails, the Episcopal authority is a cypher, and every attempt to enforce obedience is only a source of scandal and revolt.'[2]

Rival claims to the Bath mission

Baines was to find plenty of scandal and revolt in the Bath mission, which was right on the doorstep at Prior Park. He had fond memories of the mission from the days when he had been a priest there himself, and still took a great interest in what was going on there, probably more than was wise if he was not to risk upsetting the Benedictines more than he had done already. The Bath mission had been controlled by the Benedictines from its beginnings, and they claimed to own the church and the presbytery.[3] Baines, fresh from his disputes with them over the foundation of his school and seminary, the validation of monastic vows, and the withdrawal of faculties, was not averse to further battle. He was determined to stamp his authority on the mission, particularly as it was the wealthiest in the District, and he needed unlimited financial resources to develop Prior Park. And, despite the fact that he was a Benedictine himself, Baines had become a firm advocate of the right of the bishop to have some control over the founding and administration of regular missions. For many years there had been conflicts between seculars and regulars over the ownership of missions, particularly in Liverpool; the matter was not to be settled until the Papal Bull, *Romanos Pontifices*, in 1881.[4]

The position in Bath was complicated by the fact that Fr Brindle, a great supporter of Baines, who had been a missioner in the city for many years, had just become a secular priest. The Benedictines, who had always claimed the right to present priests to the Bath mission, instantly asked for his removal, but Baines refused to agree. Fr Thomas Brown from Downside wrote to the Provincial, Fr Deday, on 9 May, expressing unease at the news that: 'Dr B. is determined the Bath Incumbent shall be under his Jurisdiction only'.[5]

In spite of this, the Provincial went ahead and appointed a Benedictine, Fr Cooper, who had already been an assistant to Fr Brindle since 1823, and wrote to the latter urging him to give way: 'I require you under the precept of holy obedience that you surrender to the Rev Mr Cooper your office of principal incumbent of the Bath chapel and all documents, accounts, property and other material things belonging to it within the 24 hours next after receiving this order under the consequences which must follow from your disobedience.'[6]

Brindle, however, was now a secular priest and denied that the Benedictines had any authority over him: 'I beg leave to inform you that I cannot treat with you on the subject of the Bath mission, having surrendered whatever rights I formerly possessed to my superior, the Bishop of the District'.[7]

Brindle continued to live in the presbytery at Pierrepoint Place, hearing the confessions of his particular penitents, even though Fr Cooper was also installed there, claiming to be the mission priest. The two of them lived there together in an uneasy relationship for some months, causing a division of loyalties among the congregation.

Fr Cooper was placed in an impossible position, rebuked by the Benedictines for not making a strong enough stand against the Bishop, and by Baines for disobeying his instructions. Fr Ratcliffe wrote to Deday from Acton Burnell, expressing sympathy with the priest: 'I pity poor Cooper from my heart, as I suppose he must have a very unpleasant position at Bath, so near the Great Basher . . .'[8]

Baines was soon coming down from Prior Park to see Cooper in his room at the presbytery and demanding to know what the Provincial intended. Cooper replied that, as a result of Fr Brindle's secularization, and as the Benedictines owned the mission, he had been appointed the principal missioner of Bath. Baines protested that he would not submit to anyone, and only he could appoint a priest to Bath, where the claims of the Benedictines to own the property were very doubtful. He also raised the question of the congregation's contributions and the payment of bench rents, asserting that these should be paid to the Bishop and not to the Benedictines. In making this claim, it is probable that Baines was motivated, not only by principle, but also by his need for unlimited funds to finance his Prior Park enterprise. Fr Cooper protested, at least to the Provincial, that he had remained firm in his interview with the Bishop, and told Baines that he was resolved to obey his superiors, when their orders and those of the Bishop came into conflict.

President Birdsall unmoveable

The Benedictine President, Fr Birdsall, then entered the fray. He had already been involved in the Downside and Ampleforth disputes and the disagreement about Bishop Collingridge's will, and regarded the Bishop with extreme hostility. In fact, Baines claimed that Birdsall had been specially chosen President General, 'as the person best suited to wage war with a Bishop'.[9] Birdsall wrote to Baines in June 1830, pointing out that the conditions laid down by the Prefect of Propaganda in granting Dr Brindle's secularization was that all things held by him in the Bath mission should remain the property of the Benedictines. Baines's claim to ownership of any part of the Bath mission was completely spurious, for 'I am not at present aware that Your Lordship holds any property or foundations belonging to the mission'.[10]

Baines then responded that the validity of the Benedictines' claim to the property could only be resolved by a canonical tribunal, claiming later that: 'The Bath mission was founded, supported and served conjointly by the bishops and the monks – once for six whole years the coadjutor Bishop, served it alone. If the monks are to possess it exclusively, might they not be obliged to prove that it was founded and endowed exclusively for them – Is not the *onus probandi* on their side?'[11]

In the meanwhile, Baines reserved the right to receive all bench rents and collections made in the Bath chapel. As neither side was willing to compromise, a scandalous situation was developing among Bath Catholics, not helped by rumours that if the Benedictines did not establish the rightfulness of their claims, they would shut the doors of the chapel against the Bishop and the congregation. A Mrs Riddell and several others were said to have left the congregation 'on account of Dr Baines's conduct',[12] but, as the account came from a Benedictine source it could be biased.

Fr Birdsall then took the unwise step of resigning his faculties to protest against Baines's treatment of the Bath mission. This meant that he could no longer minister in the mission of Cheltenham, where he had been a priest for many years. It is not easy to understand what he hoped to gain by this renunciation, and in some ways he was playing into Baines's hands. Yet the President made his stand on a question of principle, claiming that he would be a traitor to the trust reposed in him, if he continued to hold faculties under such a bishop.[13]

It was to be several years before Birdsall was to have his faculties restored. And in the meanwhile, he and the Provincial, Fr Deday, planned to make a very public protest against the Bishop. They produced a pamphlet in which they declared themselves, 'the owners of the chapel' and the Benedictine missionaries in Bath 'the rightful incumbents', and ordered copies of this to be distributed on the first Sunday in Advent. This was the Sunday on which Bishop Baines, accompanied by Fr Brindle, had arranged to officiate at High Mass. As Baines walked from the sacristry into the chapel, someone thrust a handbill into his hands, and told him that copies had been left on all the benches and a man was standing on the door of the chapel distributing them to all who came in. The Bishop told Fr Brindle to go to the front door of the chapel to order him to stop, but the man took no notice, saying: 'I have received my orders and will obey them'.[14]

The congregation must have been agog at all this happening at the beginning of the mass, and they waited to see how the Bishop would react. Baines, determined to put over his point of view, wrote on the back of the handbill that a dispute had arisen between the Bishop and the Benedictines respecting the right of presentation of priests to the chapel and this could only be resolved by a canonical tribunal. If this was decided in favour of the Benedictines, he would hand over the rents of the seats and the subscriptions to the rightful owners. He ordered poor Fr Brindle to stand on top of the steps and read out the declaration to the bewildered congregation. Later, in 1835, arbiters pronouncing on the dispute between Baines and the Benedictines condemned the whole unsavoury episode, saying that: 'This would appear to be scandalous in making the congregation fully acquainted that a dispute existed between the Bishop and the Benedictines respecting the right of presentation to the chapel. This act must have been very disedifying to the pious part of the congregation'.[15]

The disregard of the Bishop's authority and the display of defiance to his face in the presence of the congregation certainly created scandal, although the Benedictines claimed that they were taking this action to protect their property. They also asserted that the dispute had become notorious long before that infamous Sunday.

Frs Brindle and Cooper continued to share uneasy possession of the Bath mission throughout the winter of 1830–1, and the latter received numbers of letters from President Birdsall urging him to stand his ground and resist Baines's demand to produce documents to establish the Benedictine right to the Bath mission: 'The Bath mission is our mission and he knows it, and we had our mission, not by the gift of the Vicar Apostolic, but by regulations laid down by the Sovereign Pontiff. These he has infringed and set at nought. There was no alternative but to complain of him to the Sovereign Pontiff and wait for redress from that quarter.'[16]

In the meanwhile Fr Cooper was urged to give away nothing, and with veiled threats Birdsall went on:

> Remember that you are by your vows under the orders of the Benedictines and them only. If I see any disposition in any monk who is a missionary to yield up any part of their right to whatever persons may ask them to do and by whatever method, I shall consider any such monks unfit to be entrusted with the guardianship of our missions and shall forthwith move him from the mission. It is not the V.A. alone who can withdraw the missionary faculties! . . . I will only add what throughout I have often admonished my confrères in this context. Endure![17]

While Fr Brindle continued as principal incumbent of the Bath mission and received the rents, there was little that the Benedictines could do, except fume against the Bishop and complain to the authorities in Rome, where the process of justice took years rather than months. Birdsall, in a letter to some unknown correspondent, was nearly beside himself with rage:

> Dr Baines continues to withhold [the mission] from us and persists in refusing the missionary faculties of a second of our body [to replace Dr Brindle]. ... Law and right and custom and privilege, all have been outraged, and set at nought in a manner revolutionary and scandalous and the Bishop of one of the Districts of England has chosen to brave the odium of every honest mind, standing as he is this 12 months before the public with the spoils of his aggression in his hands, and the plunder taken from a body of men who deserved better things of him ...[18]

From Prior Park, Baines looked down on Bath and at last decided that the situation in the mission was becoming impossible. There was no way of enforcing his authority any further, and he heard continual rumours that the Benedictines were about to close down the chapel and sell the property, a move which would have ended one of the main centres of Catholic influence in the west, as well as depriving the Bishop of income for Prior Park. The Benedictines denied that that they intended such extreme measures, but Baines was always a pragmatist, and decided that the time had come to retreat so that he might open his campaign elsewhere. He withdrew Dr Brindle from Bath to work at Prior Park, and ostensibly surrendered the mission into the hands of Fr Cooper. It was never likely, though, that Baines would stand aside and make no more demands on the mission. He still claimed the payment that had been made to him by the Bath mission since he became Bishop, and said that, as Dr Brindle could continue giving assistance in Bath, there was no need to appoint a second priest, and the salary minus the cost of maintenance could be paid to the former incumbent. Fr Cooper, anxious to end the whole matter amicably, agreed to these terms, but President Birdsall speedily intervened. He had no intention of paying any money to the Bishop and, as he now wished to appoint an assistant priest to Bath, there would be no salary available for Brindle.

The dispute over the payment of chapel rents had also not been settled, and Fr Cooper, again trying to reach a compromise, was caught in the crossfire of the endless sniping. Birdsall heard that the priest had turned down payment of bench or seat rents by members of his congregation, alleging that he dared not receive them for fear that the Bishop would deprive him of his faculties.[19] How real these fears were is not clear, but Birdsall threatened Baines with a further demonstration in the Bath chapel, if he did not agree to give up his claim to the seat and bench rents and give faculties to a second Benedictine missioner in Bath.[20] Reluctantly, Baines gave way on both these points, but Dr Brindle continued to go down to Bath to see his penitents and to hear confessions, a source of friction to members of the congregation.

During the late summer and early autumn of 1831 there was a lull in the conflict. Baines was trying to put his conduct in a good light by giving his version of events and seeking the learned opinion of a number of other bishops. Several of them declined to give an opinion, advising Baines to refer the whole matter to the Holy See. Bishop Doyle, the Bishop of Kildare and a noted writer of the day, came down on the side of the Benedictines, and in a letter which must have angered Baines told him: 'I consider your possession illegal and not equable. I think you have no right or authority whatever to threaten or to inflict the censures mentioned in your letter and that they are "*defectu vires*", null and of no effect.' Although Bishop Doyle sympathized with Baines's predicament, he was clear that 'You more than they are responsible for the scandals which have occurred and must prevail. Heal at any cost the wounds that have been made.'[21]

Fresh wounds were being inflicted by Baines's order that money was no longer to be collected at the doors of chapels in the District. The ending of the payment of entrance money to chapel was very desirable in itself, for it may have prevented some poor people from attending at all. Yet, coming at such a time in Bath, it appeared that Baines was deliberately ending an important source of Benedictine income. The Provincial, Fr Deday, told Fr Cooper to disobey the order and revert to the practice of charging one shilling admission at the door of the Bath chapel. The latter was reluctant to do this, fearing the wrath of the Bishop, who could so easily descend upon him from Prior Park. He himself had been trying to improve relations with Baines, and was going to use 'several rich crimson silk damasks presented by a penitent to adorn the Bishop's throne'. He was sorry, though, that in refusing to accept the olive branch, Baines replied in intemperate language: 'Having been violently driven from the chapel by acts and threats, I can never again enter or officiate until these are somehow recalled'.[22]

A rival chapel

From the end of 1831, Baines was trying unsuccessfully to buy a building for a chapel in the northern part of Bath, according to a

Benedictine source. An unsigned letter stated that: 'Dr Baines was offering £4000 for the Queen Square chapel. The protestants, in a fright, applied to Dr Hillcott [the minister] and, by supplying him with a sum which he wanted, engaged him to refuse to treat for the sale of the chapel.'[23]

Fr Glover, from Lancashire, writing to Birdsall, commented upon the news: 'Money now seems to be so plentiful that when he (Baines) appeals again to the public for food and rayment, I think his collections will not be so great as they have been'.[24]

Rumours about the plans continued to circulate among the congregation. A Miss Gibson had heard that the Bishop had taken rooms in a house just above her in Brunswick Place, 'where it is intended that he and Dr Brindle would attend and where mass would be said every Sunday to commence on the 4th December, 1831 until a chapel was provided'.[25]

And another member of the congregation surmised that this move had been precipitated by dissatisfaction being expressed at Dr Brindle's coming down to Bath to see penitents and to hear confessions at Pierrepoint Place. She fancied that this was a sore point with Fr Cooper and the Benedictines.[26]

Members did not consider the opening of a rival chapel to be at all wise. It was not needed from the point of view of numbers, as the accommodation in the Orchard Street chapel was quite adequate. The only advantage of an opposition was that the Benedictine priests might become a little less imperious:

> Their language ... sounds to my ears very peremptory and authoritative; 'it must be done this week and every person must show their tickets to the person appointed to take them to their seats'. ... and, 'care would be taken that no person's seat should be interfered with', and so on. This sounded to me as if the incumbent considered the congregation belonged to them instead of they belonging to the congregation, there is too much of that spirit here.[27]

The Bishop did not escape criticism, as the writer believed that such an attitude among priests had originated with Dr Baines.[28] The news that he was to open another chapel also brought wider criticism. The Benedictine Provincial wrote to Baines on 2 December 1831:

> I much regret the necessity that I am under of writing to your Lordship upon the following subject ... that your Lordship is about to open a chapel or rather some rooms for the purpose of a

> chapel in Bath. It cannot be otherwise than clear to everyone why such a proceeding is undertaken and it cannot of course tend to edify either Catholic or Protestant ... I am sorry this causes the Bath mission to become a new source of scandal to the public and endeavour thus to injure the Benedictine body. If your Lordship thinks proper to take these steps, I must candidly inform your Lordship that I think it is a duty to have resource to the court of Rome ...'[29]

Baines replied in high dudgeon:

> It is very true that I have taken a house in the upper part of Bath for the accommodation of myself and my friends, it being absolutely necessary, as you may imagine, to have some place in the city to which we can go and refer others on matters connected with the growing establishment and it being quite impossible to make use of your missionaries' house after all that has passed ... Is it on this subject that you think it your duty to have recourse to the court of Rome? If so, I can only say that the threat does not inspire me any great alarm.[30]

The house which Baines hired in Brunswick Place was said to be owned by Madam Chaussegros, the former Anna de Mendoza's other guardian; he used two of the rooms for a chapel, which would hold about sixty people, thus enabling him to continue preaching in Bath, and Dr Brindle to attend to his numerous penitents. It was the old problem stretching back to Ampleforth days – Baines found it difficult to let go of any work in which he had once been involved, and to delegate authority.

In the meanwhile, Baines continued to look around for more permanent premises, and in 1832 was more successful. He managed to lease the Portland chapel, once belonging to a Nonconformist group, on the north side of the city. He took it on a lease of ten years, with the options of purchase in the interim, or of giving it up at twelve months' notice. How he found the money to pay the rent, with all his other financial commitments at Prior Park, is unknown. Fr Cooper wrote to the Provincial, Fr Deday: 'The new chapel is announced in the *Bath Journal*, to the regret of protestants and most of our congregation. Nothing can exceed their kind feelings of regard to myself and Mr Jenkins [his new assistant priest]. I strongly suspect that Mr Burgess from Cannington is to be the priest at Portland chapel. He has been there very often lately.'[31]

More worrying to Baines was the condemnation from Rome.

Although the Pope did not decree that the Portland chapel should be closed, he wrote to Baines condemning his conduct and asking him 'what I could mean by setting up altar against altar'.[32]

In spite of all the criticism, this second Catholic chapel continued in Bath for some years with a variety of worship and lectures. The *Bath Directory* of 1837 listed the following: 'Lecture and communion mass at 8 in the morning; high mass and sermon at 11; vespers and instruction at 3 in the afternoon. Lecture at 9 in the evening on Sundays during the winter. On week-days, services every morning at 9.'

Baines also made a point of giving several courses of public lectures at the chapel, which attracted large numbers of Protestants, as well as Catholics, drawn by the Bishop's reputation as an orator and a controversial character. Six of these lectures, dealing mainly with religious issues between Catholics and Protestants, were later published. Recalling his sermon in Bradford so many years before,[33] Baines discussed Protestant objections to matters such as votive candles, the veneration of images of the Virgin Mary and the saints, and the practice in some country churches of adorning statues with garlands. This the Protestants pronounced to be idolatry, 'though the sole intention of the good people is to honour the saint merely as a servant of God, in a way which is at once natural and customary'.[34] Baines then goes into much more detail about the Catholic doctrine of purgatory and prayers for the dead, and he ends by quoting the words of an Anglican, the Caroline divine, Bishop Montague, in its defence: 'The blessed in heaven do recommend to God in their prayers, their kindred, friends and acquaintances, on earth. This is the common voice, with the general concurrence, without contradiction, of reverend and learned antiquity, for aught I could ever see or understand; and I see no reason to dissent from the Catholics touching intercession of this kind.'[35] The reference to the writings of a Caroline bishop demonstrate the width of Baines's reading and his appreciation of elegant writing, even though the author was a man of another faith.

Baines devoted a whole lecture to the even greater problem Protestants experienced over the doctrine of transubstantiation, basing his arguments on the words of Christ: 'I am the bread of life ... he that eateth this bread shall live for ever'. Protestants had chosen to interpret these words figuratively, in spite of the long practice of the Church throughout the ages.

> It is for modern innovators to show that the literal sense of scripture is to be abandoned, and a figurative one preferred. In their

> favour they have their own private judgement, at the end of eighteen centuries, but against them they have the apostolical liturgies and the universal belief and practice of the world from the very days of the apostles. If their explanation is right, all Christendom was wrong from the beginning.[36]

Renewed conflict in the Bath mission

People flocked to hear Baines speak, and it must have brought memories of the great days in Rome ten years before. Yet, in spite of all his success at the Portland chapel, Baines continued to follow closely the events of the other chapel in Orchard Street. He wrote to the long-suffering Fr Cooper that he had been receiving numerous complaints from his congregation, some of who protested that strangers were being shown into their rented seats in the chapel: 'You and Mr Jenkins have encouraged the notion that this is the result of my prohibiting entrance money. It has nothing to do with it.'[37]

Baines had also heard reports that Fr Cooper was about to introduce new regulations in the chapel, but he ordered that this was not to be done until he, the Bishop, had given his approval. Clearly Baines was going beyond the sphere of his authority in intervening in the purely domestic concerns of the chapel.

Fr Cooper replied the following day defending his actions:

> It did not at all surprise me that you had heard of various complaints in consequence of persons taking seats in the chapel being incommoded by the intrusion of strangers into their places. I can assure your Lordship that the complaints have been continually going on since the enforcement of the mandate Oct 4th, 1830. But that I have encouraged such dissatisfaction is not true; neither is it true, my Lord, that Mr Jenkins has, for when he came here he found this feeling very prevalent among the congregation.[38]

He went on to describe the new seating arrangements which he had introduced in the chapel, and hoped that Baines would approve of them; he also hoped to placate the Bishop by telling him that he had prevented a group of petitioners coming up to Prior Park to see him. They intended to ask the Bishop that:

> Your Lordship would allow the usual custom of receiving money at the chapel door, to be continued. With the exception of a very few, I don't think amounting to more than 5 or 6, it is still the general wish of the congregation. I can assure your Lordship that the

above custom was never any hindrance to persons hearing divine service, this I have often heard from protestants who attended the chapel, nor has the chapel, my Lord, been more filled upon an average since it was before the late regulation.[39]

Baines, who never liked to be contradicted, especially by a lowly Benedictine priest, replied in scathing terms. He objected to new regulations being introduced without his consent, and ordered their immediate suspension. He complained, too, of the style of Fr Cooper's letter: 'You will not I think have wished to address such a letter to your President, Mr Birdsall, and yet if you have bound yourself to obey him as your religious superior, you have bound yourself by vow to obey your Bishop as your superior in missionary concerns'.[40]

He rejected with scorn the olive branch which the priest had held out to him, showing no gratitude whatever: 'I owe you no thanks for preventing the deputation you mention, from coming up to me. I flatter myself I could have made them understand what you seem to find so exceedingly difficult of comprehension. I shall expect the pleasure of seeing you at Prior Park at 1 p.m.'[41]

The dismissal of Fr Jenkins

Relations between the two parties in Bath continued warily for the next few years, to reach an uneasy peace in the arbitration of 1835. In 1836, though, renewed controversy broke out between Baines and the Benedictines concerning the assistant priest at Orchard Street, Fr Jenkins. Baines had unwillingly agreed to his appointment in 1833 and had tolerated him for three years when, in 1836, he suddenly demanded that the new Benedictine Provincial, Fr Barber, should remove him. The latter adopted a very conciliatory tone with the Bishop, acknowledging that he had a perfect right to ask for the removal of a regular priest, without giving a reason: 'But as it seems to me desirable', he continued, 'that both parties should, if possible, act in concurrence, I will take the liberty of asking with great diffidence the grounds of complaint against Mr Jenkins, as your Lordship can disclose ... The Benedictines are not less anxious than your Lordship to avoid all future contention.'[42]

Baines refused to give his reasons for the removal of the priest, although rumours abounded. An unnamed Benedictine source interpreted the Bishop's motives in the worst light: 'You will observe how Bp Baines persists in refusing to assign any cause for the removal of Mr Jenkins and thus strengthening our apprehension of his ulterior views . . .'[43] The writer recalled the general satisfaction felt when arbitration appeared to have resolved the conflict between the Bishop and the Benedictines in 1835, 'but also our knowledge of the past and our observation of the spirit displayed more than once during the arbitration, gave us too little reason to flatter ourselves that it was likely to be very lasting'.[44]

Rumours of Fr Jenkins's relationship with three women members of the congregation spread to areas beyond Bath. Andrew Scott writing from Greenock to Fr Brown at Downside speculated on Baines's motives for removing Fr Jenkins and said that, even if there was an element of truth in the rumours, the whim of every family could not be attended to. If this came to be the case, 'I fear even the Bishop's authority might be soon weakened and the congregation begin to think that they have a right to dictate to the Bishop that such and such individual should be removed'.[45]

The first story had been circulating in Bath since 1833, and concerned two girls, Cecilia and Isabella, the daughters of a Mr English who had been Baines's solicitor. Apparently Mr and Mrs English believed that their daughters, particularly Cecilia, had become unduly influenced by Mr Jenkins, who had encouraged them to attend communion and confession frequently, and to become much more fervent in the practice of their religion than their parents. There was even the suspicion that the priest was influencing Cecilia to become a nun, a fear experienced by numbers of Catholic and Anglican parents in the middle of the nineteenth century, when many rumours of the undue influence of priests were circulating.

One of the girls described how 'Mama twisted Papa round her finger and made him think you aimed at him',[46] a reference to Mr English's accusation that the priest was attacking him in his sermons. Mr English wrote to President Birdsall, Fr Deday, the Benedictine Provincial, and to Baines who agreed to see Cecilia. Baines was in a difficult position, having employed English as his solicitor for several years, but he was also inclined to be prejudiced against Fr Jenkins, whose appointment to the Bath mission he had always opposed. He told Cecilia that he had already seen the priest and warned him not to administer communion to her or hear her confession, and wished her to attend services with her mother at Baines's new chapel in Portland Place, rather than in Orchard Street.[47]

Cecilia told Fr Jenkins of her problems at home, 'where an everlasting storm is waging against me', and complained that she was no longer allowed to go to the chapel in Orchard Street when the priest was officiating, and sent instead to say her prayers at Baines's 'detestable upper chapel, where there was only low mass, most horrid, and a quantity of English prayers. It is I assure you most shocking not to keep the Blessed Sacrament there.'[48]

Fr Barber, who succeeded Fr Deday as Benedictine Provincial later in 1833, claimed that there were faults on both sides. 'It is not unlikely that the children have been impudent in revealing Mr Jenkins' piety and direction at home and vexed their parents'. Mr Jenkins could also be blamed: 'It was highly reprehensible of him to speak of the parents checking the fervour of their children ... It was very wrong of Mr J, having given up the direction of the young ladies to pacify the parents, privately to resume it again. He laid himself open to the charge of mixing up deception with the administration of the sacrament.'[49]

Fr Barber was convinced, however, that there was nothing improper in the relationship. 'If Mr English had any real evidence against Mr Jenkins, he was too much of a lawyer not to bring charges against him ... It is clear that Mr J has done no more or rather no more than say that a child at 21 may make herself a nun in spite of her parents.'[50]

Baines's second ground of complaint against Fr Jenkins concerned a young woman called Emma Vines. She was a convert living among Protestants, but it is not clear whether these were members of her family or whether she was employed in their household. The Bishop had heard that Fr Jenkins had refused to give Emma Holy Communion as, being unwilling to reveal that she had become a Catholic, she did not wish to attend public services in the chapel. On Baines's return from Rome in 1834, Emma was called to Prior Park to explain the situation, and the Bishop was evidently annoyed that Fr Jenkins was withholding the sacrament from her. He wrote to him later: 'Since you and I cannot act together you had better resign your faculties'.[51]

Baines took no immediate action, but growing rumours about this relationship as well as stories about the English sisters, forced his hand. In spite of Fr Jenkins's reluctance to administer communion to her, Emma seems to have developed intense feelings for the priest, writing to him to offer to look after him when he was forced to leave Bath:

> Oh! I would gladly give my life to serve you and must I or anything connected with me, bring you into distress? ... Pray tell me all that you hear about your probable involvement, where you think you shall go and where you may be settled – and must I or anything connected with me, bring you into distress? – Oh! Where shall you see your little Em and is there now any hope at all that

> you can ever have her with you – I fear not ... Oh my Father if I could indeed be of any comfort to you, let me come to you if possible when you are settled! ... Your letters shall be instantly destroyed if you wish it, but for my sake write as freely as you can, and above all tell me if this business of mine is like to be brought against you.[52]

It is unlikely that Emma's feelings were reciprocated by Fr Jenkins, and both of them denied that there had ever been any impropriety; yet he kept her letters and must have given her his new address to write to, allowing the situation to get out of hand. Bishop Baines at least took a very serious view of all the rumours and reacted swiftly to remove the priest. Doing so in such an abrupt fashion was counter-productive in that it angered the Benedictines and aroused furious speculation in the mission, where Fr Jenkins was a very popular priest.

Baines was quite determined that Fr Jenkins would not have the opportunity of preaching a farewell sermon at Bath giving his reasons for dismissal. He wrote to Fr Cooper, saying, 'This I absolutely forbid ... After the mass service his function in Bath must entirely cease and I hope that his stay in Bath will not be unnecessarily protracted.'[53]

The priest left Bath on the following day, 10 October 1836, and recorded bitterly that 'it appears to be the general opinion of all in the West who dare to speak that as long as Dr Baines lives there must be confusion'.[54]

Mr Edward King, Baines's new solicitor in Bath, was most surprised to hear that the priest had already left the mission. The first knowledge he had of it was when 'several of the least influential members of the congregation came round to my house, asking me to sign a petition to the Bishop for the priest's recall'. Mr King then wrote to Fr Jenkins, telling him: 'I did not sign it, as I wished to hear from you something respecting this extraordinary measure'.[55]

Fr Jenkins replied, denying that he had been involved in any wrongdoing. Indeed he continued: 'The Bishop told me he had a high regard for me and was sorry to lose me and he even offered to employ me as a missionary in other places in his District as a proof that my character is deemed unimpaired'.[56]

This view that Baines regarded the women in the case as more at fault than the priest is borne out by his reply to the petition from the Bath congregation:

> You assign as your reason for making this petition the spiritual

> benefit and instruction you have received from Mr Jenkins, his zeal in the discharge of his sacred duties and particularly in visiting the sick and instructing the young ... it gives me great pleasure to join in commending one who I believe to be a righteous and a good priest ... there are reasons though, which render him unfit for [the mission of] Bath, and compel me to insist upon his removal.[57]

After a conciliatory beginning to his letter, Baines went on to emphasize the authority of his office and to imply that the congregation had been presumptuous to bring their petition:

> It is impossible for you to judge of my reasons without knowing what they are ... it is evident that a petition like that which you have presented wears an appearance of hostility in as much as it places your ecclesiastical superior in a most painful dilemma, for either he must yield to your petition, which would be to acknowledge that he had acted with precipitation and rashness in a case involving your spiritual interest; or he must refuse your request.

Baines ended by telling his Bath flock that they should have approached him privately and in a friendly way: 'Most certainly you would then have discovered that my conduct was not animated by unkind motives towards you, or hostile feelings towards Mr Jenkins, much less by the mean and guilty motives, which some of you, I regret to say, have most unjustly ascribed to me ...'[58]

By this period of his career, Baines was developing almost a persecution complex in believing that everyone was out to belittle and destroy him. The Fr Jenkins case is significant in showing Baines acting as he thought best, but arousing antagonism by his secrecy in not giving any reasons for his action or allowing the priest any right of reply. He became still more angry when Fr Jenkins moved to the Midland District and gained the support of Bishop Walsh in an appeal to Rome. The Benedictines believed that the case was further antagonizing the authorities in Rome against Baines. W. B. Collier, the Benedictine agent in Rome, wrote to Fr Brown at Downside telling him that Monsignor Mai at Propaganda had stated: 'We have no hope of Dr B's amendment and could expect nothing but that he would remain hereafter such as he has ever been hitherto, turbulent and precipitous, but we cannot remove him for his morals or his doctrines'.[59]

While the appeal was still going on in Rome, Baines wrote to his friend, Bishop Briggs of the Northern District, with great indignation:

> I certainly removed a regular from Bath . . . because in addition to my considering him unfit for the place [a complete contradiction to earlier statements] a most scandalous exposure must have been made of his conduct, if I had not moved him. He was received by Dr Walsh without enquiry and the latter now informs me that Fr Barber, the Provincial, and Mr Jenkins are appealing to Rome against the priest's removal, and a request that he may be restored to Bath! Dr Walsh is appointed to reconcile us![60]

Nothing came of Fr Jenkins's appeal to have himself reinstated in Bath, but his reputation was publicly vindicated and he continued his work as a respected priest in the Midland District, until some years after Bishop Baines's death he returned to Bath as priest in charge.

The Bath mission and the Bishop's authority

The long dispute over the retention of Frs Cooper and Jenkins became part of the wider controversy between Baines and the Benedictines. He had to give way on the basic issue as to whether he or the Benedictines should appoint priests to the Bath mission, but he continued to exert his authority wherever he could. He felt a proprietary interest in the mission, gained from long years of living and working in the area; he knew many of the congregation, and he and Dr Brindle had numerous penitents in Bath, all of which he believed put him in a position to understand what was best for the congregation.

As a bishop, Baines also maintained that he was defending the authority of all the Vicars Apostolic and their right to control priests in the missions, whether secular or regular. He often had right on his side, such as when he objected to his treatment in the Bath chapel on the day of the handbill incident, and in his advocacy of free admission to services in the chapel, and he obviously needed to take some action in the Fr Jenkins case. Yet he often showed an extraordinary lack of tact and a dogmatic assertion of the rightness of his own views, which antagonized many and led to unfortunate divisions within the congregation.

Notes

1 CDA, Bishops' Letters, Baines to all Priests in Missions, October 1829.
2 Ibid. Baines to Weld, 6 May 1832.
3 See J. A. Williams, *Post Reformation Catholicism in Bath* (Catholic Record Society, London, 1975).

4 CDA, Roman Documents, *Romanos Pontifices*, 1881.
5 Downside Archives, H47, Brown to Deday, 9 May 1830.
6 CDA, Baines Box Files, 4, Deday to Brindle, 1 June 1830.
7 Ibid. Brindle to Deday.
8 Downside Archives, H192, Ratcliffe to Deday, 20 January 1830.
9 CDA, Baines's Statement of Facts to the Arbiters, 11 July 1835.
10 Ibid. Bishops' Letters, Birdsall to Baines, 19 June 1830.
11 Ibid. Baines's Statement of Facts to the Arbiters, 11 July 1835.
12 Downside Archives, H163, Scott to Deday, 2 December 1830.
13 CDA, Bishops' Letters, Birdsall to Baines, 30 October 1830.
14 Ibid. Baines's Statement of Facts to the Arbiters, 1835.
15 Ibid.
16 Ibid. (quoting letter of Birdsall to Cooper, 18 December 1830).
17 Ibid.
18 Ibid. (quoting letter of Birdsall to unknown 3 May 1831).
19 Ampleforth Archives, A267 727G39, Birdsall to Robinson, 30 June 1831.
20 CDA, Baines's Statement of Facts to the Arbiters, 1835.
21 Ibid. Bishops' Letters, Doyle to Baines, 6 November 1831.
22 Ibid. Cooper to Brindle, 29 November 1831.
23 Downside Archives, H340, unsigned letter, 29 November 1831.
24 Ibid, H345, Glover to Birdsall, 28 October 1831.
25 Ampleforth Archives, A267 80 7G39, fragment of unsigned letter, giving opinions of several members of the Bath Congregation, no date.
26 Ibid.
27 Ibid.
28 Ibid.
29 Downside Archives, H374, Deday to Baines, 2 December 1831.
30 Ibid. H375, Baines to Deday, 6 December 1831.
31 Ibid. H42, Cooper to Deday, 7 March 1832.
32 CDA, Baines's Statement of Facts to the Arbiters, 1835.
33 P. A. Baines, *Faith, Hope and Charity. A Sermon preached at the Dedication of the Chapel at Bradford July 1825*.
34 P. A. Baines, *Public lectures on the Outline of Christianity* (Bath, 1839).
35 Ibid.
36 Ibid.
37 CDA, Bishops' Letters, Baines to Cooper, December 1831.
38 Ibid. Cooper to Baines, 3 December 1831.
39 Ibid.
40 Ibid. Baines to Cooper.
41 Ibid.
42 Downside Abbey, J115, Barber to Baines, 4 March 1836.
43 Ibid. J30, unnamed and undated letter.
44 Ibid.
45 Ibid. J155, Scott to Brown, 23 May 1836.
46 Ibid. J353, Jenkins to Collier, 17 October 1836 (giving information from Cecilia).

47 Ibid. I 150 (2), Cecilia to Jenkins (giving her version of events).
48 Ibid.
49 Ibid. I 153, Barber to Deday, 13 January 1834.
50 Ibid.
51 Ibid. J253, Jenkins to Collier, (reporting on letter from Baines).
52 Ibid. J239, Emma Vines to Jenkins, 5 October 1836.
53 Ibid. J253, Baines to Cooper, 17 October 1836.
54 Ibid. J161, undated fragment of letter.
55 Ibid. J241, King to Jenkins, 5 October 1836.
56 Ibid. J242, Jenkins to King, 5 October 1836.
57 Ibid. J258, Baines's reply to the Bath Petition, 22 October 1836.
58 Ibid.
59 Ibid. J306, Collier to Brown, 23 December 1836.
60 CDA, Baines Box Files, 5–7, Baines to Briggs, 12 January 1837.

10

An Uneasy Peace

'I will not put my feet under the same table as that man'
(President John Birdsall)

Bishop Collingridge's will

Disputes at Bath and Cannington were largely resolved, but other controversies between the Bishop and the Benedictines still rumbled on until 1835, a source of scandal to Catholics and Protestants alike. The longest-running of these was the matter of Dr Collingridge's will, which had still not been settled six years after the latter's death. The matter was extremely complex, as Collingridge made several wills between 1816 and 1829, and left other documents relating to the financial concerns of the District, as his biographer details.[1]

Collingridge was suspicious of Baines's profligate ways with money, and had made Birdsall the executor of his final will and also, according to Birdsall, one of the trustees of funds which belonged to the District. The news of this had greatly disturbed Baines when he first heard about it in Rome in 1829, but, in spite of opposition, he still managed to gain control of £300 of the money and invest it in Prior Park. President Birdsall protested in vain against this so-called 'usurpation of funds', and held on grimly to ground rents on certain houses in Taunton; these were part of Collingridge's private estate, but it is probable that he intended the income to be used for the benefit of missions in the District. Whatever happened, Birdsall was determined that these ground rents should not fall into the Bishop's hands and be used for Prior Park. He wrote angrily to him in March 1831:

> Having been informed that you are about to lay your hands on the portion of the property of the late Dr Collingridge, which consists of a ground rent on certain houses at Taunton belonging to Mr

> Manley, I hereby give you notice and repeat, what I have already told you, that the property is no property of the District and cannot be used by your Lordship . . .[2]

And again in June 1831: 'I have before told your Lordship that I will to the utmost of my power see carried into effect the provision of Dr C's will whatever may be your endeavours to prevent.'[3]

Baines continued to write to Birdsall directly through his Vicar General, Fr Brindle, and through his friend Miss Bettington, who also employed her lawyer in the Bishop's cause, but all to no avail. Birdsall was determined that no more of Collingridge's money would be swallowed up in Prior Park, and made his suspicions clear: 'The course you have chosen to pursue since the good Bishop, your predecessor, died has not been of a nature to induce me to commit to you the execution of my trust . . .'[4]

This last letter irritated Baines so much that he refused to have any more direct dealings with Birdsall, and wrote to Fr Deday, the Benedictine Provincial, complaining that

> The Rev President being one of my missionaries, refuses to obey a command I gave him to wind up without any further delay the executorship of the late Dr Collingridge, which he has neglected to do under various pretexts for more than 2 years and a half . . . and also to settle the executorship of Dr C without further delay. My object in thus calling upon you is to avoid the scandal which would probably be the result of my coming into contact with a person who seems to deny my authority over him as Bishop of this District . . .[5]

The question of authority was the crux of the matter, a point on which Baines felt very strongly, and on which Birdsall, particularly with his memories of Baines as an inferior at Lamspringe, was determined not to give an inch. Probably Fr Deday did not want to get too involved in the controversy, as there is no record that he replied to Baines; but in the following month, October 1831, the former President General, Richard Marsh, wrote supporting Birdsall, and referring to the £300 which Baines had managed to obtain from Collingridge's estate:

> It appears to me that Mr Birdsall was appointed trustee of certain monies by the late Dr C. and that this trusteeship has been withdrawn from him without his concurrence. As Mr Birdsall voluntarily accepted the trusteeship and pledged himself to your

late predecessor to see it executed, we are of the opinion that this trusteeship must, in the first instance be restored to him, before any other step can be taken towards the final settlement of the business.[6]

The dispute seemed to have reached deadlock, with Frs Birdsall, Deday and Marsh believing that they had right on their side, which legally they probably had. Later A. H. Lynch, a solicitor in Bath, gave his legal opinion:

> There can be no doubt under the late Act of Parliament and the decisions put upon it that eventually the plaintiff cannot succeed and that the estate of Dr Collingridge will be applied to the purpose mentioned in his instructions and in that application I think Dr Baines as Bishop of the District will and ought to be called upon to concur.[7]

If the Benedictines had decided to go to law, they could have made it extremely awkward for Baines, but they were reluctant to do so, partly owing to the expense, but more because of the scandal that would have been created among Catholics and Protestants alike. Baines would certainly not have reached a settlement out of court, as he was equally convinced of the rightness of his cause, believing that raising funds for Prior Park justified the means, however dubious. He also believed that he was defending the authority of the bishops against the growing power of the regulars. It had become a matter which could only be settled by arbitration: Baines and the Benedictines began to look to Rome to act as arbiter, both in this dispute over Collingridge's will, and in other long-drawn-out controversies between them.

The Ampleforth dispute

One of the most acrimonious of these controversies was the accusation that in 1830 Frs Burgess, Rooker and Metcalfe had removed property and money from Ampleforth that did not belong to them. Baines could not be said to be directly responsible for this, but the Benedictines considered him morally so. So long after the events of that early summer, it was difficult to get to the truth of what had really happened, especially as the stories had magnified with the years. Even at the time, we have seen that rumours were rife in York that covered wagons were secretly loaded during the night and trundled away south to Prior Park, bearing provisions, blankets and some of the treasures of Ampleforth. There were also accusations that Burgess had withheld from President Birdsall, Fr Glover and the accountants the college's pension book in which the fees paid by the students' parents were recorded.[8] In 1832–3 all these stories surfaced again, gathering momentum as they went; this was in spite of the fact that Birdsall was supposed to have reached a final settlement with Burgess in the early summer of 1830.

Baines was extremely irritated by all this and wrote to Dr Wiseman in Rome in 1832:

> I cannot understand why the affairs of my District should be mixed up with the pecuniary concerns of Ampleforth, with which I have had nothing to do and which I thought had been finally settled with Mr Burgess and his companions before Bishop Smith executed the transfer of their obedience to me. I have no objection, however, that any enquiry should be made into the affair ... though I feel confident that the gentlemen accused of robbing Ampleforth are utterly incapable of the slightest injustice ...[9]

In 1834 Baines, who was then visiting Rome, heard still more fanciful rumours of what had taken place at Ampleforth four years before. Reports reached him that Fr Brown of Downside was spreading a story that: 'Mr Burgess and his companions had carried away from Ampleforth, as had been computed by several well-informed persons £10,000 at least!!!'[10]

Baines was highly indignant, particularly as he believed that he was being prevented from knowing the details of this or any other accusation before arbitration was agreed. It is curious that the Benedictines accused Baines of purloining goods from Ampleforth, which was highly unlikely, rather than attacking him for persuading staff and students to leave the college.

The Bath mission once more

Both Baines and the Benedictines wished the controversy over the Bath mission to be put on the agenda for arbitration, although by 1834 the matter had largely been settled in favour of the Benedictines. Baines was still claiming that the mission belonged as of right to the Bishop, and the Benedictines were still angry at the existence of Baines's new chapel in the north of Bath. Both parties, therefore, wished to have an authoritative statement on the rights and wrongs of the case made by the arbiters.

The withdrawal of faculties from Downside monks

Baines also had an ongoing dispute with the Benedictines over his withdrawal of the faculties of the monks of Downside. He had withdrawn them at the end of 1829 to show his disapproval of the conduct of Prior Barber and Fr Brown, who had refused to negotiate on the question of a Catholic seminary, and then, when told that their vows were probably invalid, had gone to Rome to complain of Baines's conduct.[11] Baines appears to have believed that the suspension of missionary faculties would crush the monks at Downside; they would be too intimidated to dare to administer the sacraments in the monastery and would be soon on their knees to the Bishop, imploring his forgiveness. He could not have been more wrong, as the monks continued their life in the monastery in the same way as they had always done, celebrating their daily offices and administering the sacraments. They made no attempt, though, to take the sacraments to their Catholic missions outside the monastery, so that it was ordinary Catholic people who suffered. Baines was forced to divert priests from Taunton, Cannington and Prior Park, and even occasionally Fr Edgeworth from Bristol, to administer the sacraments in the Downside area.

All the criticism aroused by this high-handed action included a severe reprimand from Cardinal Cappellari in Rome, telling Baines that a Vicar Apostolic could not withdraw faculties from regulars except for a cause which directly concerned the hearing of confession. It is unclear what was meant by this and Baines in his 'Statement of Facts to the Arbiters' placed a large exclamation mark after it. He claimed, too, that he was perfectly justified in withdrawing faculties because of the contemptuous conduct of the monks and the need to prevent further scandals; in the stand which he was taking he naturally expected to obtain the support of the Holy See.

It was more likely, though, that Baines's action would lead to further scandals, and it proved to be one of the greatest mistakes that he ever made. He lost the support of Cardinal Cappellari, who had previously favoured him, and was left with the problem of trying to extricate himself from the situation. He noted that the Cardinal required him to desist from all controversy with the monks and find a means of reaching a settlement without losing face.[12] This was easier said than done, as the monks inconveniently refused to ask for the restoration of their faculties, and Baines did not want to make the first move. A further message from President Birdsall made him even less likely to do so: 'I feel it my duty [Birdsall wrote] to acquaint your Lordship that it has been represented to me that Religion is suffering in no small degree from the circumstances that no one of the priests there [at Downside] is in possession of missionary faculties . . .'[13]

Matters seemed to have reached deadlock, when Prior Barber of Downside, who had been Baines's *bête noire*, made a magnanimous gesture for the sake of peace and resigned from the priorship. Baines saw his opportunity and sent for the Sub-Prior, Dom John Polding, who was later to become Archbishop of Sydney, and discussed with him the matter of restoring faculties. In what could have only been an attempt at face-saving, he then told Polding that, for the satisfaction of his [the Bishop's] own conscience, he would first like to give the Sub-Prior conditional absolution from the censure he had incurred by administering the sacraments for many months without faculties from his Bishop. Polding did not want to give an immediate answer, but returned to Downside to think matters over, and probably discuss it with his colleagues. A few days later he wrote to Baines:

> At the close of the interview I had the honour of holding with your Lordship on Wednesday last, you recommended me to take into consideration the propriety of applying for a conditional absolution . . . in case I had exercised faculties in the monastery under the jurisdiction of my Regular Superior, after Your Lordship had withdrawn the faculties I held from the Bishop of the District. I have My Lord reconsidered the subject with its circumstances. I beg Your Lordship will not deem me unduly obstinate if I still object to a proceeding which I cannot persuade myself to be necessary and the propriety of which appears to me to be exceedingly dubious.[14]

Baines was again rebuffed and matters drifted on unresolved for a while longer. Then one of the Catholic flock in the Downside area became very ill and asked for the sacrament to be brought to him at home. The Sub-Prior then wrote to Baines telling him that no priest was available to minister to this person in need, but still declined to ask for the restoration of his faculties. Baines rode down to Downside from Prior Park and asked the Sub-Prior to mention any priest who would be willing to receive absolution so that he could receive faculties to minister to the sick. Polding refused to name anyone, but Baines sent for Dom John Bede Rigby, whom he had known when he was at Lamspringe, and put the question to him: 'Will you receive absolution so that I can confer faculties upon you?'

'God forbid, why should I object,' answered Rigby, bringing a refreshing common sense to the issue.[15]

Baines immediately gave him absolution and conferred faculties upon him, so that he could minister to the scattered flock round Downside. Polding, however, was very angry, believing that his authority had been undermined, and appealed to Rome. In December 1830 Baines received a strong reprimand, telling him that he had no right to insist that the Sub-Prior should receive absolution before renewing his faculties. The *sanatio* decree issued by the Vatican in April had confirmed that Downside was a monastery, so that its superiors were always entitled to administer the sacraments.[16]

Baines wrote back to Rome in great indignation declaring that, as the *sanatio* decree had not been in existence between November 1829 and April 1830, the Sub-Prior was illegally administering the sacrament during this period. In any case, he claimed that as Vicar Apostolic he was at liberty to grant faculties or withhold them. This brought a still more stinging reply from the new Prefect of Propaganda, Cardinal Pedicini, reproaching him with the public scandals he was causing. 'You may not suppose I speak from conjecture. I beg to inform you that frequent complaints which are brought here against you, prove clearly that your aversion to these religious men, causes you to over-look the propriety of religion and the salvation of souls.'[17]

Baines noted that the Cardinal had added a postscript that the Pope had made known to him his great grief at the Bishop's conduct, and his earnest wish that he should renew the faculties of the monks, etc. etc. Clearly Baines had lost all the good will he had formerly enjoyed at Rome, and he realized that the time had come to retreat. He rode down to Downside from Prior Park, accompanied by Fr Edgeworth from the Bristol mission, on whom he was coming to rely. Dr Coombes, the missioner from Shepton Mallet, and Fr Burgess from Cannington, met him at Downside, and the four of them met the new Prior, Fr Turner, to whom Baines had already given faculties without any condition. Baines was still not willing to meet the other monks, and retired to the chapel, leaving his three deputies to make peace. It was agreed eventually that the missionary faculties would be granted to two priests in the community, so that they could administer sacraments in the Downside area, but not in Bath without the sanction of the Bishop. Resentment against Baines lingered on, as he would still not grant faculties to the Sub-Prior, Fr Polding, who had greatly angered him; nor would he restore them to President Birdsall. Three of the monks wrote to the Prefect of Propaganda:

> What afflicts us is that our Father Sub-Prior, a man of great talents and piety, who has himself converted almost all our poor Catholics, is deprived of the faculty of administering to them the sacraments, and that our President General, who has done so much

> in this District for 25 years, converting to the Holy Faith many hundreds of heretics, and also by his own labours, toiling like a common labourer, has created a great chapel in the celebrated city of Cheltenham, where there was none previously, has been obliged to abandon to another the care of the mission.[18]

It was a pity that Baines was not prepared to go the whole way and grant faculties to Polding and Birdsall, which might have won back the good will of the monks, but he was still very angry, and too inclined to dwell on what he considered past insults: 'Were they entitled [he wrote] to carry their wailing and criminations to the Holy See, because I had not gone on bended knee to beg their acceptance of faculties?'[19]

He was still less inclined to do so in the case of Fr Birdsall, and here he had more right on his side, as Birdsall had actually resigned his faculties over the controversy about the Bath mission. Birdsall now wanted them back, but Baines refused to give them unless an agreement was reached about Dr Collingridge's will. Birdsall had weighty support in Rome in the person of Cardinal Weld, who told him that the Pope had directed the Prefect of Propaganda to write to Baines to order him to restore the disputed faculties.

Fr Austin Dullard, a Benedictine in Rome at the time, also reported to Birdsall that he had had conversations with Cardinal Weld about the affairs of the Western District: 'I particularly dwelt upon the great scandal caused in the convents and among the laity by Dr Baines withholding faculties for you and Mr Polding, and I plainly told him that until the faculties were restored no good would be done in the Western District'.[20]

It is interesting that Dullard also related that Cardinal Weld had sent Baines two letters, a private one commanding him to restore the faculties, and one which could be shown publicly to save the Bishop's face. Neither seems to have persuaded Baines to meet Birdsall halfway. In June 1831, Birdsall was still thundering: 'the fact was that you took them [my faculties], as indeed you took them from every priest who should use any endeavour to prevent you from possessing our property'.[21]

There is no record of a direct reply by Baines to this letter, but he wrote to Fr Deday, the Benedictine Provincial, to complain about the President: 'I should have preferred any other member of your Body for the mission of Cheltenham to Mr Birdsall, whose contemptuous disobedience to my orders in despite of the censures annexed to this violation, and repeated insolence render it extremely unpleasant to hold any further acquaintance with him'.[22]

The fact that Fr Birdsall had no faculties to enable him to minister in the Cheltenham mission meant that his congregation were deprived of receiving the sacraments. Baines, therefore, decided in November 1831 that the time had come to provide the Catholics of Cheltenham with another priest. He was willing that another Benedictine should be appointed, but Birdsall refused to allow any other Benedictine to exercise faculties in the Cheltenham mission. The Bishop then announced that, if Birdsall continued to be so obstinate, he would set up another chapel in Cheltenham and appoint a secular priest, a situation similar to the one in Bath.

As Birdsall and Baines were no longer on speaking terms, Fr Deday had to act as the intermediary. He wrote to Baines, quoting Birdsall: 'the direct attempt of Dr Baines to remove me from my mission, and his indirect one to appoint my successor, you will I am sure resist, as we are all bound to do. This mission is therefore now without a missioner and the people without a shepherd.'[23]

Bishop Walsh tried to reason with Baines to make him adopt a more conciliatory attitude: 'I cannot think that the restoration of faculties to Mr Birdsall for the sake of the Cheltenham congregation, disconnected as it is from the Bath and Ampleforth business, would in any way detract from your authority and influence over Mr Birdsall. I see much good that would arise from the restoration of faculties.'[24]

Baines, however, was now adamant that he would not make any direct concession to Birdsall, although he was prepared to negotiate with him in the presence of a mediator. For by this time Birdsall had appealed to the Pope, who, becoming alarmed at the growing warfare between him and Baines, asked the Prefect of Propaganda to arrange some form of conciliation between the two of them. The latter chose Bishop Bramston as a mediator, authorizing him to 'enquire into the unhappy differences between the parties and to report what measures he advised to put an end to them'. The choice of Dr Bramston was an unfortunate one, as he had been the other trustee of Bishop Collingridge's estate, and had been responsible for allowing Baines to obtain control of some of the money left by the Bishop. Birdsall, therefore, considered Bishop Bramston not an impartial umpire, particularly as he wished to hold the investigation at Prior Park. In his usual abrupt manner, he sent Bramston a very testy letter, which angered the recipient so much that he refused to take any further part in the proceedings. Cardinal Weld wrote to Birdsall in exasperation: 'I cannot help deploring that you should have written a letter in such a style to such a man as Dr Bramston'.[25]

President Birdsall, however, was no respecter of persons, and showed the same testiness with the second mediator appointed by the Holy See. This was Dr Wiseman, the President of the English College in Rome, who was visiting England on business. Wiseman first saw Baines at Prior Park, and then the two of them, accompanied by Fr Burgess, rode over to Cheltenham to see Birdsall. Baines was making an effort to be conciliatory, but Birdsall refused to see either him or Fr Burgess, whom he accused of the rape of Ampleforth: 'See Dr Baines and Mr Burgess I would not. Dr Wiseman asked me if I would, to which I answered I would, if the Pope ordered it, see Dr Baines . . . Dr Wiseman throughout the whole acted more like the advocate of Dr Baines than an umpire.'[26]

Arbitration the only solution

As Birdsall also protested 'I will not put my feet under the same table as that man [Baines]', it was clear that the only kind of mediation that might be successful was an official board of arbitration set up by the Holy See, at which the main opponents would not have to confront one another. It was agreed that the subjects for discussion were Bishop Collingridge's will, the Bath mission, the Ampleforth affair and the withdrawal of faculties, but Baines protested in May 1834 that an additional subject was being added without his knowledge, namely, the problems of the ownership of the Bristol mission. He discovered this during a visit to Rome in 1834, having decided to go there to protect his own interests over the arrangements for the coming arbitration. He stated in a letter to Bishop Briggs that:

> The question respecting the Bristol mission (long since given up by the Provincial of the Jesuits) had been ingeniously introduced for the purpose of showing that I was the general enemy of the regulars and in order to restore peace to the congregation of Bristol inconsolable for the removal of one of the last Jesuits, Mr Rowe, by submitting the case of the Bristol mission to the same arbitration which it was proposed should be appointed to settle or rather examine the Benedictine dispute.[27]

It was quite untrue for Baines to say that the Jesuits had abandoned the Bristol mission. They still regarded it as their own, although they had had no priest there since the removal of Fr Rowe by Baines in 1831. His dismissal had caused much resentment among some of the congregation, where there was still much support for the Jesuits. The issue, however, had no bearing on the dispute between Baines and the Benedictines and, with the Bishop's insistence, it was removed from the agenda. There were enough problems to be confronted over the composition of the panel of arbiters and the location of the place of arbitration.

Matters were so delayed that, even though both sides had agreed upon the principle of arbitration by the end of 1832, it was 1834 before things really started moving. Each side was trying to marshal support. Baines wrote to Lord Clifford in plaintive mood:

> I do not assert that all I have done was the best that could be done, but my motive has always been good and I have always acted to the best of my humble judgement. I have done nothing through passion, though I have not been without feeling. I shrink from no enquiry. I court the strictest investigation. I implore as the only favour, that those who accuse me on what ever matter may be summoned to meet me, and that I may have a fair opportunity of self-defence.[28]

Baines seems to be acknowledging here for the first time that he had made mistakes in his many disputes with the Benedictines, but he genuinely believed in the rightness of his cause; it was his judgement and lack of tact that can most be called into question. Bishop Walsh of the Midland District in replying to a letter from Baines also questioned his motives:

> Charity urges me to be candid with Your Lordship. In one part of your letter you request me to remain neutral: in another part of the same letter you intimate that it is a conscientious duty on my part . . . that I should admit a measure seriously affecting the character of one who has always behaved in my district as a most zealous exemplary missioner. Justice also demands that I should hear Mr Birdsall's statement.[29]

Both protagonists were born along by their mutual dislike, almost hatred, of one another. Baines, by this time in Rome, was trying to persuade the authorities to command Birdsall also to journey to Rome to answer the Bishop's accusations. Birdsall was most indignant, writing to Bishop Walsh:

> My Lord, this attempt by Dr B. at making people believe at Rome that I decline to meet him, will no doubt be successful with many! We have twice, My Lord, had members of our Body at Rome since this injurious and arbitrary infliction upon us began. Had Dr B. wished to confront me, or be confronted by us at Rome, then

would have been a convenient time to bring that about. We on our part did not presume to dictate the journey to Dr B. . . .[30]

Choice of arbiters

In any case the time for personal meetings had passed, and by May 1834 Baines was immersed in negotiations for arbitration. He agreed willingly when it was proposed, that the arbiters should be Vicars Apostolic or other bishops, but then Fr Brown of Downside proposed that the five arbiters should be chosen by the parties to the dispute. This was accepted, and it was agreed that two should be chosen by Baines and two by the Benedictines, allowing the four arbiters to choose a fifth. Baines was concerned about the kind of arbiters the monks might choose, and protested indignantly: 'I will not appear before a tribunal of laymen and inferior orders of clergy'.[31]

This fate was averted and Baines wrote to tell Bishop Briggs of the Northern District that the decree had been modified at his insistence, and that the arbiters chosen must be 'ecclesiastics par grandee'.[32]

In spite of this success, Baines was still worried about the growing influence of the regulars at Rome and feared that they had prejudiced the Secretary of Propaganda against him. He wished that the other Vicars Apostolic would speak out against them, 'for whilst I alone speak openly and all the rest remain silent, my candour must pass for hostility and my courage for independence'.[33]

This was unlikely, as though some Vicars Apostolic had difficulties with the regulars in their own districts, they were reluctant to antagonize them; after all, they did reply upon them to minister in many of their missions. In Rome, too, the impression had grown that Baines was a determined foe of the religious orders and, according to Cardinal Weld, was making a bold push to get rid of them as '"bishops" of the west'.

Back in England in the autumn of 1834, Baines started to make his own arrangements about the arbitration. He wrote to Birdsall in early November, giving him his interpretations of the decisions made. Birdsall was not very pleased, judging by a letter written on 13 November: 'By the decision of the Sacred Congregation referred to you in your letter, I am to bring forward my case *sine prejudicio*, which cannot be done while you continue to inflict more injury upon me for nothing but what has grown out of these disputes, which are to be determined by chosen arbiters.'

He ended sarcastically: 'If it is to be the intention of the Sacred Congregation that I come before the court in fetters, I shall be told it by them'.[34]

Baines replied a few days later, ignoring the jibes, but informing Birdsall that he had appointed Bishop Briggs as his first arbiter, and now wished to know whom the President wished to appoint. He was annoyed that Birdsall was still bringing up past grievances and ended by saying: 'Will you please inform me what is the severe injury which I continue to inflict upon you; if you are referring to missionary faculties, it is an injury inflicted by you yourself'.[35]

The tone of the letters did not augur well for the coming arbitration, particularly as Birdsall was refusing to inform Baines of the name of the bishop he proposed to nominate as an arbiter. Baines wrote to his ally, Bishop Briggs, on 23 November asking him whether, as he had not obtained any satisfaction from Birdsall, he was justified in refusing to restore his faculties until the investigation had taken place. There is no record of any reply to this, but it does make clear that Baines was contemplating retreat.

In December, he wrote a more conciliatory letter to Birdsall, saying that he would agree to restore the faculties as soon as the five arbiters had been appointed and the day of their first meeting had been fixed. He was still not prepared to admit that he had been at all in the wrong, going on to say:

> In making this concession I am actuated solely by an anxious desire that the investigation ordered by the Holy See may be made with as little delay as possible, but I do not admit the justice of your demands, nor do I intend to absolve you from any censure which you have incurred by your appeal in the Bath chapel and other proceedings . . .[36]

It was sufficient, though, to start the ball rolling until five arbiters had been appointed. Besides Bishop Briggs, Baines nominated Dr Yoens, a missioner from his native Liverpool: Birdsall nominated Bishop Walsh of the Midland District, and Fr Brooke, the Jesuit Provincial. It is significant that he chose the latter, demonstrating that an alliance was developing between the Benedictines and the Jesuits to resist the Bishop's encroachment into what they both considered to be their legitimate interests.

Baines was equally determined that the growing power of the regulars had to be resisted and viewed the coming arbitration as a means of doing so, for

> I consider this investigation as an affair of the greatest possible importance not only to the District, but to the whole English mission, for upon it must depend whether the authority of the

> Bishops or that of the regulars is to go on *indefinitum*. If it shall be found that they are wrong in that instance, they will be more cautious in future how they assist us; but if they triumph our difficulties will be exceedingly increased.[37]

The fact that the four arbiters chose another bishop, the Vicar Apostolic of the Western District of Scotland, as the fifth arbiter, encouraged Baines to think that the result would be favourable to him.

The choice of venue

More argument then developed over the venue for the arbitration. Baines was anxious that it should be Prior Park, but Birdsall would have none of it. Bishop Walsh wrote to Birdsall: 'I have signified to Dr Baines and Dr Briggs that Bath, Prior Park and Wolverhampton will be objectionable as the site of the investigation'.[38]

Eventually a decision was reached to hold the arbitration in a large house in Royal Crescent, Clifton, Bristol. This was the impressive terrace of Georgian houses, now known as Royal York Crescent. This was not the end of the delays, as even the date caused problems. The arbiters wanted 8 July 1835, but Baines objected to it as being the day of the oral examination and prize-giving at Prior Park. He won his point and the date was at last agreed upon for 10 July.

Fr Edgeworth was given the task of finding accommodation in Bristol for the arbiters and the witnesses. He rented a house in Clifton where all the arbiters could stay, and the monks were put up in one of a row of houses near the new Catholic chapel, which had just been built in Bristol, Fr Brown obtaining another room for the celebration of mass. Fr Edgeworth arranged for other witnesses to be put up in houses belonging to members of the Bristol congregation. Fr Burgess arrived on 8 July and told Baines that he was staying with an acquaintance in Park Street. Baines himself was not arriving until the night of 9 July, and probably stayed in the presbytery with Fr Edgeworth.

The arbitration and the report

The arbitration went on for several weeks, with two arbiters interviewing all the witnesses separately and then making their decisions after a lengthy discussion. The proceedings were not published, but the arbiters sent a report to the Sacred College of Propaganda, and issued a brief announcement for the benefit of the general public. They first discussed the long-running argument about the executorship of Bishop Collingridge's will and queried Birdsall's claim to be a trustee of the estate, as well as an executor, so that he could not object to Bishop Baines using the disputed £300 as he thought fit; the sum was already swallowed up, probably in the purchase and alterations to Prior Park. As to the rest of the money, some of it consisting in ground rents of houses in Taunton, it seemed this was entirely Collingridge's own money and therefore should be applied according to the wishes of the testator. The arbitrators proposed that Dr Collingridge's library of books should be valued and the value added to the money left to be paid out for the foundation and assistance of missions in the Western District. Bishop Baines and President Birdsall were to have some discretion in the choice of missions, although the needs of Wrexham and Merthyr Tydfil were particularly mentioned.[39]

The acrimonious dispute about the affairs at Ampleforth was next on the agenda, and had gained most publicity, for all could understand the accusation that the Bishop and his associates had stolen thousands of pounds from Ampleforth, if they could not appreciate the complexities of the other issues. It was an accusation that was very difficult to prove, for not only had the supposed crime taken place five years before, but some of the accounts were no longer available. Birdsall had made the mistake of not thoroughly examining the accounts on his visit to Ampleforth in September 1829, and again in April 1830, when he signed a legal agreement exonerating the three ex-monks, Burgess, Metcalfe and Rooker, from all future demands on them. He and the Benedictines were therefore in an impossible position when they tried to resurrect the whole matter. Nevertheless, they raised several points which they regarded as particularly suspicious. The first of these was the question of the Pension Book, which Burgess had taken away with him. This was supposed to be a complete list of the 'pension', or fees, paid in by the students during the last year and a half in which Burgess was in charge, but the ex-Prior had entered these amounts '*in globo*', so that it was completely impossible to make out whether all the moneys received for pension had been credited to the college account. At the arbitration Burgess claimed this pension book was a private book and that he had copied from it all that was necessary to be known. As the Benedictines could not produce any document to show that it was binding on a Superior to leave the pension book for his successors, the arbiters ruled that Burgess was justified in withholding it. It was a lasting point of aggravation for Birdsall and the monks, but something they were forced to accept. On two minor matters, though, they gained some satisfaction, as Burgess was forced to agree that a painting of St Jerome taken away from Ampleforth was in fact the property of the college, as was a sum of £100 which Burgess had thought was his own.[40] He was obliged to return both, but in general the arbitration was regarded as a complete rebuttal of the wild charges of theft and exploitation at Ampleforth against Burgess, Metcalfe and Roper, and indirectly by Baines. If the arbitrators had looked into the question of inveigling students and staff away from the college, they might have reached a different conclusion.

The other two items of dispute were largely resolved by the time the arbitrators met. Bishop Baines announced before the first meeting that he would restore faculties to President Birdsall and Fr Polding, the Sub-Prior of Downside, a matter which would have been settled long before if it had not been for the obstinacy of the two main protagonists. The Benedictines had already rebuffed the Bishop in the quarrel over the Bath mission, so that Baines had been obliged to withdraw his missioner to Prior Park,[41] but both parties still wanted the arbitrators to rule on the rights of ownership. They came down mainly on the side of the Benedictines, confirming their ownership, dating back to the late seventeenth century. Then the building known as the Bell Tree House had been held by lay trustees on behalf of the monks, as religious orders could not hold property openly. On the other hand, there were peculiar circumstances to the mission, as the Vicars Apostolic had lived there for forty-five years during the eighteenth century. The factor was not necessarily relevant in itself, as all three of these, Bishops York, Walmesley and Sharrock, had been Benedictines, but it was a point to be taken into consideration. More relevant, the arbitrators thought, was the claim that a large number of Catholics, who were not Benedictines, had contributed to Bishop Walmesley's appeal for a new chapel after the Gordon riots. The arbitrators thought, therefore, that it would be an equitable arrangement if the Bishop had the right to appoint the second missioner in Bath. This clause remained only a recommendation, which seems to have been ignored, as Fr Jenkins remained in Bath for another two years and was succeeded by another Benedictine. Bishop Baines continued to run his rival chapel at Portland Place for another few years, when the expenses became too much, and the Benedictines regained full control.

The public declaration made after the end of the arbitration on 22 August 1835 dwelt entirely upon the Ampleforth affair, which had created the greatest scandal throughout the Catholic world. This announced that in the opinion of the arbitrators:

> No part of the property of the monastery of Ampleforth was taken away by Messrs Burgess, Metcalfe and Rooker, nor received by Dr Baines, except a picture of St Jerome, which was removed under an erroneous impression that it had been given to Mr Burgess, and a sum of about £150, which was taken through an unintentional error; which error having been discovered by Mr Burgess during the course of this enquiry, the sum has been repaid by him. Of these mistakes Dr Baines could not have had any knowledge. The arbitrators further add in general terms that in the course of their enquiries they have not met with any thing to impeach the character of either Dr Baines or Messrs Burgess, Metcalfe and Rooker.[42]

The results of arbitration

So what was achieved by this long drawn-out procedure, ending with such a statement, which some of the Benedictines considered a white-wash. If nothing else, it cleared the air, so that relations between Bishop Baines and the Benedictines were never to be as strained as they had been in previous years. In 1836, Dr Walsh was continuing to promote further reconciliation between the parties, by talking with Baines and the new Benedictine Provincial, Fr Barber, about the desirability of the Bishop officiating again in the Downside chapel. Fr Andrew Scott wrote to Fr Brown at Downside supporting this idea:

> I think the proposal agreed to by Mr Barber would bury into oblivion all the old disputes provided that Dr Baines would agree. In my opinion he would best promote his own interests, as well as the interests of religion by officiating occasionally in your chapel and delivering his lectures there ... Dr Walsh also told me that you have not yet taken down the episcopal throne in your Bath chapel. If I were a member of the Benedictine Body, I would vote for its not being taken down ...[43]

The prospect of arbitration had also concentrated Baines's mind so that he was forced to restore faculties to Birdsall and Polding before the arbitrators met, and the arbitrators persuaded both him and Birdsall to accept a compromise on the question of Bishop Collingridge's will; it meant, too, that the long-drawn-out rumours about the Ampleforth affair were largely laid to rest, although some of the Benedictines continued to argue that they had been unfairly treated. On the other hand, the monks gained official recognition of their claims to the Bath mission, and there was no mandatory requirement on them to allow the Bishop to appoint the second missioner.[44]

Yet the overall impression remains that an unsuitable amount of time and energy was expended in this affair, which the Bishop and the monks could have used much more profitably. Solutions could surely have been reached years earlier, if the two main protagonists had agreed to meet in a spirit of Christian reconciliation; unfortunately, though, such a spirit was non-existent.

Long after these events, however, there came evidence of at least the show of public goodwill in the August of 1835. A note was found in the papers of a monk of Downside, who reported that: 'After the conclusion of the synod, as a public act of friendship and open testimony of satisfaction at the result of the investigation, the Rt Rev and Rev Arbitrators dined with both parties at Prior Park and the following day at Downside College. *Sic finitur ad majorem Dei gloriam.*'[45]

It is not revealed whether President Birdsall was one of the party.

Notes

1 J. B. Dockery, *Collingridge*, pp. 315–19.
2 CDA, Bishops' Letters, Birdsall to Baines, 12 March 1831.
3 Ibid. 26 June 1831.
4 Ibid.
5 Ibid. Baines Box Files, 5–7. Baines to Deday, 30 September 1831.
6 Ibid. Marsh to Baines, 6 October 1831.
7 Downside Archives, I 438, Legal Opinion, 15 June 1835.
8 See above, chapter 6.
9 CDA, Bishops' Letters, Baines to Wiseman, 19 November 1832.
10 Ibid. Baines Box Files, 5–7, Baines to Briggs, 13 May 1834.
11 See above, chapter 6.
12 CDA, Baines Box Files, 5–7, Baines's Statement of Facts to the Arbiters, 1835.
13 Ibid. Bishops' Letters, Birdsall to Baines, 16 June 1830.
14 Ibid. Polding to Baines, 29 June 1830.
15 Ibid. Baines Box Files, 5–7, Baines's Statement of Fact to the Arbiters.
16 Ibid.
17 Ibid.
18 Ibid.
19 Ibid.
20 Downside Archives, H219, Dullard to Birdsall, 11 March 1831.
21 CDA, Bishops' Letters, Birdsall to Baines, 28 June 1831.
22 Downside Archives, H296, Baines to Deday, 26 July 1831.
23 CDA, Bishops' Letters, Deday to Baines, 6 November 1831.
24 Ibid. Walsh to Baines, 21 August 1831.
25 Ampleforth and Downside Archives, 'Lives of the English Benedictines', Weld to Birdsall, 29 September 1832.

26 Ibid. Birdsall to Brown, 26 November 1832.
27 CDA, Bishops' Letters, Baines to Briggs, 13 May 1834.
28 Ibid. Baines to Clifford, 27 January 1834.
29 Ibid. Walsh to Baines, (date not known).
30 Ibid. Birdsall to Walsh, (date not known).
31 Ibid. Baines Box Files, 5–7, Baines to Briggs, 13 May 1834.
32 Ibid. 10 November 1834.
33 Ibid. 22 May 1834.
34 Ibid. Birdsall to Baines, 13 November 1834.
35 Ibid. Bishops' Letters, Baines to Birdsall, 19 November 1834.
36 Ibid. 1 December 1834.
37 Ibid. Baines Box Files, 5–7, Baines to Briggs, 10 November 1834.
38 Downside Archives, I 415, Walsh to Birdsall, 30 April 1835.
39 Ampleforth Archives, A268 89 7G39, 1835.
40 Ibid.
41 See above, chapter 9.
42 Ampleforth Archives, A268 89 7G39, 1835.
43 Downside Archives, J72, Scott to Brown, 23 January 1836.
44 Ampleforth Archives, A268 89 7G39, 1835.
45 James Shepherd, *Reminiscences of Prior Park*, p. 139.

11

Prior Park 1835–1841: Years of Triumph and Disaster

A disastrous visit

While Baines was involved in disputes with the Benedictine monks and with the nuns of Cannington, he awaited the fulfilment of his hopes for the future of Prior Park as a university with the arrival of Nicholas Wiseman from Rome. In the summer of 1835 Wiseman came to Prior Park amid great hopes and expectations. He had heard unfavourable reports of the college from some quarters, but was disinclined to believe them; he was looking forward to working with Baines in creating the first Catholic university in England since the Reformation. What was it that went so tragically wrong?

Baines left no account of what had happened, although his view of Wiseman's conduct is strongly expressed in his correspondence with the future Cardinal. Wiseman wrote to John Bonomi many years later referring to the episode and his separation from Baines:

> One cause of our separation is too painful for me to recount, but the decisive one was my unfortunately presuming on what I thought confidence, and offering advice which I thought would be most useful. This produced such a rebuff as I have never received before and never since. It was by letter; but if my answer was preserved among the Bishop's papers, I should not mind all the world seeing it. I closed it by saying what may seem prophetic, that if anyone should hereafter record his life, I hoped he would not draw his character from his letters.[1]

John Bonomi, a student at Prior Park, and later to be a great defender of Bishop Baines, said that he knew of the dispute, and was sorry for it, but had no idea of its cause. He admitted that Baines was quick-tempered and liable to make hasty decisions, which he later regretted,[2] but he never made any serious efforts to resolve this dispute.

Bernard Ward in his *Sequel to Catholic Emancipation* concluded that Wiseman had objected to Baines's change of plans for him – that is, the possibility that he might take up a position at Prior Park provisionally, while still retaining his post at Rome. This gave Wiseman the idea that Baines did not have full confidence in his abilities, and there was also the feeling that the Bishop should have pressed harder at Rome to obtain the coadjutorship for him. Baines himself believed that the latter was the main cause of the initial disagreement.[3]

Wiseman in an angry mood left Prior Park in a great hurry, but at this stage the disagreement did not appear to be insoluble. The cause of their lasting estrangement is to be found in the events that followed. Wiseman went on to stay with the Earl and Countess of Shrewsbury at Alton Towers and, while there, was highly critical of Baines and the way in which he ran his college. The stories reached the Bishop, who resented such criticisms and wrote to Wiseman to tell him so in no uncertain terms. Wiseman with extreme lack of tact replied to Baines giving his impressions of 'the lack of order, discipline and spirituality' he had found at Prior Park, and going into details about the small numbers communicating, comparing them unfavourably with other colleges; he also criticized the fragile financial basis of the college, a particularly sore point with Baines, and pointed out the risk of pouring out so much money on an expensive style of building without much prospect of return. 'All seem to think', he wrote 'that you have command of princely wealth and that you risk the interests of your diocese'.[4]

Baines was outraged at these criticisms, particularly as they came from a younger man of inferior position, and answered them in his usual forthright manner. He accused Wiseman of no longer acting towards him as a friend:

> You lost no opportunity of letting me know how much you could do for me, although without an effort, but you also gave me very clearly to understand that the fulfilment of my 'earliest intentions' was the only condition on which you would do it. You could raise 25,000 pounds in France any day – but you would not do it. You could do more in Germany, but you would not do it. You could procure professors, and I requested you to do it as a favour as you came through Germany, but you did not do it. I requested from you some trifling assistance at Prior Park, which you acknowledged that you could easily give, but you would not give it . . .

All this would have been provocation enough, but Baines went on to refute the criticisms of Prior Park by turning them back on Wiseman himself: 'Suppose that when I was last in Rome I had collected reports from your own disenchanted subjects and had told some distinguished family in Rome (I will suppose the Shrewsbury family themselves) the following story ...'

Baines then went on to imagine visiting the English College in Rome, where Wiseman was Rector, and noting every possible criticism. Some of his account was greatly exaggerated, but Wiseman, his friends and critics must have recognized home truths behind the colourful language. Comparable criticisms could be levied against the English College as those which Wiseman had directed towards Prior Park and Baines made this clear:

> There is a deplorable want of discipline in the Eng College. Some of the young men do not communicate at all regularly and none of them so often as they do in such and such colleges. There have been so many disorders that Dr W. was obliged to expel I don't know how many, and the remainder, though he thinks otherwise, are by no means united or so satisfied with him as he imagines ...

Baines then went on to make more subtle jibes at Wiseman's reputation for obscure learning:

> Dr W. is constantly engaged in giving them [the students] lectures on subjects which are of little purpose, which few of them understand and which produce little effect but to make them conceited – that it is much to be feared that their principles may be shaken by the new learning and the quantities of heterodox books which he puts into their hands ...

Baines also made much play on Wiseman's love of entertaining and being entertained, his vanity and love of show:

> It not infrequently happens that the college is left without a rector or vice-rector both being out at some dinner or evening party from which they do not return until a late hour at night; that of all the rectors in Rome, Dr W. is the only one that is seen ... at all the gay assemblies, that of course his expenses are much increased by them and similar means, which may account for the college not maintaining more than two thirds the number it did in Dr Gradwell's time; that Dr W. pretends that he has improved the farms, but the only improvement which can be seen is in his own

> apartments (which are very much improved) and in some of the galleries in adorning which he has spent great sums of money which 'can make no return'.

Baines then went on to raise the suspicion that Wiseman was advancing the prospects of his own relations and raising money by unscrupulous means:

> Nay, it has even been whispered by some of his best friends that some of his relations have been somehow or other supported or endowed by him, and that he is making a private purse out of the means of the college by keeping in it a number of secular young men . . .

Baines was quick to end by remarking, 'This is of course false', but Wiseman would have known that his cousin, Charles Macarthy, had been one of a small number of lay students at the English College.

Finally Baines drew attention to Wiseman's known liking for the company of women:

> It is also regretted [he said] by some of his best friends that he allows the college to be inundated with ladies, several dashing young ladies having been seen strolling about the galleries and even coming from his own private apartments. There is not the slightest suspicion that Dr W. himself means any harm by this, but it is a pity the ladies, if he admits any at all, should not be of a matronly character etc. etc. etc.

And Baines ends by urging an imaginary Lord Shrewsbury, 'But of all this say nothing till you get back to Alton, then write to him a friendly letter of serious warning'.[5]

Baines then urged Wiseman to return to Prior Park and discuss matters, 'for', he wrote, 'I have not time to set you right in details, but if you will favour me with a call on your way back to London, we will examine on the spot into the truth of the statements made to you and into the accuracy of the opinions you have formed'.[6] After such a letter, this was most unlikely. Wiseman defended himself and his criticisms of Prior Park in a letter to Baines,[7] but never visited the college again.

This dispute may not have been the only reason for Baines's doubts about Wiseman, judging by a letter to Lord Shrewsbury written about this time.

> Would W. be content to be second to me? [he asked]. Would not parties be formed? Should I not find myself compelled either to yield to all his views or quarrel with many of my friends here? I have not yet known an instance of a person who has been an absolute superior becoming a good subordinate one. Would W. be an exception?[8]

Whatever the reasons for the separation, the result of the estrangement was an enormous setback to the future of Catholic higher education in England. Both men were brilliant, but both were also tactless and obstinate, and Baines especially regarded criticism as a personal insult. He showed no regret at the episode and continued to talk about his plans for a Catholic university. In reality all prospects of such an establishment disappeared with the departure of Wiseman. He would have brought an international reputation for scholarship to Prior Park, and without him or figures of comparable stature, attracting students of calibre was always going to be difficult.

Luigi Gentili at Prior Park

Fr Gentili, who arrived at Prior Park from Italy the same year as Wiseman, was to stay much longer, but his first impressions of England and of Prior Park were almost as depressing as Wiseman's had been. His description of arriving in London was very similar to that of Baines himself when returning from Rome in 1829:

> We seemed to be really entering the city of Pluto: black houses, a black sky, black ships, and black looking sailors – filthy to an extreme – the waters of the Thames were tinged with a colour between black and yellow, and emitted a highly offensive stench: on land there prevailed a confused noise, with horses and carriages of every description running and crossing each other's path – in fine, to make a long story short, here the devil is seen enthroned, exercising a tyrannical sway over wretched mortals.[9]

Gentili's first impressions of Prior Park was not much better. Although he appreciated the magnificence of the building, he was dismayed that it showed no signs of being a Christian institution, let alone a Catholic one. There were pagan statues in front of the mansion, but no image of the Virgin or the saints; there was no rosary, no prayers in which she or other saints were invoked, and not even a lighted lamp left in the chapel. Bishop Ullathorne coming to Prior Park ten years later gained the same impression:

> Unfortunately Prior Park was stamped all over, inside and out, with a secular tone. The only cross visible from the outside of that vast range of buildings was one put up by the Protestant, Bishop Warburton, upon the gable of the chapel, when he possessed it, as the heir to the wealthy founder, whose daughter he married. Inside the statue of a saint, even of the Blessed Virgin Mary, was not to be found. Mr Vaughan told me that when he was appointed President of St Paul's, he put up a statue of the B.V.M., and that one of the superiors came up and said, 'Let us have no Romanising here. Take it away!'[10]

In spite of all the time that Baines had spent in Rome, he was still against many of the new forms of worship coming from the Continent, and preferred to follow in the traditions of the English Catholic Church with its subdued form of devotions. And although attitudes were changing since Catholic Emancipation, English Catholics were still afraid of antagonizing their Protestant neighbours with too much ostentation, although this does not seem to have worried Baines when he organized the great processions for the feast of Corpus Christi.

Gentili was also disconcerted to find that the Catholic clergy did not wear clerical costume, but this was a practice which had continued since the time of the penal laws when it had been illegal for Catholic priests to wear clerical dress out in the streets. Bishop Brown later told one of Gentili's disciples that at Downside 'the only habit worn by the Benedictines was blue stockings, knee breeches and a long dark blue coat. It was still customary for priests to wear blue coats, and some of them continued the practice well into Queen Victoria's reign'.[11]

More to the point was Gentili's criticism of the priests at Prior Park as being so obsessed with their work as schoolmasters that they hardly had time to perform their real duties as priests. These doubts and criticisms did not enamour Gentili to other members of staff, and relationships became very strained, especially with Fr Rooker and Peter Hutton, the novice, who had also come from Ampleforth.

In spite of all this, Gentili and his fellow Rosminians settled into the work at Prior Park and made a considerable difference to the teaching in the college and its spiritual life. Baines appointed Gentili to teach Italian and Philosophy, Rey to teach Theology and Belisy, French. He also made Gentili spiritual director, and the latter began to organize ceremonies and to develop the choir. By Passion Week in 1836, Gentili was arranging the spiritual exercises for teachers and students, basing these on the methods of St Ignatius Loyola, in which everyone took part in a week-long retreat, with a regular timetable of meditation, spiritual reading, prayers and sermons. Gentili preached several times and enhanced the dramatic effect of his discourses by speaking from a specially-erected platform in the chapel, with windows darkened all around.

The first retreat was so successful that Gentili felt that he could introduce further innovations, such as the wearing of holy medals and scapulars among the boys. This was not so popular among parents and members of the old clergy, and many complained to Baines, who eventually had to stop the practice.

Gentili became well-known among boys and staff for his eccentricities, and stories about him were passed down by word of mouth. He was determined to take action against the pagan statues outside the main mansion, and recruited a chain of boys to remove the massive figure of Hercules. He himself put a rope round the figure and directed the boys to hold the other end: 'When I say the third time, come down you great monster, all of you pull together'.

Gentili gave the signal, once, twice and then as he raised his arm for the third time, Dr Baines put his head out of the window and stopped the destruction.[12] Baines himself then thought he had better do something about the statues, and had them painted with draperies to disguise their nakedness. Heavy rains undid the good work and restored the statues to all their pagan nudity.

The first winter after Gentili's arrival was very severe; the lake froze over and staff and students were able to enjoy skating on the thick ice. Gentili had never seen anything like it before, and from the edge of the pond began preaching that it was a mortal sin to go upon the glass, as he called it; he began running about to entreat them to come off the 'glass' before it gave way, and was very excited and prepared if necessary to absolve and give the last blessing. They only laughed at his fears, as the ice was so thick and strong; but even Dr Rooker, who was a good one on the skates, could not convince him that there was no danger. James Baines then ran up to his uncle, the Bishop, to tell him what was going on. Baines, who prided himself on his skating prowess acquired in Germany and on the Gilling pond near Ampleforth, came down, borrowed his nephew's skates, and soon was skating about on the ice 'with his purple feraiola flying in the air, and inviting Dr Gentili to come on the ice and he would conduct him round the pond'.[13]

The fire of 1836

In spite of all the vicissitudes 1836 dawned fair for Prior Park – the numbers had increased, Gentili, notwithstanding his eccentricities, had improved the standard of teaching and earned the respect of the students and most of the staff, and the College of St Paul, which was to house the episcopal seminary of the Western District, was nearing completion. Baines even had time to show a Baroness and a party of other visitors round the mansion. Emily Smith, who came with the Baroness, described her impressions: 'The chapel is small and elegant with a sweet organ. There are some fine pictures and pieces of sculpture. The Baroness and I visited Bishop in his private apartments. His manners are delightful.' Baines would have been flattered to hear such compliments, but not so pleased by Miss Smith's further remarks. 'What a pity', she said, 'that a man of such talent and learning should be enlisted under the harness of such a fearfully corrupt Church as that of the Roman Catholic. May the Lord open his eyes and make him a true convert to the Faith of the Bible.'[14]

Such pleasant occasions were far from Baines's thoughts on 30 May 1836, when calamity struck Prior Park. A small boy noticed smoke coming from the roof of the mansion and pointed it out to one of the prefects, who took no notice. A few hours later, though, as Baines was sitting down to dine, the alarm was given, and it was obvious to all that there was a major fire. The *Bath and Cheltenham Gazette* later reported:

> About sunset the wind suddenly rose and having about half past eight veered round to the N.E., the sight of the immense body of flames which rushed out at the back and S.W. corner of the edifice was awful in the extreme ... from this time the hope of rescuing any portion of the edifice was utterly abandoned, as in a short time the whole of the apartments on the library floor were with two exceptions involved in the conflagration. ... The flames spread so quickly to the upper part of the mansion, that the roof of the chapel was speedily consumed and serious fears for the safety of the organ were entertained. The engine belonging to the west of England fire-office played with great effect on the dangerous parts adjacent to the valuable instrument ... On the first intimation of danger, and when it was found impossible to save the chapel entire, the tabernacle and other notable parts of the altar, composed of jasper, statuary, lapis lazuli, and black and gold, were taken to a place of safety. At about a quarter to nine, the fire had extended to the first floor ... the reflection of the flames on the various trees, and on the vast crowd of persons who had assembled on the rising ground to the rear of the building, presented a very magnificent spectacle. Soon after their appearance in the first storey of the splendid building, the flames spread through it from end to end, and in a short

> time Bishop Baines's private chapel in the west extremity of the mansion was destroyed. ... About ten o'clock nearly the whole of the floors had fallen in and the work of destruction was completed. The engines, however, continued to play on the ruins until about half past one, when the supply of water became extinguished ...[15]

Baines was at his best in a crisis and directed the fire-fighting operations until the fire engines made their way up the steep hill from Bath. Later he was to advise Bishop Briggs of the Northern District to be sure to have his own fire engine on the spot to protect his buildings, for Baines had learned his mistake the hard way in the calamitous losses at Prior Park, made worse by the lack of water after the ponds had been pumped dry. He had been very successful, however, in directing the rescue operations to save the contents of the mansion, and most of the valuable things were saved.

The operation had been joined by large numbers of local people and Baines was touched at the great sympathy shown, particularly by the city's representatives, the gentry and clergy. The *Monthly Intelligence* reported that:

> the Mayor rode up on horse-back, and reached the spot at half past six, and, by his own personal exertions, and the influence of his example, rendered important service. A great number of the clergy and gentry, with other inhabitants of the city, to the number it is conjectured of 10,000, were present at this calamitous spectacle, and not only evinced the warmest sympathy towards the highly respectable and amicable individuals, whose abode and property were thus exposed to the destructive ravages of the flames, but made the most strenuous, and, in many instances, intrepid and daring exertions, to secure the moveable portion from the general wreck. ... Immense crowds of visitors, attracted by a desire to see the ruins of this noble pile, have daily resorted to the spot, as well as a very large number of the most distinguished gentry and respectable inhabitants, to leave their cards, as is usual in such cases of trying calamity.[16]

Baines was particularly impressed by the sympathy shown by Protestant clergy, especially Dr Moysey, with whom he had had an acrimonious dispute. He wrote a letter of thanks to the editor of the *Bath and Cheltenham Gazette*:

> Allow me to express the deep sense of gratitude I feel to the numerous individuals, who valiantly lent me their valuable aid on

> the late distressing occurrence at Prior Park. It was no small consolation to me, under the heavy affliction, which it pleased an all wise and all bountiful Providence to send, to witness the charitable sympathy expressed, and the zealous exertions made on my behalf, by persons known and unknown, sometimes not without considerable personal risk.

He then went on to refer to Dr Moysey indirectly, as the Protestant clergyman had not wanted his name to be revealed: 'I should have been happy if permitted, to mention the name of a highly respectable clergyman of the Established Church, whose conduct on this occasion showed that the parable of the Good Samaritan had not been lost on him'.[17]

All this was of great consolation to Baines demonstrating, as he believed, his own reputation in the community, and the increasing stature of Prior Park and the Catholic Church. It was also an indication that the relations between Catholics and Protestants were a great deal more amicable than they became later in the century. Soon, though, he had to concentrate on the enormous problems created by the fire. These were increased by his failure to insure the building properly, believing that fire was impossible in such a massive stone mansion, so that the losses were found to be £10,000 above the amount insured. Even this realization and the knowledge that he had lost his own home did not break Baines, or shake his belief in the future of his great enterprise. And providence, in the shape of his old friend, the Hon. Miss Crewe, came to his aid in providing him with a house. She moved out of the Priory, her own home in the grounds of Prior Park, and lent it to the Bishop until the mansion could be rebuilt. Thus rehoused in pleasant surroundings, Baines turned his attention to rebuilding the mansion for which he desperately needed more funds. He tried another public appeal, writing to Bishop Briggs: 'I am requesting all the Bishops to put their signatures to the enclosed appeal ... This is an awful business. Thank God it happened in the day hours which enabled me to save most of the property, and no lives were lost ... Pray for me, my dear Lord.'[18]

Like other appeals, this one brought in very little and Baines was forced to increase his debts still more by borrowing. In his papers there are records of his taking out a mortgage for £11,000 plus interest to Lady Acland on an area of land called The Beeches, which was part of the Prior Park estate, and another note mentioning the payment of £25 for negotiating a loan of £10,000, although it does not mention the source of the loan.[19]

He was soon full of plans for restoring the mansion, making it even more palatial than it had been before. It happened that Hound Street House, a large eighteenth-century house near Shepton Mallet, was being taken down about this time, and all the fittings and contents were up for sale. He seized the opportunity to buy ornamental plaster work, mahogany doors, pilasters, a staircase and bannisters, chimney pieces and oak boards, and had them all transported to Prior Park, which must have been a big expense in itself.[20]

He also made some changes to the interior of the mansion, opening up the hall ceiling, which had been partly destroyed anyway, and building an ornate balcony, from which visitors could view the ceremonies below, and those beneath could see the magnificent ceiling high above. Lady Arundell, Baines's old friend from Wardour, now a widow, gave most of the new furnishings, and the Hon. Miss Crewe gave a magnificent collection of paintings.

The opening of St Paul's College

Baines also went on with his plans for opening the ecclesiastical seminary in the autumn of the year. Fortunately the building was almost completed by the time of the fire, which did not touch it, so no further expense on this was involved, and some of the staff were able to stay there. The College of St Paul was opened with great ceremony on 21 November 1836, beginning with High Mass at which the Bishop officiated:

> After mass a procession consisting of 50 of the clergy and older students in the appropriate costume followed the Bishop and his attendants, and the younger students and numbers of visitors proceeded from the chapel through the principal apartments and the exhibition room ... here the bishop delivered the constitution of the college to the Very Rev. Dr Brindle V.G. ... and having appointed the Rev. Dr Gentili president and nominated the principal officers of the college, his lordship delivered an address. The procession then returned to the chapel and the ceremony finished with a solemn Te Deum.[21]

Unlike the complete lack of preparation which had accompanied the opening of St Peter's, Baines had prepared detailed regulations to be ready for the opening of the new college, the work of H. E. Goodridge. These started with instructions as to how staff should conduct themselves towards students, showing kindness and affability at all times. 'One well turned remonstrance is worth a hundred angry or teasing scoldings'; followed by details of religious exercises, including the instruction that no confessions were to be held anywhere except in the confessional except in the case of sickness, a practice which was still not general in England. And Baines went on to issue precise regulations about conduct in the dormitories and lavatories for the boys in St Peter's:

> The Vice-President wakes students at 6 – they must have sufficient time to wash themselves and brush their teeth, hair and cloathes. By 6.15, the President must be in the play-room, keeping order and seeing that each student as he descends from the dorm goes straight to the lavatory. As he returns, he should be carefully inspected as to the hands, face and teeth, particularly those of the younger students not under the matron . . .[22]

Gentili resented all the close supervision he was required to do, reducing the time he wanted to give to his true work of evangelism, and extending his hours from 4.30 in the morning to 10 o'clock at night. Yet he always supported Baines, defending him against the attacks of his critics. One of these wrote to the Pope in February 1837, giving him a very unfavourable account of Prior Park, and urging that the establishment should be closed down. Hearing of this through Cardinal Weld, Gentili replied to the criticism. While he admitted that Prior Park did not have teachers of the calibre of some of the Roman schools, Gentili thought the classical authors were taught as well as they were in Rome. Although he agreed, too, that the college finances were not sound, he rejected the idea that Bishop Baines was living in luxury in the midst of it all.[23]

The idea of sumptuous living was also rejected by Lady Arundell, who came to stay at Prior Park while the mansion was still being restored:

> . . . as to the poor Bishop's building palaces. Before the fatal fire he lived in handsome rooms because he took the house as he found it. The flames gutted the whole of the house, everything except the chapel, and the handsome stucco ceiling of that was destroyed – he at last completed a small sitting room, which opens into a literal cell, with an uncurtained bed in it for himself. Opposite to this is a drawing-room, as he saved most of the furniture from the fire, which leads to the chapel gallery. Under this on the ground floor is a plain dining room . . .[24]

And Ambrose Phillipps de Lisle, in a letter to Gentili, reported the favourable impression of Fr Bernard, later Abbot of Mount St

Bernard's Abbey, on St Paul's:

> Fr Bernard says that in the college there is a piety, a regularity, a recollection, a seat for the honour of God and the advancement of the Catholic faith, which he can never think of without feeling his heart ravished with excessive joy. Fr Bernard says that Bishop Baines is one of the most glorious Bishops in the whole Catholic Church. He cannot speak of him without tears of joy to God for having raised up such a man in England.[25]

Growing problems at Prior Park

In spite of these favourable impressions, Baines was having new problems of staffing. Dr Rooker, who had been an excellent teacher and a stabilizing influence since he came from Ampleforth, decided that he could no longer work with Gentili, and left. Peter Hutton, the former novice from Ampleforth, was also becoming more and more resentful of Gentili, so Baines sent him to the University of Louvain to complete his studies and become ordained. Dr Logan, who was the foremost scholar at Prior Park, left to join the staff of Oscott, whither he was probably lured by Wiseman. Baines was very angry at what he considered a betrayal, and wrote protesting letters to Bishop Walsh, but Dr Logan left nonetheless. Baines was becoming very worried at the increasing competition of Oscott, and tried in vain to get teachers of the same calibre as those he had lost. He approached Dr Lingard, the historian, without success, but Lingard recommended a Dr Dunham, who proved to be a disaster, a hopeless teacher and a laughing-stock with the boys; he finally brought Prior Park bad publicity by being imprisoned for debt.

Baines continually pressed Gentili to persuade his order to send more men and eventually, in July 1837, two more priests and three lay brothers came. Gentili did not approve of the new arrivals, whom he described as looking so odd that the boys laughed at them, and not offering the subjects most needed – mathematics and German. He felt that the Institute had let Baines down, and actually sent one of the priests back to Italy without Baines's permission. Rosmini also sent his deputy, Loewenbruck, to assess the situation at Prior Park; he reported that the venture ought to be strongly supported, because it was so important for the whole of the west of England. Yet he had his reservations: 'The Bishop [he said] is very distinguished in many ways, but he is a swash-buckler, a despot. He often acts on angry impulse, and is capable of suddenly conceiving and executing extreme measures that really require time to mature.'[26]

By 1837 Baines was very concerned that numbers had started to drop, and the school, which provided the main income for the whole concern, was reduced to fifty. There were various reasons for this, including the problems of staffing (Dr Dunham's activities alone were said to have led to the withdrawal of fourteen boys), the rumours that Prior Park was facing imminent bankruptcy, the strict regime introduced by Gentili, which some parents, especially aristocratic ones, objected to, and there was also the increased competition of the new Oscott, which had such teachers as Wiseman, Pugin and Logan. The fundamental reason, however, was that there were not enough Catholic students to fill all the colleges, so only the best of them prospered.

Baines tried desperate measures, first by trying to persuade the Pope to designate Prior Park a Catholic University, although there was no longer any possibility of it reaching that standard, and then trying to persuade Bishop Walsh of the Midland District and Bishop Griffiths of London that Oscott and St Edmund's colleges should become purely lay schools, and that all church students should be sent to Prior Park. When all this failed, he decided to take the only action within his power, first reducing Gentili's authority in the college, and then finally getting rid of him altogether. Baines could be ruthless when he had set his mind on a course of action, and seemed to care little about the feelings of those who had served him well. Gentili first reported to Rosmini in April 1836 that: 'It is now forbidden to give the boys books of devotion, scapulars, rosaries or anything of that kind without permission of the Vicar General [Dr Brindle]'.[27]

This was a direct slight to Gentili, and there were other stories, such as one about a boy who brought a scapular to be blessed by Gentili and had it taken from his neck and trampled on. As soon as he was seen to have lost the Bishop's favour, Gentili was insulted and mocked continually. Both he and Moses Furlong, the former novice from Ampleforth who had joined the Institute of Charity, were not allowed to preach until their material had been censored. Then at the end of the summer term of 1838, Baines sent Gentili away, first on a temporary mission to the nuns at a convent at Stapehill and then to a convent at Spettisbury near Blandford to act as a confessor to the nuns there. It is typical of Baines, though, that he required Gentili to come back to Prior Park for a short period to prepare students for the Christmas exhibition. Publicity for the college was all-important, no matter what the feelings of those involved.

Rosmini was forced to appoint one of the newcomers, Dr Pagani, as superior of the Institute of Charity at Prior Park, and finally withdrew Gentili back to Italy for a time. He suffered a great deal of pain and humiliation over the episode but, in a new and spectacular career as a missioner in the Midland district, he was able to put all this behind him.

The end of a dream

Later Baines appeared to regret his decision to get rid of Gentili, and he gained nothing from it in the end. At first numbers rose again, only to fall once more in the 1840s, as continued rumours of bankruptcy spread, and Baines became involved in a long dispute with the papacy over his 1840 pastoral, which further reduced confidence in his judgement. In the last three years of his life, it became obvious to many that the college could not survive much longer without complete reorganization.

Baines's ideas for Prior Park were magnificent, imaginative and ahead of his time, but the flaws in his character, and misfortune, prevented their successful execution. Prior Park is the story of what might have been, if only Baines had proceeded more slowly, so as not to burden himself with mounting debt; if only he had not antagonized Dr Wiseman, who could have enhanced the academic stature of the college, and other members of staff who had served him so well; if only there had not been the calamitous fire of 1836, or Baines had taken out adequate insurance. Today only a few elements of his great plan survive. The Catholic school, now run by a private trust, and of which its head and members of staff are now lay teachers, stands on the same spot. Its grounds, which run down from the school towards Bath, now belong to the National Trust, which is gradually restoring them to their former magnificence. Baines's vision of a great church proclaiming the glory of Catholicism can be glimpsed in the fine building designed by J. J. Scoles, which is now used as the school chapel. This building, started in 1844 in memory of Baines, was endowed by one of his great admirers, Miss Bettington. Unfortunately funds soon ran out, leaving the unfinished building roofless and derelict for many years – until its completion in 1882, thanks mainly to the generosity of Bishop Clifford. The magnificence of the church symbolizes all Baines's aspirations for Prior Park.

Notes

1 Ampleforth Journal 1910, Wiseman to Bonomi, 11 May 1858 (quoting from CDA letters, but reference cannot be found).

2 Ibid. Bonomi to Wiseman, 15 May 1859.
3 Bernard Ward, *Sequel to Catholic Emancipation*, pp. 59–64.
4 CDA, Miscellaneous Letters recently received from the City of Bristol Record Office, Wiseman to Baines, 2 November 1835. See also Richard Schiefen, *Nicholas Wiseman and the Transformation of English Catholicism*, pp. 55–61.
5 Ibid. Baines to Wiseman, 11 November 1835.
6 Ibid.
7 Ibid. Wiseman to Baines, 21 November 1835.
8 Ibid. Baines to Shrewsbury, undated letter.
9 Ibid. Denis Gwynn, *Luigi Gentili and his Mission* (Dublin, 1951), p. 90.
10 William Ullathorne, *An Autobiography* (London, 1868), p. 226ff.
11 Denis Gwynn, *Luigi Gentili and his Mission*, p. 90.
12 J. Roche, *Prior Park*, p. 158.
13 Ibid.
14 Margaret Smith, *From Victorian Wessex: The Diaries of Emily Smith, 1836, 1841, 1851* (Norwich, 2003).
15 *Bath and Cheltenham Gazette*, 3 June 1836.
16 *Monthly Intelligence*, 1 July 1836.
17 CDA, Prior Park File 7.
18 Ibid. Baines Box Files, 5–7, Baines to Briggs, 9 June 1836.
19 Ibid. Prior Park Files, 21–4, 11 October 1836.
20 James Shepherd, *Reminiscences of Prior Park* (Bath, 1886), p. 34.
21 CDA, Prior Park Files, 21–4, November 1836.
22 Ibid.
23 Claude Leetham, *Luigi Gentili, A Sower for the Second Spring* (London, 1965), p. 91.
24 CDA, Baines Box Files, 12–17, quoting from *The Radcliffian*, vol. 2, no. XXI, Mid-Summer, 1892, Lady Arundell to her son, Ambrose.
25 Bernard Ward, *The Sequel to Catholic Emancipation* vol. 2, Phillipps de Lisle to Gentili, 22 June 1837.
26 Claude Leetham, *Luigi Gentili, A Sower for the Second Spring*, pp. 88–9.
27 Ibid.

12

Baines among his Peers

A time of change

Baines became Vicar Apostolic at a time of great change in the Catholic Church in England, reflecting changes in society as a whole. The shift of population from the country to the towns was destroying the influence and patronage of the great Catholic landowners, whose private chaplains ministered to the scattered flock in their neighbourhood. New missions were developing in the urban areas, where there was a struggle for control between the priests and the laity, many of whom were members of the rising class of tradesmen, merchants and industrial entrepreneurs. By 1829, when Baines succeeded, the priests had gained the ascendancy and were exerting more and more control over their congregations, tending in some instances to question the authority of the Bishop.[1] At the same time the Catholic population was growing dramatically so that, even in the Western District where the number of Catholics had always been small, there was a substantial increase; this was particularly so in the city of Bristol, where the Catholic population increased from about 1,000 at the beginning of the nineteenth century to over 6,000 in 1830. The main cause of the rise was the influx of the Catholic settlers from Ireland, which was steadily increasing in the 1820s and the 1830s and reached a flood in the 1840s, but was also due to the growing number of converts.

All these developments meant that the old relaxed administration of the four Vicars Apostolic in England and Wales was incapable of meeting the challenges of a new age, which demanded greater professionalism and control.[2] Baines was at the forefront in seeing the need for change and pressing for it with his usual vigour. He persuaded the other three Vicars Apostolic to meet more regularly than the annual Low Sunday meetings, which had developed since 1825. Although any decisions made at such meetings had to be referred to Rome before they could be implemented, Baines believed that regular meetings and consultation were essential if the bishops were to present a united front. Baines appears to have acted as a secretary to the group, writing to Bishop Briggs in December 1836 that he was proposing that the next meeting should be held in London on 24 January 1837, and 'Dr Griffiths kindly offers us hospitality during our stay'.[3] Each bishop was asked to suggest topics for the agenda, and among Baines's proposals was 'the expediency of adopting some more effective means of acting in union and concert in the government of our districts'.[4]

Baines was a lover of Rome, Roman architecture, Roman music, and the Roman way of life, and recalled nostalgically his golden years in Rome, when he had been a favoured son of Leo XII. Yet as Vicar Apostolic, he was prepared to question Roman decrees and cast doubts on whether the Prefect of Propaganda and some of the cardinals really understood the situation of the Catholic Church in England. He was not afraid of increasing the unpopularity which he had already incurred in Rome by his long disputes with Downside and with the nuns of Cannington, and in 1838 he launched into an attack on new Roman decrees concerning indulgences and the regulars.

The decree on indulgences

The granting of indulgences for sins for all manner of pious observances had long since been a feature of the Catholic Church on the Continent, but had been little practised in England since the Reformation. Baines, who had grown up in the old English tradition, regarded such practices with disfavour in themselves and likely to arouse even more criticism from the Protestant majority. He was therefore dismayed when in 1838 Rome decreed that a larger number of indulgences should be granted for religious practices of all sorts, 'many of which are not suited to our climate and the crisis in which we are now placed'.[5]

He and the other Vicars Apostolic were also concerned that the decree gave the regulars special rights to attach indulgences to prayers and devotions, rights that the secular clergy would not have. As a result they feared that the people would be more attracted to the chapels of the regulars.

Baines poured scorn on the whole practice. There was, he believed, 'no end to the pranks which we shall have played in our churches by regulars and seculars of more piety or more wrongheadedness than good sense'.[6] He was particularly against indulgences granted for veneration of the Sacred Heart, a practice which he opposed anyway. In contrast to Bishop Milner who supported the devotion, he was fearful of what ruses some of his clergy might adopt in order to satisfy their flocks: 'Only think what hearts will be hung up in our public chapels for the veneration of the faithful and the ridicule of protestants, copied as one to my knowledge was, most recently, from a cow's heart borrowed from a butcher'.[7]

Baines urged his fellow bishops to send a joint petition to the Pope,

> expressing great alarm to the alteration made to the decree in the constitution of Benedict XIV, stating that there never was a time in which it was more necessary than it is at present to take care that every public and private exercise of religion should not only be conformable to faith and good morals, but suited to the practice and circumstances of the country and that we foresee many serious inconveniences to our clergy, division among the faithful and scandal . . . we humbly pray His Holiness graciously to suspend the execution of the said decree till the Bishops shall have had time to take it into consideration . . .[8]

The decree on regular missions

At first Baines did not realize the full implications of the second decree concerning the regulars, which authorized them to establish missions in any part of the country they wished. He blamed this on Bishop Griffiths of the London District, who had written to him about the substance of the decrees, and whose writing Baines found very difficult to read. He had only managed to decipher part of it and gathered from this that the regulars were only authorized to restore and expand their present missions. Even this he regarded 'as an encroachment upon our authority. We should send a joint petition to the Pope that no alteration should be made in our regulations without the previous knowledge of the Bishops, and if this is not granted, to tender our resignation as a body.'[9]

Realizing that this could be interpreted as a direct attack on the Pope, he retracted a little: 'The Pope means well, but he is easily prevailed upon to do indiscreet things by those about him.'[10]

When he understood the full import of this decree, Baines was even more angry: 'The decree is in fact equivalent to granting the regulars permission to establish new parishes wherever they please in spite of the Bishop, whose judgement is thus subject to theirs. It is taken for granted that the regulars are right, and we shall have no redress but in proving them wrong at Propaganda'.[11]

He tried to rally the other bishops to the cause. At first all three of them supported him in a letter to the Pope protesting against the decrees, being particularly suspicious of the growing influence of the regulars in their Districts. As time went on, however, and Baines became more belligerent, advocating a formal petition and an agent at Rome to put their case, Bishop Walsh of the Midland District and Bishop Griffiths of London became more uneasy. They were upset by reports of Baines's growing unpopularity at Rome and criticism at home from the senior Catholic aristocracy, such as Lord Shrewsbury and Lord Clifford. The latter wrote to Baines in December 1838, telling him that: 'If you feel that you cannot meet the wishes of His Holiness, you should immediately in a respectful but decided manner, offer your resignation'.[12]

Baines was not subdued by this or a similar letter from Lord Shrewsbury. He told his friend, Bishop Briggs: 'I have written very strong letters to Lords Shrewsbury and Clifford, who appear to think we are all rather wrong-headed and unmanageable. Be assured that the Jesuits are at the bottom of all this and will leave us no peace until they get their own ends.'[13]

The latter remark reveals that Baines was beginning to consider the Jesuits, rather than the Benedictines, his main enemy at Rome, and had changed his opinions from the time in 1829, when he supported Bishop Collingridge in obtaining legal authorization for the Jesuits' recognition in Britain. In the meanwhile, in January 1839, Bishop Griffiths, the senior Vicar Apostolic, had received a letter from Rome urging the execution of the papal decrees, to which Baines advocated an immediate and robust response: 'The time has come to buckle on our armour, for depend upon it either the Pope will confirm the decrees, in which case I think we should tender our resignations, or he will assent to our demands, but will give us a tremendous lecture . . .'[14]

By this time Bishop Griffiths, who did not want a fight, was regretting that he had ever involved himself with Baines, and Bishop Walsh was becoming more influenced by Lord Shrewsbury, Pugin and Ambrose Phillipps de Lisle, who all opposed Baines's belligerent attitude. Lord Clifford also supported Bishop Walsh's new views, writing to Baines in January 1839:

> Bishop Walsh has taken a right view of the best, not to say the only course, which the V.A.s can take in honour or as gentlemen, if they intend to retain their offices. I should at once advise Your Lordship to retire from so inglorious a conflict, where victory on either side would not benefit the R.C. Religion and the prosperity in England.[15]

Baines had no intention of retiring from the conflict and would have equally ignored other critics writing in the same tone. Dr Brown of Downside wrote to the Catholic historian, George Oliver, saying that on one of his regular visits to Wardour Castle, Baines had made no secret of the very strong remonstrance he and the Rt Rev B.B. (Bishop Briggs) had made: 'He talked very big, threatening to throw up the mitre rather than to submit to such proposals.'[16]

Dr Brown criticized Baines particularly for giving such a bad example of obedience to the laity: 'What would the Duke of Wellington have said and done if he was treated as cavalierly by a subaltern as the Vicar of Christ is here by his delegate. This is too bad.'[17]

Baines was more concerned at the growing apprehension of Dr Briggs, who he feared would desert the cause and refuse to sign the petition against the decree. He wrote to him on 2 February 1839:

> As Your Lordship has not yet written retracting your signature respecting the decrees, I most earnestly implore you to allow a little delay before you take a step, which will cause fatal and lasting schism in the English Catholic Church ... Alas I was in hopes that the frightful scandals, which have long desecrated the English mission, arising from one Bishop opposing his private opinion to that of his colleagues, had been put an end to by our meetings and by entering into concert on all points, where uniformity is so essential.[18]

Baines must have carried his point with Bishop Briggs, as in the following month they were both discussing further appeals to Rome. Baines wrote on 26 March:

> Between us I think we shall be able at Prior Park to get a good quiet statement written in the Italian language and feeling by an Italian professor of Theology, who is an elegant writer and most holy and admirable man. This may be something, but not much, for there is an evil principle actively at work, whispering in the ears of His Holiness ...[19]

In the following month, April 1839, Bishop Briggs was making the long journey to Prior Park to discuss the situation of the regulars. Baines asked him to bring with him an exact account of regular missions in his district with the dates and manner of their foundation. He suggested that they should both have a plan ready of all the places in their districts where they would be willing for the regulars to build chapels at their own expense, stressing that they could permit no unauthorized foundations. On the lighter side, Baines joked that Bishop Briggs would not receive the lavish treatment at Prior Park, which he usually provided in his own district: 'Don't be afraid that you will be too well fed at Prior Park ... you will have a joint, or two, and a pudding or two. You will have a marsala during dinner and port and brandy after, but you will not be expected to sit very long after it.'[20]

A minor triumph

Baines's ideas of economy may seem curious, but Bishop Briggs was well satisfied with his visit to Prior Park, and their planning and appeals to Rome seem to have been effective. In June, Baines rejoiced that the decrees had been modified:

> It appears to me that the sting is entirely removed from the Decree about chapel building, which was the one upon which our strong remonstrances to the Pope were founded and to which was attached the intimation of our resignations. The matter now stands exactly as it did before with the difference that now we are I believe expected to write to Propaganda every time we refuse the regulars permission.[21]

Baines regarded this settlement as a triumph, although it still left the relationship between bishops and regulars in the same grey area where they had been for many years, not to be resolved until the Constitution *Romanos Pontifices* of 1881. He was also reasonably pleased with the mitigation of the decree on indulgences, which now gave the bishops a greater say in deciding what indulgences should be offered to their congregations. He felt, though, that the English bishops should follow up this success by a further petition to Rome that: 'The regulars shall not publish any peculiar indulgences without the express approval of the Bishops, a regulation which the peculiar condition of the clergy justifies ...'[22]

Baines and Bishop Walsh

During the next two years, Baines's relations with Bishop Walsh of the Midland District became more hostile, thus straining the already fragile alliance between the Vicars Apostolic. He had a dispute with him about Dr Logan who had been a lecturer at Prior Park, and whom Baines claimed Bishop Walsh had enticed away to take up a post at Oscott College. Baines also disapproved of Walsh's support for the movement to return to the vestments, ritual and architecture of the medieval Church, and the campaign for the conversion of England.[23]

Finally he had a dispute with Walsh over money, claiming that the Bishop had deprived him of funds which could have been used at Prior Park. This was a disagreement which also included Bishop Briggs, as Baines claimed that Walsh had promised to give as much as £5000 from a legacy for use at Ushaw as well as Prior Park. Baines's expectations may not have been based on fact, as he was inclined to exaggerate claims to funds to finance his great project at Prior Park. Bishop Walsh was exceedingly irritated by the rumours he heard and wrote to Baines in June 1839:

> I regret to inform Your Lordship that I have lately heard from more than one individual, that in consequence of your declaration on the subject, it is said in Bath and was a few days ago reported in London, that I had pledged myself to give Your Lordship £5000 and that relying on this pledge, you had incurred expenses, which you would not otherwise have ventured upon.[24]

Bishop Walsh denied that he had ever made any definite promise to Baines, and certainly would not have given him more than £1000. Baines hastily denied the report and said that he would be very grateful for the £1000 towards the enormous expense of Prior Park. Yet at the same time he was writing to Bishop Briggs, asking him to try to recall the exact import of Dr Walsh's promise to them both at a meeting at York, and stating categorically that Walsh had promised the two of them £5000 each for Ushaw and Prior Park colleges. There were no conditions laid down, he claimed, except that Bishop Walsh should obtain a large property from a promised legacy.[25]

Baines also wrote to Dr Griffiths, Vicar Apostolic of the London District, seeming to rebuke him for not criticizing Walsh's conduct in paying £1000 only to Ushaw and Prior Park colleges, instead of the £5000 originally promised. Such insinuations did not make for harmony between the bishops and prevented them from forming a united front over the difficult problems to come: the expansion of the Vicariate and the campaign for the conversion of England.

The expansion of the Vicariate

The expansion of the Vicariate was long overdue and the bishops had recognized the necessity for many years. They linked such expansion, though, with the long-held desire for the establishment of a Tridentine form of episcopal government which had at least some independence from the Vatican. When, therefore, Cardinal Franzoni, Prefect of the Congregation of Propaganda, proposed an increase in the number of Vicars Apostolic to eight, the four bishops met in June 1838 to consider their reply. They drew up a series of requests to become known as *Statuta Proposita*, which they submitted to Rome.

While they agreed to the proposed increase, the bishops advised delay so that other vital matters might be considered. They asked particularly that, while they retained the title of Vicars Apostolic, they were allowed to exercise the faculties of diocesan bishops and to appoint a chapter of canons to administer and assist the administration.[26] This was restoration of the hierarchy by the back door and was not acceptable to Rome. Likewise, the proposal to give the Vicars Apostolic a greater say in the new appointments was frowned upon, although Baines and Briggs particularly were determined to make their opinions felt.

Baines believed that Propaganda had little knowledge of the requirements of the mission in England and Wales, and the kind of men who would be most suited to fill the individual sees. He also wanted the bishops to voice their views on how the present districts should be divided: 'In making a division of Districts there are other considerations beside the number of catholics, which must be attended to, viz:- the number of missions, the extent of the country over which the Bishop has to travel, the mode of conveyance whether by land and sea, the state of the roads, the rank or condition of the people ...'[27]

Opposition to regulars as bishops

Above all, both Baines and Briggs were opposed to the appointment of any regulars as bishops. This was an irony in view of the fact that, had the rule operated in 1823, Baines himself would never have been appointed a bishop. His views had completely changed in the years since, and he had made himself the champion of secular priests. The secular priests themselves were naturally on the side of the bishops in this matter and were becoming vocal in opposition to the appointment of regular bishops in the Western and London Districts, objecting also to the fact that they had not been consulted. In the Northern District, Bishop Briggs was sounding out opinions among priests in the missions and wrote to Baines in February 1840:

A memorial has gone off to His Holiness from the Manchester

> clergy and its neighbourhood against the appointment of a Benedictine Vicar Apostolic. Another will follow to Cardinal Franzoni on Monday next from Yorkshire priests and another on Tuesday from the secular priests of Durham and Northumberland ... I wish Rome to see that the secular clergy feel strongly in these matters and are quite aware what is going on.[28]

Thus the bishops were not averse to encouraging the militancy of the secular clergy when it suited their purpose, although Baines on other occasions lamented the high-handed behaviour of some of the priests in his missions.

Nothing, however, was likely to prevent the appointment of Dr Thomas Brown, a Benedictine, to the new vicariate of Wales. Baines gradually became reconciled to the idea. In the first place he was not averse to losing Wales from the Western District, for the long distances, difficult terrain and poor roads had made administration and pastoral work very difficult. He had changed his opinion, too, of Dr Brown, whom he had once regarded as an enemy during the long dispute with Downside, but now considered as a priest of outstanding qualities. He was determined, though, to continue his opposition to the appointment of any other regular bishops, and still more so to the return of Dr Wiseman to be the coadjutor to Bishop Walsh in the Midland District.

Opposition to Wiseman

Baines had long opposed the idea that Dr Wiseman should return to England. As early as 1838 he was writing about the possibility as likely to injure his own interests and those of Prior Park. Two years later, in an unusually pessimistic letter, he implored Dr Briggs:

> Pray turn your attention to the district of the west, and see whether something cannot be done for it. If not, it is hopeless. I begin to be quite worn out and do not think I can stand the wear and tear much longer. I do not mind labour nor suffering, but to toil and endure for no other purpose than to lose all powers of attention to more important concerns is wrong and I must put a stop to it. If Dr Wiseman is to become a coadjutor in a neighbour's district and a rival against this establishment organized with overflowing funds, I have no chance and I will abandon the contest ...[29]

Baines did not remain in this state of mind for long, and was heartened by the fact that Bishops Briggs and Griffiths both opposed the return of

Dr Wiseman to England as a bishop. Bishop Griffiths mistrusted him and would not have him as coadjutor in the London District; Bishop Briggs and many of the secular clergy opposed Wiseman's appointment because he had little experience of England, and no experience at all of work in the missions. Baines also agreed that Wiseman was completely inexperienced on the mission and unknown to the English clergy, but added:

> He is also a person who had done many imprudent things and who might do more if invested with additional powers, in which case his high respect as a scholar would put him at the head of a party and it would be impossible to control him. Of all places I think the proposed Midland District the most objectionable for him if he is to be a Bishop.[30]

At that time the Midland District was probably more important than London for the life of the Catholic Church. It was supported by the wealth and patronage of Lord Shrewsbury, who was encouraging the genius of Pugin, and financed the building of churches. The Midland District was also the home of Oscott College, one of the four Catholic seminaries in the country, and of the University of Oxford, then at the height of the movement which was to bring converts into the Catholic Church. To the Vatican, therefore, the Midland District seemed to be an ideal setting in which the scholarship and exuberant personality of Dr Wiseman could flourish. Baines had other ideas of Wiseman's suitability, urging Dr Briggs to write to Rome to object to such an appointment:

> [You should] strongly object to his appointment over any portion of the Midlands because such appointment would give a fearful preponderance of the fanatical party and to the college of Oscott, both of which preponderate too much already. I have suggested that his appointment should be deferred till his character is both known and till his principles have acquired greater consistency ... I am in fear that the great influence he exercises by his writing in the public mind, might render him difficult to control. [And again] I have strongly recommended *if he must be Bishop* that he should not be appointed in the Midlands ... He has come back to England as an unmitred appendage of Oscott, soured with disappointment and, conjecturing that I have opposed him, he may injure P. Park more than he has done.[31]

Baines's good opinion of Wiseman once lost, as it had been in 1835, was never likely to be regained, but as neither he, Bishop Briggs or Bishop Griffiths wanted Wiseman in their District, and Bishop Walsh appeared to do so, it was very unlikely that Baines was going to be able to prevent Wiseman's appointment to the Midlands.

Consultation vital

Baines also corresponded with Bishops Briggs and Griffiths about the appointment of the four new Vicars Apostolic: the bishops were mainly concerned that they should be consulted before any final choice was made. Bishop Briggs thought that the bishops should reach a unanimous decision in considering the possible candidate for the new post but, at the same time, it was not advisable to give the appearance of working in concert, or hackles would rise at Rome. The great fear of all the bishops was that the whole matter would be arranged before their opinion was asked.

Baines and Briggs conducted a lengthy correspondence into the merits of likely candidates. Dr Briggs dismissed Dr Baggs, who had spent most of his ministry in Rome, for the same reasons he had rejected Wiseman: 'There is strong feeling amongst the clergy of my district in England against having anyone placed over them as V.A., who is not immediately committed to their District.'[32]

Fr Spencer, who started the campaign for the conversion of England, was dismissed as unfit for promotion: 'an enthusiast, of no prudence'. Mr Weedall, the Vice-president of Oscott, was also unfit in the eyes of Briggs and Baines: 'in danger of losing his head if a mitre with its solicitudes is placed upon it'. Two candidates were rejected because they had strong associations with the Jesuits, and two others because they were physically unfit for the work. Bishop Briggs referred to George Brown, the late President of Ushaw, as a man of uncertain temper, whose 'constitution has been shattered', and a Mr Newsham of being quite unfit, 'by the firing of a gun through part of his right hand [so that he always has to] wear a glove to cover his shattered hand'.[33] And poor Mr Thompson was dismissed as being 'too old, and by the loss of his teeth, his articulation is very indistinct'.[34] Baines considered proposing the candidature of Dr Lingard, the historian, and Fr Husenbeth, a secular priest and writer, well known at the time for this life of Bishop Milner, but was not very hopeful that Rome would be willing to accept such appointments.

He also discussed the possibility of Dr Brindle for Wales; he was hesitant about proposing the latter as he did not want to lose Brindle from Prior Park, and in any case believed that Dr Thomas Brown was almost certain to be appointed.[35] The only impediment to this was Dr Brown himself, who was a very reluctant candidate. Fr Collier, a Benedictine, was very concerned about this, writing to Dr Brown just before the appointment was made, 'It is of great consequence that we should have one of our brethren among the Bishops who will defend our interests and support our rights among his episcopal colleagues'.[36] And again with more urgency: 'His Holiness is not willing to listen to any excuses for you refusing the Welsh Vicariate'.[37]

In the end Dr Thomas Brown was prevailed upon to accept the appointment, but at least the bishops and the secular clergy were successful in preventing the appointment of any other Vicar Apostolic from the regular orders. Baines and his allies were not so successful in securing the rejection of other candidates, particularly in the Midland District, where Dr Wiseman was appointed as coadjutor to Bishop Walsh and president of Oscott College. Baines relieved his feelings by sketching the new president of Oscott striding along in the wake of his acolyte, both adorned in the medieval vestments with huge lawn sleeves, which Baines himself so ridiculed.

The division of the Districts

Dr Briggs was also not at all happy about the division of his former Northern District. His jurisdiction was confined to Yorkshire, while candidates he objected to were appointed to other parts, George Brown to the new Lancashire District and Dr Weedall to a new district in the far north consisting of Cumberland, Westmorland, Northumberland and Durham. The latter was never enthroned, as he petitioned Rome to be relieved of his appointment, and a Dr Mostyn, whom neither Briggs nor Baines knew anything about, was appointed in his place. Rome may have wished that it had taken more notice of the objections to George Brown, as he proved to be a martinet in office, and caused more clergy appeals to Propaganda than even Baines had done. Pope Gregory XVI declared that he had more trouble in the administration of church affairs in his province called England, than he had with church affairs in the whole universal church.[38]

Dr Griffiths was the only one of the three bishops who did not have strong cause to complain, as the London District was little changed, only losing Bedfordshire and Buckinghamshire to the new Eastern District, where Dr Wearing, formerly of Oscott College, had been made Vicar Apostolic, another appointment which was said to be the result of the need for a clear-out at Oscott to make room for

Dr Wiseman. Dr Griffiths, however, agreed with Baines that the whole operation was premature and should have been postponed until a restoration of the hierarchy: 'I do not believe that we shall be Bishops in ordinary in ten years'.[39]

Financial implications

There were financial repercussions to the changes, as Propaganda had apparently made no provision for salaries to be paid to the new bishops. Dr Briggs was worried because his neighbouring bishops were trying to claim revenues provided for him. Baines wrote to him urging him to take a stand:

> The new V.As cannot claim any portion of the revenue provided for the former V.A. Of all the counties comprised under the new Vicariate you asked for no relief from your charge. If others thought proper to take a portion from you, it was their own affair ... if you are called upon to give up part of your income to them, say 'No. Give me back my work, but don't diminish my salary, which I cannot spare'. Let the Propaganda allot something for the propaganda ... Don't budge on this head, my Lord. I won't, I assure you.[40]

Baines himself was being asked to contribute something to the salary of the new Welsh Vicariate, but refused. He was working upon Dr Griffiths, who had greater resources in the London District, and asking him to contribute something to Dr Brown in Wales. What the outcome of this was is not known, but the Welsh Vicariate remained even poorer than the restructured Western District, where besides Wales Baines had lost the border counties of Worcestershire, Hereford and Shropshire.

So Bishop Baines, in spite of his declaration that he was giving up the unequal struggle, was battling still. In fact, in 1840 he was embarking on his greatest conflict, which he was to describe as 'the war of the pastoral', a conflict which was to lead to great repercussions throughout the Catholic Church in England and Rome.

Notes

1 Edward Norman, *The English Catholic Church in the Nineteenth Century* (Oxford, 1985); and Bossy, John, *The English Catholic Community 1570–1850* (London, 1975).

2 Ibid.

3 CDA, Baines Box Files, 5–7, Baines to Briggs, 16 December 1836.
4 Ibid. 1 November 1836.
5 Ibid.
6 Ibid.
7 Ibid.
8 Ibid.
9 Ibid. 12 November 1836.
10 Ibid.
11 Ibid.
12 Ibid. Clifford to Baines, December 1838.
13 Ibid. Baines to Briggs, 15 January 1839.
14 Ibid.
15 Ibid. Clifford to Baines, 20 January 1839.
16 Downside Archives, K162, Brown to Oliver, 1 January 1839.
17 Ibid.
18 CDA, Baines Box Files, 5–7, Baines to Briggs, 2 February 1839.
19 Ibid. 26 March 1839.
20 Ibid. 1 April 1839.
21 Ibid. 13 June 1839.
22 Ibid.
23 See below, chapter 13.
24 CDA, Baines Box Files, 5–7, Walsh to Baines, 5 June 1839.
25 Ibid. Baines to Briggs, undated letter.
26 Ibid. Roman File, 17881855, unsigned comments on new division of the Western District, probably written by Baines.
27 Ibid. Bishops' Letters, Baines to Briggs, 8 February 1840.
28 Ibid. Briggs to Baines, 2 February 1840.
29 Ibid. Baines to Briggs, 8 February 1840.
30 Ibid. 12 February 1840.
31 Ibid.
32 Ibid. Briggs to Baines, February 1840.
33 Ibid.
34 Ibid.
35 Ibid. Baines to Briggs, 20 January 1840.
36 Downside Archives, K361, Collier to Brown, 3 April 1840.
37 Ibid. K373.
38 CDA, Bishops' Letters, Griffiths to Baines, 5 February 1840.
39 Ibid.
40 Ibid. Baines Box Files, 5–7, Baines to Briggs, April 1840.

13

The War of the Pastoral

Bishops' pastorals seldom cause a stir, or merit even a line in the local newspapers. Bishop Baines's Lent pastoral of 1840 was one of the exceptions. All the people who listened to it would have recognized their Bishop's usual forthright language and flamboyant style, but a few of the more educated would also have wondered about his choice of subject matter. He seemed to be questioning the policy of a fellow Vicar Apostolic, and even a campaign which had been blessed by the Pope himself.

The converts

Baines's mistrust of religious activities in the Midland District went back to the mid eighteen-thirties. Then Ambrose Phillipps de Lisle, the convert son of a member of the gentry who lived in Grace Dieu Manor in Leicestershire, gained the support of Bishop Walsh and the patronage of Lord Shrewsbury for holding missions and retreats in his neighbourhood, and introducing innovations such as devotion of the Sacred Heart, the doctrine of the Immaculate Conception and the use of medals and scapulars in worship. At his chapel at Grace Dieu, Phillipps insisted on elaborate ceremonials, not seen in Catholic churches since the Reformation.[1] All this was anathema to Baines, who had been brought up in the traditions of *The Garden of the Soul* in which the old Catholics practised a restrained form of worship and tried to avoid antagonizing their Protestant neighbours by adopting the more extreme continental forms.

In 1840 Phillipps appointed Fr Gentili as his chaplain and for missionary work in the area. Gentili was so successful that he converted several hundred people to Catholicism, arousing the wrath of local vicars and dissenting ministers.[2] These conversions were to stand the test of time, as many of the descendants of these villagers are still Catholics. Gentili's appointment was another irritation to

Baines, although as he himself had dismissed him from Prior Park, he was not justified in asserting that the priest had defected to the Midland District.[3]

Baines was still more suspicious of the work of another Catholic convert, Augustus Welby Pugin, one of the greatest architects of the Victorian era, and the champion of the Gothic Revival. Pugin believed that Catholics and Gothic architecture were inseparable and that the Reformation had started a decline in architecture, when the classical style came to be more and more used in church and domestic architecture, a style which Pugin considered to be pagan and corrupt. This judgement was anathema to Baines, who loved the classical styles of Rome, and did everything he could to discourage the building of more Gothic churches in his District.

Pugin gained the patronage of the wealthy Earl of Shrewsbury, who was an enthusiastic believer in the architect's principles, and backed him financially. He helped him to create a number of church buildings, one of the most important of which was St Giles, Cheadle, in Staffordshire, which the Earl considered to be 'a text book for all good people'.[4] It is extremely ornate, with a profusion of colour, reds, blues and gold, an ornate reredos and a rood screen, which Pugin was to insist upon in all his churches. To Pugin, the sanctuary had to be the most highly ornamental part of the church, as it was the most important, and the presence of the rood screen increased the air of mystery for the congregation, who were thus distanced from the sacrifice of the mass.

Pugin was not only an architect but a designer, who insisted on being responsible for all the decoration and furnishings within the church, and the design of the vestments worn by the priests. He waged a campaign for the restoration of Gothic vestments in England, the return of the full and flowing lines of those used before the Reformation. On the Continent, as well as in England, vestments had changed so much as to be almost unrecognizable from their medieval counterparts, and Raymond James, in his history of Roman liturgical vestments, described how: 'the chasuble . . . was no longer wide as charity, all embracing as love: the dalmatic, stiff now, short and inelegant . . . the stole and maniple, now fat and stumpy, where once they were slim and graceful . . .'[5]

Pugin wanted to change all this and he persuaded Lord Shrewsbury, and through him Bishop Walsh, of the rightness of his views to such an extent that Bishop Ullathorne described how:

> On my return to England I assisted at the opening of Oscott College, at which the Bishop and a hundred priests were present. It

> was on that occasion that the French style of vestments and surplices were changed for those of ampler form. Pugin with his eyes flashing through his tears, was in raptures, declaring it the first great day for England since the Reformation.[6]

All this added fuel to Baines's resentment, believing as he did that such ostentation would only increase the fears of Protestants. He strictly forbade the wearing of Pugin's vestments in the Western District, but it is noticeable that, if the Bishop's vestments were not Gothic, they were certainly magnificent, judging by the inventory for the sale of Prior Park in 1856. Lot 41, for example, described a set of all-white vestments for priest, deacon and sub-deacon, with gold edgings, the chasuble richly embroidered with gold; Lot 59, 'an antique purple chasuble embroidered with the Crucifixion and emblems of the Trinity': and Lot 66, 'a superb cope of richest cloth of gold woven with flowers and wheat ears, the cope with emblems of the Trinity'.[7]

Pugin and Ambrose Phillipps de Lisle wanted to return to the use of Gregorian chant, widely used in all English churches before the Reformation and hardly heard since. Baines again strongly opposed this development, feeling that it was abandoning the traditions of his early life, and in particular those of his years in Rome, where church music was becoming almost operatic with instrumental accompaniment. He encouraged this form of music in all the big churches in the Western District, where he could exert his influence and did not have to give way to the wishes of wealthy patrons.

The campaign for the conversion of England

Above all, Baines hated and feared the campaign for the conversion of England, which first developed in the Midland District. It was started as a campaign of prayer for the conversion of Christendom, and was brought to England by another Catholic convert, Fr Ignatius Spencer, the youngest son of the second Earl Spencer of Althorp, who had travelled widely on the Continent. The inspiration for the campaign came almost accidentally at a meeting between Spencer and the Archbishop of Paris. Spencer told the Archbishop that what was wanted most in England were good prayers, and asked that the French should unite in prayer for the conversion of England. He had not intended that any formal arrangement should be made, but the Archbishop proposed that all priests in his diocese should pray for the conversion of England every Thursday. This favourable beginning encouraged Spencer to approach other archbishops, bishops and leaders of religious houses throughout France asking them also to offer up prayers for the conversion of England on one day in each week; from there the campaign spread to be supported by Dr Wiseman in Rome and blessed by the Pope. Spencer returned to England to tell the Vicars Apostolic of his success on the Continent and ask for their support.[8]

Bishop Walsh was enthusiastic and sanctioned the crusade throughout the Midland District. Bishops Briggs and Griffiths mistrusted the idea of formal prayers and were decidedly lukewarm. There is evidence that the latter was personally reprimanded by the Pope for being sceptical about the campaign, and that Gregory XVI wrote a letter to the London clergy to denounce him.[9] Bishop Baines was anything but lukewarm, burning with anger at what he considered to be the crass folly of the whole idea. He determined to wage war against the crusade and all the other religious innovations coming out of the Midland District.

Throughout 1839, Baines was writing to Dr Briggs on the subject. As early as February, he noticed that Dr Griffiths, Vicar Apostolic of the London District, had also mentioned The Association of Persons for the Conversion of England in his pastoral, although not in the same vehement terms as Baines himself was to do in the following year. He told Dr Briggs: 'I dislike the thing greatly. It rests upon a false and fictitious supposition that England has to be converted in some supernatural and miraculous way, and this supposition is founded upon the alleged prophecy of some passionist monk in Italy, and on which Messrs Spencer and Phillipps lecture, but in which I believe not.'[10] In August 1839 Baines travelled into the Midland District himself, saying that 'There is a spirit of mischief afloat in this District, which can be dissipated only by actual contact'.[11] To develop this contact, he visited Lord Shrewsbury and stayed at Alton Towers, writing hopefully to Dr Briggs: 'Lord Shrewsbury is candid and open to conviction and is of vast importance, as he has now become a resident of Rome for half the year'.[12]

By September, Baines had moved on to stay with Lord and Lady Arundell at Wardour Castle, so Prior Park could not have seen much of him that summer. He was still concerned about the developments in the Midlands, and suggested to Dr Briggs that he should not attend the opening of a church where the new vestments were to be used, 'lest by your presence [you] countenance the use of such vestments'.[13]

He gave it as his opinion, repeated from Monsignor Rey, that: 'A Bishop cannot sanction the use of such vestments, even though he can prove they were formerly in use in the diocese'.[14]

He went on to send an appeal to Rome, illustrated by sketches of the vestments, protesting against their use in churches. The Prefect of Propaganda, Cardinal Franzoni, appears to have supported Baines at this period, writing to him in October 1839: 'I ought most highly to commend the prudent diffidence with which you have entertained the too dangerous innovations which the pretext of returning to the ancient practice or customs of the Church, might introduce into the sacred ornament and the Sanctuary Tabernacles and likewise into other things of great importance regarding the Divine Worship'.[15]

The Cardinal went on to inform Baines that he intended to write to Bishop Walsh to tell him that he ought to act like his colleagues and prevent the new innovations, whatever his personal inclinations. This support over the vestments gave Baines renewed confidence to continue his opposition on all fronts and embark on what he was to call 'the war of the pastoral'.

Social problems in England and Wales

On 24 February 1840, Baines began his famous pastoral by comparing some of the problems of the day in England and Wales with those of the early Christians in the Roman empire. The British empire had attained the height of its prosperity and was beginning to show some of the symptoms of national decay, such as enormous wealth and luxury for the few, and poverty and destitution for the many. This had brought some civil unrest, particularly in South Wales, still part of the Western District. Baines was referring to the Chartist risings in 1839 where there were outbreaks among the Welsh miners, which led to the imprisonment of some of their leaders. He rejoiced that none of his Catholic flock had taken part in these risings:

> Yet many of you are far more distressed than those taking part – you are exiles and unwelcome here, toiling to procure for yourselves and your families the necessaries of life. Act upon the example of the early Christians. Never attempt to correct heaven's laws by violating the divine ... never listen to those wicked or deluded men who would urge you to break the laws of your country, and offend God, for any purpose whatever.[16]

Hostility to Catholics

In describing the social problems of his day, Baines was drawing upon observations made in travelling to the poorer missions of his huge district, and reading the detailed letters of his priests. He also came to realize the fear and resentment felt by Anglican and Nonconformist ministers to the growth of Catholicism. If he did not understand this before, it was made very clear to him by a priest from South Wales, who advised him to travel incognito when visiting a particular mission.[17] In his pastoral Baines went on to tell his flock that the clergy of the Established Church and some of the Nonconformists were showing a similar hostility to Catholicism as that shown by the pagan priesthood to the growth of Christianity. He hastened to make clear, however, that he was not suggesting that the clergy of the Established Church were a pagan priesthood. He pointed out that:

> Our traducers refuse to listen to our statements, and continue to reassert the fables which it is thought in their interest to believe . . . if we are not to be delivered to the lions, as were the ancient Christians, it is because the liberality of our governors and the honesty of the people have outstripped the candour of their religious leaders.[18]

Generally Catholics had remained silent under all the abuses heaped upon them by their clergy, but Baines regretted that some of the new converts had begun to answer back and to call their attackers 'heretics' and 'separated brethren'. They cloaked their motives under an extraordinary zeal for the truth, but should really model their conduct on the advice of St Peter of 'not rendering evil for evil, not railing for railing, but contrariwise blessing'.

Baines, brought up in the traditions of the *Garden of the Soul* preached, although he did not always act accordingly, on the principle of 'turning the other cheek' and exhorted his flock:

> They call you idolators, blasphemers, enemies of God and man. What then? these unjust charges do not make you so. But they injure you and your holy cause, and they involve you in injustice, if they provoke you to retort upon the adverse party even the milder reproach of heretic. This term may be unjust and, if applied to all in error, is certainly so . . .[19]

Criticism of converts

Baines then went on to criticize the converts in more detail, claiming that most of the problems they experienced arose 'from the difficulty of eradicating from their breasts the vices which held sway over them before their conversion ...' Some of them were filled 'with the presumption of their ancient sect' and were 'strangers to the humility of the religion they have embraced, commencing their careers by dictating to their spiritual rulers the conduct they ought to pursue in the government of the Church'.[20]

He was particularly critical of the converts' adopting practices of piety and devotion not customary in the practice of the Catholic Church in England, and which were 'peculiarly obnoxious to Protestants', and which belong not to 'the code of defined dogmas'. He condemned the converts' pride in thinking they knew best for the Church they had adopted, for 'disdaining to walk among the crowd or the lowly and beaten path of Christian simplicity and humility, they soar into the clouds and attempt to pry into the hidden councils of God'.[21]

Baines condemned above all the efforts of the converts to obtain sanction for the weekly offering of public prayers for the conversion of England, which they represented as an event likely to occur. Baines stated that, even if he believed general conversion to be a possibility, he would hesitate to adopt such a public display, which would give unnecessary offence to Protestants; he believed, however, that the event was what he described as 'morally impossible'. It was as impossible as 'the return of the negro's skin to its antediluvian whiteness'.[22]

Baines believed that prayers for conversion should only be made in the general way, as they had always been used in the office of Good Friday, when Catholics prayed that God 'would purge the world of all errors, remove sickness, dispel famine, open all prisons, loosen every bond, grant a happy return to all travellers, and a safe port of safety to all at sea'.[23]

In his usual forthright language, he went on to condemn the campaign:

> So far, therefore, from approving this novel and extraordinary project, we disapprove it, and strictly forbid any of our clergy to offer up publicly in their churches and chapels the weekly prayers above mentioned. At the same time we pray, as has been customary, for all spiritual and temporal blessings in favour of our country, and for the conversion of such erring souls, as God in his mercy may be pleased so to favour, and of whom, we doubt not, there will be a great and increasing need.[24]

Nine years later John Lingard, the historian, praised Baines's enlightened attitude:

> In consequence of the Catholic Emancipation [he said] I trusted that the Catholic Church in England would throw open its portals to draw within it men of influence and education, which I thought would never take place if we insisted on practices calculated to enforce on the minds of protestants that much of our religion consisted in superstitious or fanatical practices. But of the then Bishops there was not one who could be persuaded to see the matter in this light excepting Dr Baines.[25]

Prayers for the Queen and the Prince Consort

As if he had not created great enough controversy already, Baines ended his pastoral by urging his flock to offer up prayers 'for our beloved Queen' and for Prince Albert, whom she had just married, and upon whom 'her happiness depends'. In this he was ahead of his times, in encouraging a closer union between the head of state and her Catholic subjects.

Rumours in Rome

Baines sent copies of his pastoral off to the other Vicars Apostolic and did not appear to be worried about the repercussions it might cause. He continued his campaign against those he referred to as 'fanatics' in the Catholic Church and regretted in a letter to Bishop Briggs on 11 March that the latter had said nothing 'of the petition about the vestments, nor about my manifesto against the fanatics'.[26] Perhaps Bishop Briggs was becoming wary of giving Baines too strong support, now that rumours were beginning to come from Rome that Baines's activities were being viewed in an unfavourable light. It was too early for a copy of the Lent Pastoral to have reached Rome by this time, but by late April 1840 it is certain that one had been sent there, possibly by Bishop Walsh, or taken there by one of the converts visiting the Holy See. Baines's nephew, James Baines, was in Rome at this time, and wrote to warn his uncle:

> I hear (your pastoral) is much spoken of in the city and not in any favourable terms by many who are not your Lordship's friends. Some have gone so far as to pronounce it heretical. It has been translated into Italian and perhaps not very justly in order to be presented to his Holiness, whose opinion of it I have not yet heard. He most probably has expressed it to Dr Wiseman, who I believe was sent for on the occasion. I am sorry also to say that the Earl and Countess [of Shrewsbury] are not pleased with it. The ladies

look upon it as an indirect attack upon his Lordship, who almost considers himself the patron of Mr Pugin . . .[27]

The summons to Rome

Baines could not have received this warning by the time the summons to Rome came at the beginning of May. He wrote to Bishop Briggs expressing his bewilderment at a letter from Cardinal Franzoni, Prefect of Propaganda, and Mgr Cadolini, Secretary of the Sacred College, informing him that: 'Affairs of the highest importance which are under consideration at Rome require indispensably your presence in this city, and the sooner you can present yourself thus, the greatest gratification you will afford to the Sacred College and his Holiness himself'.[28]

Baines thought that the summons might relate to the role he had played in opposing the Roman decrees in 1838 and 1839, and never considered that Propaganda might have moved so quickly to condemn his pastoral. He was forced to abandon all the problems of Prior Park, the care of his huge district and his campaign against the Midland 'fanatics' and start the long journey to Rome on 14 May 1840.

Before leaving, he urged Bishop Briggs to send him on as many examples as possible of 'the fanaticism of the day'. He had also been busy in getting his priests to send him details of the number of conversions throughout the Western District over the past few years, and proposed to make use of these figures in his defence. He told Bishop Briggs, 'I foresee that [the returns] will demonstrate clearly that to convert my District, as things are now going, will require at least 7,000 years! I really wish you would produce such returns. They are demonstration of the folly of fanatics.'[29] By 28 May Baines, accompanied by his secretary, Fr Bonomi, had reached Auxerre in southern France, from where he confided to Bishop Briggs: 'I am more puzzled than ever for what I am going to Rome . . . my nephew has told me that he heard Dr Wiseman speak of me as the person to send to compose the difficulties in the Ionian Islands . . . I cannot believe that such an idea will be entertained, but that of getting me out of Wiseman's way might.'[30]

On his journey through northern Italy, Baines called in to see an old friend of Roman days, Cardinal Odescalchi, once a power in the papal court in the days of Leo XII and Pius VIII, but then living as a virtual recluse in a hermit's cell. Odescalchi was delighted to see Baines, but grieved to hear of all his troubles and the fears of what awaited him in Rome. He said to him: 'Alas! Monsignor, you should never have left Rome. You made the great mistake of your life, when you declined that generous offer I was ordered to make you. Ah, now you remember! Eh?' Baines wept as he heard these words and turned to Bonomi: 'You understand, John, what he said?' And Bonomi answered, 'Perfectly, my Lord'. To which Baines rejoined, 'Then never forget it'. These words implied that Pius VIII actually renewed Leo XII's offer of the cardinalate to Baines, although Cardinal Wiseman later disputed this.[31]

Baines hurried on to Rome after this nostalgic meeting, arriving there on 8 June, and began to believe that his nephew's fears were justified. He wrote to Bishop Briggs: 'My suspicions regarding Dr Wiseman are a great deal more than realized now ... A plot has been formed to get rid of me ... Wiseman had instantly recommended me the fittest person for the Ionian Isles.'[32]

Baines was also worried by the coldness the Pope showed towards him on his arrival:

> The audience was of a good hour's length, the Pope standing all the while, notwithstanding my instruction that he should sit down. The moment I entered the audience room I knew that something was amiss. He put on an air of coldness that I had never seen before ... he then gave me to understand that I was sent for as one of the Vicars Apostolic of whom he had the most serious occasion to complain.[33]

Baines defended his own conduct and that of the other Vicars Apostolic, and said that he was sure that no bishops could be more attached to the Holy See. When this matter was raised, he also went on to defend his Lent Pastoral telling the Pope that its doctrine was correct and its language justified by the facts. At the end of the audience, Baines claimed that the Pope appeared more favourable to him and invited him to come again when he liked.

At last on 2 July 1840 Baines was given a full list of charges made against his Lent Pastoral, and retreated to his apartments in the Via Nicosia to prepare his defence. In a letter to Bishop Briggs he attributed all this to the enmity of Dr Wiseman:

> Since my last letter, I have been regularly called upon by Propaganda to answer a number of charges made against my Pastoral Letter by the converts of England, that is, by Dr Wiseman in their name ... This is all the work of our worthy agent, who also endeavoured to prove the pastoral heretical! ... I have been not considered on any single subject, but they shall have my opinions whether they ask for them or not ...[34]

Baines's defence of the pastoral

Bishop Baines spent the next few weeks preparing a long letter to Cardinal Franzoni, Prefect of Propaganda, in which he stated his very strong opinions in no uncertain terms. He began by going into greater detail about the unrest in England, which had been mentioned in his pastoral. This had created new tensions between the ruling classes and the proletariat and, combined with the continuing fears of many Protestants over the granting of Catholic Emancipation, made it desirable that 'all public boasting and inadequate triumphs should be avoided and quiet and conciliatory tones adopted in relation with Protestants . . .'[35]

Unfortunately some of the new converts had not seen the wisdom of this traditional Catholic policy in England and, exaggerating the number of conversions in the past few years, boasted that in a short time Catholicism would become dominant in England. Most damaging was the campaign for the conversion of England, which had been started by a priest from a noble Protestant family, with the support of foreign ecclesiastics. It was a campaign, however, which was not supported by three out of four of the Vicars Apostolic. It was particularly inflammatory because English Protestants knew that many Congregational prayers adopted by the Church of England had been used for political purposes: they would believe that Catholic public prayers would be used in the same way.

The movement had increased anti-Catholic feeling throughout England and Wales and led to the creation of Protestant Associations for the purpose of resisting the Catholics. Many itinerant preachers toured the country challenging the Catholic clergy and vilifying their faith. Baines could quote particular instances of this in his own District, where in Bristol huge anti-Catholic meetings had been held. He believed that the only way of appeasing the storm was for 'catholics to resume their quiet and peaceful demeanour'.

The converts, though, had other ideas and were resolved on 'open war with the heretics'. They tried to shelter under the protection of a bishop when they could, but when they could not, claimed that they were supported 'by foreign bishops, by the Holy See and even Heaven itself', and demonstrated this by quoting prophecies and miracles. Chief of these prophecies quoted was one by a Cistercian lay brother in the Midland District, who claimed to have constant visions relating to individuals and the nation. He was finally dismissed by his superior as a madman or imposter.

Medals were often used, and were stated to possess greater efficacy than all the sacraments. Baines regarded the use of many of them as complete superstition, and they and the prophecies only increased the torrent of ridicule poured upon Catholicism by Protestants. Instead of remaining quiet the 'controversialists' heaped more abuse on the Anglican establishment, and this was causing embarrassment to the Government and especially to political friends, who had supported the Catholic cause in Parliament, and were now becoming reluctant to do so.

Baines then condemned other practices of piety used by the converts, which may have been suitable in Catholic countries, but were certainly not in England and Wales. Some of these practices had been deformed 'by ignorant and tactless individuals'. Baines also criticized the use of medieval vestments, as supposed to have been used in England four or five centuries before. The 'fanatics' had introduced a chasuble nearly 6ft in width, hanging in ample folds, and more resembling a large shawl. He no longer recognized them as vestments used in the rest of the Catholic Church.

Baines objected also to the communion rail being omitted in many of the new churches, and the reserved sacrament being suspended from the ceiling by a chain or cord in a silver dove, all practices foreign to the English tradition. Then the Roman missal was being gradually set aside and the old English missal of Salisbury, not used since the Reformation, substituted in its place.

The final affront was for the converts to distribute to the different districts, without the consent of the Vicars Apostolic, certain forms and prayers to be used in public worship throughout Catholic churches in England and Wales. They believed that, as the Pope had sanctioned similar prayers, the bishops would not dare to condemn them. Baines himself, however, had forbidden all such prayers, although he had no objection to private prayers for conversions, or such prayers as the Litany of Loretto, in praise of the Virgin Mary, as prescribed in the Catholic prayer book which he had ordered to be used in all chapels where there was not High Mass.

Later, in a letter to his friend, Sir Charles Wolseley, Baines mentioned that ever since he was a child he had been in the habit of reciting the Litany of Loretto daily, a rare glimpse into his personal devotions. He had also arranged for the litany to be sung weekly at Prior Park, so could not be accused of abolishing it altogether; he had only expressed a dislike to the conduct of those who selected the one 'epithet' out of all the others, which was likely to cause offence to Protestants.[36] It is likely that Baines was referring to the doctrine of the Immaculate Conception, which was already being taught long before the promulgation of 1854. Since, however, the invocation 'Queen conceived in orginal sin' was not added to the Litany until the time of the papal definition in 1854, it remains a mystery as to what particular 'epithet' Baines was alluding.

Baines then turned to the particular accusations which had been made against him, allegedly by converts, although he believed that the charges had been concocted in Rome 'by some individuals, whose activity in this affair is well known, and whose want of sympathy towards me admits of no doubt'. He named no names, but was probably referring to Dr Wiseman, whom he had regarded as an enemy since 1835, and leaders of the Jesuits who were opposed to him because of disputes in the Bristol and Bangor missions. The accusations were many and some obscure; the most dangerous to Baines accused him of 'being little friendly to Roman maxims and devotions, being far more hostile to them that patronize them than to heresy itself'. Baines claimed, however, that in the Western District, 'the essential doctrines and discipline of the Catholic Church were universally received and all that concerns the exterior of religion is scrupulously fashioned upon the Roman model'. He pointed out that for three years he had assisted at the Pope's throne in Rome, and was therefore well versed in all the ritual and ceremonies.

The charges accused him of objecting to a book dedicated to the Immaculate Conception, but Baines pointed out that 'this doctrine did not belong to the code of defined dogmas, and may therefore be rejected by Catholics without censure'. It was a doctrine which English Protestants particularly disliked and Baines declared that 'whilst I am endeavouring to convince some unfortunate Protestant of the Divinity of Christ and the real presence, he interrupts with clamours about the Immaculate Conception'.[37]

Baines dealt with criticisms of his opposition to other religious innovations in similar style: 'Till the Protestants have learned to digest the simple dogmas of Faith, they should not be compelled to swallow the more highly seasoned dishes . . . What the converts wish to insinuate is that in spiritual matters, I am too fond of simple furniture and plain wholesome food for their refined taste and luxurious habits.'[38]

Baines then went on to challenge the criticism of his opposition to the crusade for the conversion of England. He stressed again that he had not objected to private prayers for conversion but, as he considered 'the immediate notional conversion of England as morally impossible, we should content ourselves with praying for the conversion of England in the way that has been customary: viz, on the understanding that our prayer should be heard in the manner and at the time most consistent with the inscrutable providence of God'.[39]

He saw no signs of a great conversion in England and, on present returns received, calculated that it would take 2,617 years for the conversion of England; the conversion of the Western District, with its comparatively small number of Catholics, and its extreme poverty, would be the most difficult.

A bishop's pastoral was the customary medium through which he gives instruction to his flock and the means by which 'he contradicts erroneous assertions, refutes false principles, opposes dangerous innovations and lays down suitable regulations for the conduct of his flock'. It was not the province of new converts to teach a man who has been a priest for thirty years and a bishop for seventeen years what is edifying to put in his pastoral.

Finally Baines referred to the criticism of his decision to authorize a prayer for the Queen and her new consort. His accusers say that

> my only solicitude is to gain the favour of the Government and the Protestants . . . there is no reason to suppose though that the Queen ever saw a copy of my pastoral. She did, however, see a copy of the pastoral of the Vicar Apostolic of the London District, which contained the same form of prayers as my own, and expressed her great satisfaction.

The converts had not made the smallest attempt to attack Dr Griffiths.

A long delay

Baines ended his letter by appending to it letters of support from other bishops and ecclesiastics, although no names are given. On 18 August he delivered it to the home of Cardinal Franzoni, who was out at the time. He waited impatiently for a few days and then returned to find that the Cardinal had not even read his letter, but had sent it on to the Secretary of the Sacred College, Monsignor Cadolini. The Cardinal then told Baines to his considerable annoyance that there would be a long delay in making a judgement on the case, as the Pope had ordered that a special congregation of cardinals should consider the question, and they could not meet until the end of September. It was unlikely that Baines would be able to return to England until after the winter. The Bishop complained bitterly about this delay, and the adverse effect his absence would have on Prior Park and the Western District, but all in vain. Roman procedure was slow and cumbersome and Baines had to wait around with as much patience as he could muster.

In September he was in better spirits, as he had met the Pope again and Gregory XVI had greeted him with far greater warmth, and had actually invited him to spend a day with him at the monastery of Camaldolese, where he was making a retreat. At dinner Baines was given a place on the Pope's right hand and 'reposed afterwards with the Pope in his own apartments on one of the hermits' straw beds. Before he left, I thanked him for the honour and satisfaction of the day. He said many kind and flattering things in return, patting me on the head at the time, a proof I should think that he considers me a good boy!'[40]

Baines thought this change of attitude was significant and it was likely that the Pope had been reading his 'Defence of the Pastoral' and was looking upon it in quite a different light. By October he was not so sanguine as he had still heard nothing about the judgement of his case, although he had been remonstrating strongly with Mgr Cadolini about the long delay. He had another appointment with the Pope at the end of the month and told Bishop Briggs that 'I shall complain grievously of the treatment I have received from Propaganda, which I consider as an insult upon the majority of the English Vicars Apostolic'.[41]

It was not until November that Baines was given information about the procedure which had been set up to examine his case. His pastoral translated into Italian, with comments upon it, Baines's defence of his pastoral and the comments of a consultor of Propaganda on the whole affair were laid before a special congress of cardinals who would make a final decision. Baines then applied to Monsignor Cadolini to be allowed to see the printed documents, but was refused, nor was he allowed to know the names of the cardinals who were to form the congress. He protested that the congress was like the Inquisition, a secret tribunal, and Monsignor Cadolini did not dispute this. He told Bishop Briggs that he had requested a further audience with the Pope: 'I shall complain [to him] of the mode of procedure and beg him to interfere to prevent any censure of my pastoral'.[42]

Problems from home

The months of delay were even more frustrating, as Dr Brindle was writing long letters from Prior Park, telling Baines of all the financial problems accumulating in his absence. The money that Baines had paid into the bank for the payment of bills would soon run out, and Dr Brindle was relying on Baines to arrange the studies for the coming academic year to enable Prior Park to compete with other colleges, particularly Oscott. The situation exposed the weakness in

Baines's system of administration in holding on to all the reins and refusing to delegate more than he was obliged. Dr Brindle was also faced with new problems in the missions owing to the redistribution of the districts in 1840, particularly the separation of Wales from the Western District, and this was something which only the Bishop could make a decision about.[43] He wrote also to tell Baines the unwelcome news that Dr Brown, the new Vicar Apostolic of the Welsh District, was to be consecrated in the Bath chapel, and Brindle had been asked if the reception afterwards could be held at Prior Park. He had agreed to this and hoped that Baines would not disapprove, hastening to reassure the Bishop that he would not have to bear any expense whatsoever. There is no record of whether Baines agreed to this, but he would not have liked to be absent at a time of such great events and celebrations in his own home.

As the weeks went on and the term at Prior Park got going, Dr Brindle related that he was having a problem with various students at the college, and widowed Lady Arundell, who had installed herself in rooms there, was being a nuisance: 'She is exclusive in her invitations, never asking some people to her tea parties at all, and concentrating on those she wants to draw into her circle; some she invites much too frequently'.[44]

A decision is reached

Baines, overwhelmed with troubles in Rome, could probably have done without hearing the minor irritations faced by Dr Brindle at Prior Park. His frustrations increased as the weeks went by, and it was not until the week before Christmas that the select congregation of cardinals met to decide on Baines's case. Even after they had reached their verdict, he was not told until some time afterwards, but wrote to Dr Briggs:

> I have however had information from one of the most important judges that I may keep quiet and dismiss my fears, that all goes well in this curious, I had almost said amusing case. The unknown accusers have been driven from every point, all sorts of underhand expedients have been adopted to make out more charges and swell the previous indictments ... To acquit me is to condemn themselves, to condemn me is to raise opposition, which they fear. I have denied the right of the Cardinals to entertain the charges, and have got some of the most influential on my side. I feel confident that the business will do an infinity of good ... It was so outrageous that it has disgusted many here. The proceedings of the

> Jesuits, as is well-known, are at the bottom of this and of all the late manoeuvres.[45]

Finally Baines received the decision of the congregation in a letter from the Pope on 18 January 1841, stating conditions which he wished the Bishop to accept before the matter of the pastoral could be closed. He had to make certain declarations, such as saying that when writing his pastoral letter, he had no intention of alluding to the Decree of the Sacred Congregation issued on 29 September 1838; that he would endeavour to repair any scandal that may have arisen out of the pastoral by declaring that he fully approved whatever the Holy See approved relating to the devotion of the Sacred Heart and the Immaculate Conception. He also had to declare that he had not disapproved of prayers for the conversion of England and much less those authorized by the Pope, and that he never wished to deny that Protestants were heretics in as much as they denied the articles of the Catholic Faith and were separated from the centre of Catholic unity; he had only wished to signify that some of the Protestants, as erring without obstinacy, were not heretics in the strict and formal sense of the term.[46]

Baines would have made these declarations extremely reluctantly, as the whole gist of his pastoral showed that he had very different views, but he had no other option if he was to remain a bishop. Then on 19 March 1841 the Pope sent for him again and gave him a letter which he could show to his critics in England, demonstrating that Baines had faithfully complied with the conditions laid down and that the declarations he had made satisfied 'both the decision of the Sacred College and our own exhortations'. The Pope ended by urging Baines 'to preserve the bonds of sacerdotal concord and unity of spirit with your colleagues, the Vicars Apostolic and other Pastors of souls'.[47]

As Baines feared that many of his critics in England would not believe that the affair had been satisfactorily concluded, and would be inclined to put out their own version, he asked the Pope's permission to publish a new edition of the pastoral, with the substance of the Declarations appended. According to Baines, the Pope agreed to this and added, as he later told Bishop Briggs: 'But take notice, you have not been asked to retract anything'.[48]

The return to England

Baines's life seemed to have come full circle when he returned home to Prior Park on 21 April 1841. We know that he feared that his life's work had come to nothing, but he took heart when he saw the cheering students waiting for him at the bottom of the hill and 'he was drawn by the whole assemblage to the foot of the splendid steps leading to the mansion.'[49] He had been away from his work for nearly a year, most of his time being spent in kicking his heels waiting for decisions in Rome. He felt humiliated by the long proceedings, over a pastoral which expressed his deeply held convictions, and which he believed to be the common-sense way of reacting to the difficult situation in England at the beginning of the Victorian era. The great welcome of students and staff made him forget all his troubles for a while, as his carriage was drawn through the grounds by cheering students and the whole college proclaimed his welcome in song, the effusive words written by Dr Rooker:

> He comes, and let youth with a fervent devotion
> In rapture unbounded his welcome proclaim;
> Let age with a calmer but deeper emotion,
> With eyes beaming pleasure, repeat his dear name.
> He comes, on his head Heaven's blessings be pouring;
> Henceforth may his struggle and sufferings cease;
> For him are the pure and the grateful imploring.
> His welcome be whispered by Angels of Peace.[50]

Baines was overcome with emotion as he was drawn up to the foot of the splendid steps which he had had built, to be welcomed by Dr Brindle and all the clergy, and in the midst of 'one hearty congratulatory group', moved up to the portico, where he was met by one of his most steadfast woman supporters, Lady Mary Arundell, and his great benefactress, the Hon. Miss Crewe. They all proceeded into the chapel where a solemn Te Deum was sung and 'the peals of the noble organ, the hundred voices joining in one heart felt prayer to Almighty God and the solemn pontifical blessing which followed, was such a scene as an indifferent spectator could not have witnessed unmoved'.[51]

A new history of the pastoral

Baines, a man much swayed by his emotions, took heart from this, and determined to silence his critics, whom he heard were now repeating their own version of recent events in Rome. He wrote to Bishop Briggs, telling him to take notice of the malicious stories that were going around:

> Look carefully at the facts which your Lordship knew from His Holiness's own pen to be true. He sends you a copy of the Declaration ... now what does the declaration contain? Any retraction of falsehood, mistatements, erroneous doctrines or anything that could imply that the pastoral had been condemned out-and-out or condemned at all? Certainly not. It merely declares what I meant in certain passages and what I did not mean in others ...[52]

The latter statement was not completely accurate, but Baines was always inclined to remember the past as he wanted it to be. It would have been better if he had left the matter there, but this was not Baines's way; if he believed that he was in the right, he was always eager to fight no matter what the consequences and he was telling Bishop Briggs in July: 'We must absolutely defend ourselves, or we are ruined by this wicked and powerful body ... If we hold together, the foxes could not come near us.'[53]

He composed a history of the whole pastoral affair and sent it, with his version of the declarations made in Rome, to the other Vicars Apostolic and friends who were concerned over the controversy. Unfortunately, however, Baines's version of the declarations differed radically from the original. A study of the two versions shows a considerable difference of emphasis and some omissions in Baines's later transcript. For example, in the Roman version, of which there is a copy in the Clifton Archives, Baines promised that: 'I solemnly engage that as soon as a favourable opportunity shall present itself, I will carefully endeavour to repair any scandal that may have arisen out of the pastoral by declaring that I most fully approve whatever the Holy See approves relative to the devotion of the Sacred Heart and the Immaculate Conception'.

In Baines's version of the History of the Pastoral Letter he says only: 'I declare that in no part of the pastoral did I mean to disapprove of the Devotion to the Sacred Heart as far as it has had the approbation of the Holy See'.

There is no mention of trying to prevent any scandal, and the doctrine of the Immaculate Conception is not directly mentioned here, although Baines claimed later that he had always approved of whatever the Church or its organ, the Holy See, approved. The two versions relating to prayers for the conversion of England also show considerable differences. According to the Roman manuscript, Baines promised that

> I will, in like manner, declare that I by no means disapprove of

> prayers for the conversion of England and much less those which the Pope has approved, and I never presumed to condemn them, but in my pastoral letter I only disapproved of a mass proposed to be celebrated every week, without the consent of the Vicar Apostolic ... for the immediate and general conversion of England.

In the later version, Baines declared that:

> I did not in the pastoral disapprove of prayers in general for the conversion of England, some of which I ordered, much less did I disapprove of any particular prayer which the Holy See had approved; that the only prayers I prohibited in the Pastoral ... was a weekly mass proposed to be celebrated publicly for the immediate national conversion of England.

Again there is difference in emphasis, for in the first version Baines made his declaration in the present tense, 'I by no means disapprove of prayers for the conversion of England', while in his own version he used the past tense, and qualified his disapproval; 'I did not in the pastoral disapprove of prayers in general for the conversion of England, some of which I ordered': he also failed to use the phrase, 'I never presumed to condemn them'.[54]

The letter to Sir Charles Wolseley

There are similar discrepancies between the two versions throughout. It is likely that Baines chose to recall his declarations made in Rome in the most favourable light, rather than that he deliberately set out to deceive. A moment's thought should have made him realize that he could not get away with it, particularly when he compounded the offence by sending an open letter to his friend, Sir Charles Wolseley, in which he again related his history of the pastoral affair, with his own version of the declarations. He also made an emphatic claim, which was likely to anger Rome: 'I hereby publicly declare that, neither on the subject of the pastoral, nor any other, have I been required to make the slightest apology or retraction and that therefore neither the slightest apology nor the slightest retraction will I make'.[55]

If this had remained as a private letter, all might have been well, but Baines had it published by the Prior Park press and it was eagerly purchased by friend and foe alike. It was inevitable that one or other, or both of the publications, would reach Rome.

The gathering storm

By September 1841, it was clear that the storm was about to break in Rome. Baines wrote to Bishop Briggs:

> As I supposed, the war of the Pastoral is not ended ... You will see from Dr Baggs' letter [the new English agent in Rome] that I am again about to be attacked. The danger is great that the Pope may be teased and bullied into some hasty decision. Mgr Cadolini is furious against me, so are the priests and so is Cardinal Lambruschini, the Secretary of State. Mr Ambrose Phillipps declared to Sir Charles Wolseley that my letter would cost me another journey to Rome.[56]

At the beginning of October Baines was agreeing with Bishop Briggs that it would be better if the latter wrote a personal letter to the Pope supporting the pastoral, rather than raise a petition among the Vicars Apostolic. He told Briggs that he had looked through his letter to Sir Charles Wolseley again and could not understand what all the furore was about. He maintained that the Pope had given him leave to express the declarations in any way he chose and, showing a disregard for the strict truth, maintained that he had repeated the original almost verbatim.

Apart from Dr Briggs, the other bishops were keeping their heads down, not wishing to become involved in Baines's conflict with Rome. The latter referred to them as 'cautious and prudent Vicars Apostolic, who will be quietly put down one after the other'. They were so timid that they only stood by when Ambrose Phillipps de Lisle insulted him, regarding it, not as an insult to the cloth, but as Baines's own personal affair.

'*O tempora, O mores*!' Baines bewailed in his letter to Bishop Briggs. He was suffering at the time, not only from mounting stress, but also from an infection of the stomach and liver, which laid him low in late October and early November. Events at Prior Park on 5 November, when a corn stack was set alight in the yard and an attempt was made to fire twenty others, convinced him that he had taken the right stand over the pastoral. He told Bishop Briggs that the local people had been inflamed by the Anglican clergy to an extraordinary degree, thanks in part to the provocation of 'our Midland friends'.[57]

Baines's mood soon changed to a more jocular one and he told his friend, Briggs, that, with the coming of Advent, he might try to gain some new laurels in the pastoral way; on the whole, though, he thought he had better restrain his ambition, 'and leave to others the records which my courtly talents must have won'. He thought that perhaps a pastoral on charity would be safer than a follow-up of last year's effort. Even a letter from his nephew in Rome did not depress him unduly. He wrote to Bishop Briggs that James had told him that: 'My enemies are hard at work and he fears will not stop till they have ruined me. This is cheering ... but I have no fear if my friends will endeavour to dissipate the idea, which my nephew tells me prevails, that the world is against me.'[58]

Baines was still in playful mood in early December, telling Briggs that he might have conformed so much that: 'I have joined Br Joseph in praying for the Queen's conversion', but not to the extent of calling 'the good little lady a bloody persecutor and comparing her to Nero and Domitian', as apparently one of his critics in the Midlands had done. Later in the month he was in a more sober frame of mind, urging Briggs to fulfil his promise of writing a letter of support to the Pope, and practically dictating the words he should use.[59]

The Pope's condemnation

Yet it was too late, for on 6 December 1841 the Pope had written to all the English Vicars Apostolic, condemning Bishop Baines in stinging words:

> Since, however, the Bishop of Siga, instead of responding to our clemency as he should have done, has published new pamphlets in which he perverts almost every fact, and, quoting one letter of ours, that dated 19th March, after he had made his Declarations, omitted other things which had happened before, and finally, as if celebrating a triumph, endeavoured to persuade his own people that the Pastoral letter in question, written by him, had been held to be free from the taint and suspicion of error and not worthy of censure, we feel it due to our office that we should by no means permit such boasting and untruthfulness from which great dishonour to the Apostolic See and the Christian Religion might arise to prevail against the truth. Here we have thought well to send the aforesaid documents to your fraternity, as well as to your colleagues, the Vicars Apostolic of England, that you may learn the whole matter and, at the same time, take measure according to your wisdom to guard against all scandal, and reasonably and prudently to inform those whose ignorance of these things might be harmful ...[60]

It was a crushing blow to Baines, a proud man, who always believed optimistically that the Pope was on his side and would support him against his critics. Although he had made some errors of judgement and had strayed from the truth, he had been standing up against the 'innovators', and those who sought to destroy the *modus vivendi* between English Catholics and the Protestant majority. It was a blow from which he never fully recovered, clouding his last tragic months, and leading to his premature death in 1843.

Notes

1 See Margaret Pawley, *Family and Faith* (Canterbury Press, 1993).
2 Denis Gwynn, *Father Luigi Gentili* (Dublin, 1951), pp. 140ff.
3 See above, chapter 11.
4 Augustus Pugin, see Paul Atterbury and Wainwright, *Pugin: a Gothic Passion* (Yale University Press, New Haven and London, 1994).
5 Raymond James, *Origin and Development of Roman Liturgical Vestments* (Exeter, 1926), p. 26.
6 William Ullathorne, Archbishop, *An Autobiography* (London, 1868), p. 142.
7 CDA, Inventory for the Sale of Prior Park.
8 Pius, the Rev Fr a Sp Sancto, *The Life of Fr Ignatius Spencer* (Dublin, 1866), pp. 24ff.
9 CDA, Baines Box Files, 5–7, Baines to Briggs, February 1839.
10 Ibid. 4 February 1839.
11 Ibid. 16 August 1839.
12 Ibid.
13 Ibid. 26 September 1839.
14 Ibid.
15 Ibid. Franzoni to Baines, 26 October 1839.
16 Ibid. Collection of Baines's Pastorals, Baines's Lent Pastoral, 1840.
17 See above, chapter 8.
18 CDA, Baines's Lent Pastoral.
19 Ibid.
20 Ibid.
21 Ibid. Roman Documents, Baines's Defence to the Vatican, 1840.
22 Ibid.
23 Ibid. Baines's Lent Pastoral.
24 Ibid.
25 Ushaw College, Walker Papers, Folder 8, John Lingard to Walker, 22 July 1850.
26 CDA, Baines Box Files, 5–7, Baines to Briggs, 11 March 1840.
27 Ibid. Bishops' Letters, James Baines to Peter Baines, 27 April 1840.
28 Ibid. Baines Box Files, 5–7, Baines to Briggs, 12 May 1840.
29 Ibid. Bishops' Letters, Baines to Briggs, 12 May 1840.

30 Ibid. Baines Box Files, 5–7, Baines to Briggs, 28 May 1840.
31 Ampleforth Journal, May 1910. Correspondence between Canon John Bonomi and Cardinal Wiseman is reproduced, based on printed copies obtained from the Clifton Archives, by kind permission of Bishop Burton. The originals of these letters cannot be found and were possibly lost in the several moves of the Clifton Archives since 1910.
32 CDA, Bishops' Letters, Baines to Briggs, 8 June 1840.
33 Ibid.
34 Ibid. 5 July 1840.
35 Ibid. Baines to Franzoni, no date.
36 Ibid. Public Letter, Baines to Wolseley, (Prior Park, 1840).
37 Ibid. Roman Documents, Baines' Defence to the Vatican, 1840.
38 Ibid.
39 Ibid.
40 Ibid. Bishops' Letters, Baines to Briggs, 14 September 1840.
41 Ibid. 29 October 1840.
42 Ibid. November 1840.
43 Ibid. Brindle to Baines, 20 October 1840.
44 Ibid.
45 Ibid. Baines to Briggs, December 1840.
46 Ibid. Roman Documents, and in Bishops' Letters: the Pope's Declaration on Baines' Lent Pastoral, 18 January 1841.
47 Ibid. Bishops' Letters, Pope Gregory XVI to Baines, 19 March 1841.
48 Ibid. Baines to Briggs, 30 April 1841.
49 See chapter 1, p. 1.
50 J. S. Roche, *The History of Prior Park and its Founder, Bishop Baines*, p. 167.
51 *Tablet*, April 1841.
52 CDA, Bishops' Letters, Baines to Briggs, 30 April 1841.
53 Ibid. 14 July 1841.
54 Ibid. Baines Box File, 13, Baines's History of the Pastoral with Latin translation.
55 Ibid. Baines to Wolseley, (Prior Park 1840).
56 CDA, Bishops' Letters, Baines to Briggs, 28 September 1841.
57 Ibid. 27 November 1841.
58 Ibid.
59 Ibid. 21 December 1842.
60 Ibid. Bishops' Letters, Pope Gregory XVI to the English Vicars Apostolic. The letter is in Latin and the translation used is from B. Ward, *The Sequel to Catholic Emancipation* vol. 1, (London, 1915), p. 219.

14

The Last Fight

The aftermath of the pastoral

There was an uncanny silence from Baines in the early weeks of 1842. His letters, which he wrote almost daily from his early years at Ampleforth to the end of 1841, suddenly ceased. Letters were his safety valve, in which he poured forth all his hopes and frustrations, his plans for the future, and his criticisms of those he felt were leading the Catholic Church in the wrong direction. Yet there are no letters describing Baines's reactions to the severe rebuke of the Pope in December 1841, or the rumours that he was soon to be replaced as Vicar Apostolic of the Western District. One can only conclude that he was so overcome by the condemnation and so humiliated by the whole situation that he had no heart to write to any of his friends, still less his critics.

There was also the factor of Baines's ill-health, made worse by constant worry and tension. It was no surprise that in March 1842 he suffered a severe stroke, and for some weeks his friends despaired of his life. Baines was ever a fighter, however, and was determined to overcome his illness; a few weeks afterwards, a visitor to Prior Park was surprised to find the Bishop crawling up the main staircase on his hands and knees determined to reach the top, symbolic of the way in which he always approached life.

The return to problems

By 4 July Baines was well enough to preside over the annual exhibition and prize-giving at Prior Park, and soon after this event went to Cheltenham Spa for a short period of convalescence. He was back again later in August to be confronted with new problems of staffing at the college, with the news that Fr Rosmini was withdrawing the Fathers of Charity to form a new foundation in the Midland District. Their members had recently been increased by the decision of Frs Furlong and Hutton, two of Baines's most loyal supporters who had come from Ampleforth, to join them. Baines had reluctantly agreed, knowing that their allegiance would be divided, but he realized that he would lose them anyway. On 12 August Fr Pagani, who was already at Loughborough, wrote to tell Baines that all members of the Institute would be withdrawn from Prior Park. Fr Brindle wrote to Pagani, on Baines's behalf: 'The Bishop expressly told you that such a removal could not take place . . . without very serious injury to this establishment and scandal to the public . . . His Lordship has expressed no wish for the removal of any of your members, but for this he most certainly calls – that all the 3 English members may continue at the college . . .'[1]

On his return to Prior Park, Baines put strong pressure on Frs Hutton and Furlong to stay; they had made up their minds to go to Loughborough, but were fearful of confronting Baines directly. Finally the two of them decided to make a secret getaway:

> The evening before their departure the Bishop having some suspicion of their intention sent a written protest to their rooms . . . their minds, however, were fully made up, and hastily packing up a few necessaries for the journey, they literally fled from the college on Wednesday morning, August 24th, and reaching Bath proceeded thus to Bristol, the very day after the railway between these two places had been opened.[2]

With the Fathers of Charity went Lady Arundell, who had adopted Fr Furlong as her spiritual director, and was later to found a convent in Loughborough. She had been a devoted supporter of the Bishop since his early days in the Bath mission, and Baines felt her defection sorely. He was soon at work, though, labouring to replace staff; he tried to persuade Dr Rooker, now Bishop Brown's Vicar General in Wales, to return to the college, but without success; he brought priests in from the missions as teachers, but they were often not qualified for the work and the standard of teaching declined. Monsignor Shepherd in his *Reminiscences of Prior Park* described this period, 1841–2, as the period of decline of Prior Park: 'Its excellent professors were disappearing from the scene in a dissolving view – not all at once, but still completely'.[3]

Later the Rosminians relented and wrote to offer the service of one other priest, but Baines told Brindle to write and reject the offer, telling him that the college was now fully staffed. In spite of all his troubles he still had intense pride, and would not accept favours from people he believed had let him down.

Although still far from well, Baines began to assume his wider duties, going out into his huge district to visit missions and administer confirmations. On 28 May 1843 his last confirmation, at Poole, was of a young girl called Rose, who later became a nun; she recorded her memories of Baines on his visits to her aunt:

> He would come about the grounds and call at my aunt's, enter into conversation – the last time he was less cheerful, gave us four views of Prior Park, told us to pray hard for it – shedding tears. My aunt made the remark that she hoped all would go well – 'Well we hope so,' said the Bishop . . . he was very sad and spoke of his life's work as a failure.[4]

A church for the future

At other times, however, Baines was still planning for the future, supporting the decision of Fr O'Farrell of St Joseph's, Bristol, to buy a new church for Catholic use from the Irvingites. The magnificent church was renamed as St Mary's on the Quay and converted for Catholic worship. It was built in the classical style by a local architect, Richard Shackleton Pope. The *Bristol Mercury* praised the splendour of the church:

> The entrance to the building is by a magnificent portico, supported by columns upon the plan of one of the most exquisite models of antiquity, the Diogenes Lantern at Athens. The interior which is cruciform, contains about 4,000 superficial feet and is capable of containing some 600 persons. The sanctuary, which is supported by four elegant corinthian columns is situated at the north west extremity and on its right and left are the statues of Sts Peter and Paul, the former holding the keys, the latter holding the sword; over the altar is found a crucifix, with the Saviour in burnished gold, surrounded by a halo gilt with the same precious metal . . .[5]

It was a church after Baines's own heart, classical, magnificent in style, and in a prominent position on the waterfront in the centre of Bristol. The ships would sail up the river almost to its door, and all the world would pass by and note the glory of the Catholic Church. He urged Fr O'Farrell to buy, in spite of the cost, and the priest put down a deposit of £500 for the building, the remaining £4,500 to be paid in instalments. It was a big financial burden for a congregation which had a large number of poor in its midst, but as usual Baines thought the price worth paying. He agreed to dedicate the new church on 4 July 1843.

Baines also had new plans for raising money to ease the financial problems of the Western District, and particularly of Prior Park. He wrote to all the priests in his district, asking them to do a census of their congregation, estimating the income level of its members. He then planned to write a special pastoral urging his flock to contribute, according to their ability to pay. He wrote to the *Tablet* explaining his plans, and the letter was published after his death.[6]

On 3 July Baines once more presided at the annual exhibition at Prior Park, and this time presented the prizes. It was a long and exhausting ceremony for a man who was still in very poor health, and could only get up and down steps with difficulty. There was no chance for rest and recovery on the next day, Sunday, as he had to be up early to travel to Bristol for the dedication of St Mary's on the Quay, a great event in the city and district.

Baines and his chaplain and clergy travelled on Brunel's railway, which had only recently been opened, and then by carriage to the great church. The *Bristol Mercury* described the magnificent procession, which entered the west door:

> The Sub-Deacon, Rev H. Astropp, habited in his gorgeous vestments of cloth-of-gold, with richly embroidered stole, bearing a cross of silver gilt.
>
> Four torch-bearers with lighted tapers
>
> Four acolytes.
>
> The thurifer with the incense
>
> The Bishop's attendant.
>
> The Rev J. Bonomi, of Prior Park College, who was the conductor of ceremonies within the altar.
>
> Between 30–40 priests, including some monks from Downside Abbey, in their robes, walking two by two.
>
> Rev D. Brindle, Vice-Rector of Prior Park, and V.G. of the Western District.
>
> An attendant bearing the Bishop's crozier of silver, richly jewelled.
>
> An attendant bearing the Bishop's mitre.
>
> The Deacon, Rev H. Woolat, in vestments of cloth-of-gold.
>
> The Rev Patrick O'Farrell, officiating High priest, also habited in vestments of cloth-of-gold.
>
> Rev Mr Rooker, officiating as conductor of the ceremonies within the chapel.[7]

Bishop Baines did not join the procession until it reached the high altar, when he entered from the vestry, 'habited in his purple cope with hood of ermine . . . attended by his chaplain'.

The service began with the Revd P. O'Farrell singing in English a prayer from the breviary, 'Let us Adore the God of Glory' . . . leading into High Mass, *coram pontifice*. Bishop Baines took his seat under a canopy on the west side of the altar, where 'he was unrobed of his cope and habited in far more gorgeous vestments, his mitre, richly jewelled being placed on his head'.[8]

The Bishop preached on the theme of 'The Four Marks of the True Church'. Usually he did not write out his sermons, but relied on note headings and a long period of meditation which, with the stimulus of a large crowd, bore him up to the heights of oratory. This time, racked by illness, he could not rely on his memory or his oratorical powers, and partly wrote out his sermon himself and partly dictated it. His language, though, was as forthright and as colourful as ever, as he contrasted the disunity among Protestants where 'they agreed with each other in nothing', with the unity of the Catholic Church:

> Travel where you will and ask the catholic pastor in regions the most remote, what you are to do to be saved, what are the doctrines and the duties commanded by Christ, you will receive the same answer. If you enter a catholic place of worship, whether it rivals in magnitude and splendour the dome of the Vatican or resemble the thatched house of the wandering Indian, you will find yourself at home.[9]

The ending of Baines's sermon was more provocative than usual, considering that he was preaching in a strongly Protestant city, where many felt great apprehension about the renewal of Catholicism. He ended by deriding the Anglican Church's claim to be part of the Universal Church:

> You unhappy children of a revolted sect, on whom the Church's anathema fell near three centuries ago; you who at first gloried in your separation, renounced the see of Peter, and the glorious promise annexed to it; yielded up your title of Catholic to which no one recognized your right, and pronounced yourselves the Church of England, now vainly and not very modestly attempt to recover the title you have lost and to be, what you will never be again, till God give you that grace to return like the prodigal, to the loving parent you forsook, and be again admitted as a member of his great and happy family.[10]

This was like the language of the Midland District, rather than Baines's usual more diplomatic way of addressing Protestants, and perhaps illness and exhaustion affected his judgement. It is no wonder that the Tory press of Bristol later railed against his sermon. At the time, though, nothing marred the joy and magnificence of the occasion: 'At the conclusion of the mass, the bishop and the priests surrounded the altar and chanted the *Te Deum*, after which the procession was reformed and preceded his Lordship, habited in Episcopal vestments, bearing his crozier and wearing his mitre and jewels, around the aisles ... the ceremony of the opening thus concluded, the company left the church'.[11]

As Baines went out of the church, Dr Brindle reported that: 'The poor with whom the bishop was a special favourite, crowded upon him and were seen to kiss the hem of his *cappa magna* as he passed'.[12]

The crowds liked a colourful personality and, even when they did not understand what he was saying, they were carried away by his fine delivery and vivid language. When he spoke to them afterwards, he had the power of being all things to all men, whether low or high.

The final drama

The whole ceremony lasted until 2 o'clock in the afternoon, when the choir went off to a free lunch at a nearby hotel, and the clerical party returned by train to a dinner at Prior Park that evening. Mr Edward King, Baines's solicitor who travelled with them, joked about being the exception among so many black coats. Baines himself must have been exhausted, and Dr Brindle persuaded him to go to his own room to rest. Later in the evening, though, he came down to join the assembly for a short time: he seemed quite his usual self and joined in the college Latin song, singing the last verse himself:

> '*Ubi sunt qui ante nos*
> *In mundo fuere?*
> *Transeas ad Superos*
> *Abeas ad inferos,*
> *Hos si vis videre*'

Monsignor Shepherd, once a student at Prior Park, translated it, and the words of the song later gained a sad irony:

> Those who lived before us, where are they now?
> If you wish to see them

Amidst God's Angels you must seek them
or find them in the realms below.[13]

At 9 o'clock Baines retired to his room, took a little cold chicken and a glass of wine, telling his servant that he felt better. He must have had another stroke in the early hours of the morning, and just after 6 o'clock the servant found him dead in bed, but looking as if he had fainted. Dr Brindle was sent for and administered the last sacrament, in the hope that life was not quite extinct. It was thought that the Bishop could not have suffered much, as he had made no attempt to ring the bell beside him, and the clothes of his bed were undisturbed.[14]

The drama of Baines's sudden death affected critics and friends in different ways. In Bristol, where he had preached his controversial sermon the day before, the editor of *Felix Farley's Bristol Journal* felt that he had to modify his criticism of the sermon a little, combining it with a reference to the Bishop's death. Nevertheless he said: 'We would be failing in our duty if we did not say that [the sermon] was not only a meagre specimen of pontifical oratory, replete with perverted views of scriptural truth, but fraught with misrepresentations of the Church of England ... We are not sitting in judgement on Dr Baines; he has gone to an infinitely higher tribunal ...'[15]

A member of the Catholic congregation in Bristol, who disapproved of Baines's treatment of the Jesuits, had no such inhibitions, writing: 'The Bishop came from Prior Park with his clergy, and his splendid vestments, and seemed to triumph over all opposition, but the next morning he was found dead in bed ... and the coroner pronounced the sentence of the law: Died by the visitation of God.'[16]

At Prior Park, though, all was silence. A visitor coming up from Bath on the day of the Bishop's death could find no one, and the silence was oppressive. All had gone to their rooms to cope as best as they could with their founder's sudden death at a comparatively early age.

For two days before the funeral his body lay in state under a canopy in the great hall of the mansion; on the first day, 3,000 people, and on the second day up to 10,000 people struggled up the hill and filed past the catafalque to pay their respects. J. S. Shepherd recalled that the crowds were excessive and 'fashionably dressed ladies struggled for admission with the utmost earnestness, and with the most perfect indifference, not only to their dresses, but even as to the safety of their persons'.[17]

There were Catholics and Protestants, the poor and well-to-do; some were friends and admirers, and others may have come from curiosity, as they had done before to watch the Corpus Christi processions, the fireworks after the annual exhibition, and even the great fire of 1836. All must have felt, though, that a colourful personality had gone from the scene, and life would be duller without him. And when the great doors were shut on the night before the funeral, there were still 2,000–3,000 waiting outside, some of whom had come from as far as Nottingham.[18]

The funeral service was held at Prior Park on 13 July and was attended by four bishops and about forty clergy, but there was no Bishop Walsh, no Bishop Wiseman. The *Tablet* described how: 'During the greater part of this most impressive funeral service, there was, so far as we could observe, hardly a dry eye, and the deep grief of those who had known the good Bishop most intimately and who had indeed loved him as a father, was, at times, almost painfully discernible'.[19]

Baines's friend, Bishop Briggs, who had stood by him through all his later trials, preached the sermon. Referring to the pastoral controversy, he explained that: 'Whether he was mistaken or not mistaken in these addresses, he had no other view in them than the Glory of God, the propagation of His truth, and the cause of our Holy Faith, and he never wished to wound the feelings of any member of the household of Christ . . .'[20]

Dr Briggs ended, with great emotion: 'O! I loved him and will never abandon him; but will accompany him with my thoughts and prayers until he reaches the tabernacles of eternal bliss'.[21]

A flawed genius

Controversial in life, Baines remained controversial in death. Fifteen years afterwards, Cardinal Wiseman was still trying to explain the inconsistencies of his character:

> He had a power of fascinating all who approached him, in spite of a positive tone and manner which scarcely admitted of difference from him in opinion. He had sometimes original views upon a certain class of subject; but on every topic he had a command of language, and a clear manner of expressing his sentiments, which commanded attention, and generally won assent. Hence his acquaintances were always willing listeners, and soon became sincere admirers, then warm partisans. Unfortunately, this proved to him a fatal gift. When he undertook great and even magnificent works, he would stand alone: assent to his plans was the condition of being near him; any one that did not agree, was soon at a distance; he isolated himself with his own genius, he had no coun-

> sellor but himself; and he who had, at one time, surrounded himself with men of learning, of prudence and of devotedness to him, found himself at last alone, and fretted a noble heart to a solitary death.[22]

There is truth in the early part of this appraisal, in that Baines used his charm and good looks to persuade people to follow the course he wanted, as he did with the students at Ampleforth in 1829. He was so talented, too, that he believed that no one could do things as well as he himself, so that he liked to keep everything under his own control. This was something that he could not possibly do, and he only succeeded in antagonizing others and exhausting himself. He was also inclined to abandon people when he believed that they had failed him, or when he had no further use for them, as he did with Fr Gentili. The loss of some of his other able staff owed most to the unfortunate rivalry with Bishop Walsh and Oscott College, where a brilliant mathematician such as Dr Logan thought that he would have better opportunities.

It was certainly not true, though, that almost everyone deserted Baines in his last days. Dr Brindle, whom Baines often took for granted, remained loyal to him for thirty years, and Fr Bonomi, once a student at Prior Park and later his chaplain and secretary, was still defending his reputation twenty years after the Bishop's death; Dr Briggs, too, never ceased to stand up for Baines in the height of the pastoral controversy, when it would have been more expedient to remain silent. And Baines inspired life-long devotion in numerous women friends, such as Miss Bettington and the Hon. Miss Crewe, who lent him vast sums of money on dubious security, the latter keeping a scrap book of the Bishop's ministry and writing on a copy of the sermon of 4 July, 'the dear padre's last sermon'. There were other less exalted women, such as Rose's aunt in Poole, who welcomed Baines into their homes on his many visits to the missions, and listened to his confidences; and above all there was his ward, Anna de Mendoza, who never ceased to admire him and to help him whenever she could, although she too must have felt taken for granted.

Wiseman's implication that Baines's life was a failure also does not stand up. Granted that he failed in his main enterprises: his seminary lasted only a few years after his death, and his dreams of a Catholic university were stillborn; yet the school, which he started mainly as a money-raiser, survived, although it has gone through many incarnations and the mansion which he bought for the Catholic Church and adorned, still stands in its magnificent grounds, which are now being restored by the National Trust.

Baines had once planned a great church above Prior Park, on a site dominating the skyline; it would proclaim the glory of the Catholic Church. The new church would be cruciform, surmounted by a great dome and with Corinthian porticos. As with many of Baines's dreams, however, his plans never reached fruition because of lack of funds. Yet part of his vision remains in the magnificent church designed later by J. J. Scoles.

What then were Baines's main achievements? He was far from being a saint, and some of his financial transactions, particularly, were unworthy of his calling. Although he preached forcefully of God, there is little mention of his own devotions in all the hundreds of letters that have survived, or his Ampleforth and Bath diaries. He was not a theologian, and left no lasting works behind him. He was, however, according to many observers, one of the foremost preachers of his age, and Protestants as well as Catholics flocked to hear him. Many of his sermons were printed, far outnumbering those of any other Catholic preachers of his time. J. S. Roche maintained that they showed the originality of the man, the fullness of his knowledge of both men and books, his skill as a controversialist, and his fervent desire to win over others to that Faith, which in himself was so deep. His most famous sermon, 'Faith, Hope and Charity', preached at Bradford in 1825, was translated into three or four European languages and reached a circulation of 25,000 in addition to the copies printed at Prior Park. This was a large circulation for religious books in his day.

Yet even this sermon can give little impression of the brilliance of Baines's oratory, the power of his delivery. Men such as James Shepherd and John Bonomi remembered his words years afterwards, but the long-term effect of these sermons and lectures on the thousands of poor and uneducated people who listened to them can never be measured.

As an educationalist, Baines was far in advance of his day. He experimented with new teaching methods, such as those of Professor Fenaigle and, in great contrast to the practice of the big public schools, and of the Irish Christian Brothers who followed him at Prior Park, he dissuaded his teachers from using corporal punishment. The syllabuses he planned at Ampleforth and Prior Park were wide-ranging and enlightened at a time when Harrow and Eton were teaching little but the classics.

As a bishop he had considerable influence in persuading the vicariate to present a united front ten years before the restoration of the hierarchy. He could not always carry the other bishops with him in his efforts to convince the Papacy that the Catholic Church in

England and Wales had particular problems, which required sensitive treatment. Yet in his campaign against the papal decrees and in 'the war of the pastoral' he made a valiant stand for what he believed was right.

Baines's greatest achievement was to raise the profile of the Catholic Church in England, just emerging from the repression of the penal laws – his sermons and lectures, and his splendid ceremonies at Prior Park all contributed to this, as did the importance he placed on church buildings. He founded his college on a hillside, so that all Bath could see, and persuaded his priests to move their churches from the back streets to the centres of communities, where all the world would pass by. Above all, he made his influence felt by the force of his personality and, although Wiseman claimed that this was a dangerous gift, it brought riches to the Catholic Church as well as failures. Many people admired Baines, and others loathed him, but it was impossible to ignore him.

Notes

1 CDA, Bishops' Letters, Brindle to Pagani, 12 August 1842.
2 J. S. Roche, *A History of Prior Park and its founder, Bishop Baines*, quoting from a memoir of Joseph Hurst (London, 1917), p. 72.
3 James Shepherd, *Reminiscences of Prior Park*, p. 24.
4 Ibid.
5 *Bristol Mercury*, 5 July 1843.
6 *Tablet*, 5 July 1843.
7 *Bristol Mercury*, 5 July 1843.
8 Ibid.
9 CDA, Baines Box Files, 25, Documents left to Bishop Clifford by the Hon. Miss Crewe, 1879.
10 Ibid.
11 *Bristol Mercury*, 5 July 1843.
12 J. S. Roche, *A History of Prior Park*, pp. 169ff.
13 Ibid. (quoting James Shepherd's translation).
14 Ibid.
15 *Felix Farley's Bristol Journal*, 8 July 1843.
16 John Smith, *Jesuitism and Friarism in Bristol* (Bristol, 1845), p. 57.
17 *Tablet*, 15 July 1843.
18 Ibid.
19 Ibid. and J. S. Shepherd.
20 Ibid.
21 Ibid.
22 Cardinal Nicholas Wiseman, *Recollections of the Last Four Popes* (London, 1858), p. 325.

Epilogue 1909

In 1856, when Prior Park was up for sale, two monks were wandering through the buildings. They came to the uncompleted chapel, where work had ceased for lack of money, and were startled to find four coffins in a side room. Among these were the coffins of Bishop Baines and his nephew, James, who had died a short while after his uncle. Originally it was intended that they should be buried in the new chapel when it was finished, but it had never reached that stage. Now the future of the chapel and Prior Park itself seemed so uncertain that, as both Baines and his nephew had been Benedictines, it was decided to bury their remains in the cemetery at Downside.

Here Bishop Baines lay for over fifty years until in 1909, soon after the choir of the great Abbey Church of Downside was completed, a titular abbot Kindersley decided that the time had come for reconciliation. He wrote to the Bishop of Clifton, George Ambrose Burton, and suggested that Baines should be re-interred in the abbey, and this was agreed upon. On 2 August 1909, Abbot Kindersley wrote to Bishop Burton: 'I have at last managed to bring the Bishop of Siga into our church and I hope, that having done, he will rest in peace and bring us peace as well . . .'[1]

Grave robbers had been at work over the years and it was revealed that, when the coffin was opened, the Bishop's ring and his pectoral cross were missing. The ring was said to have been given to Baines by Pope Leo XII.

Downside raised the money to complete Baines's marble tomb, but their magnanimity did not extend to providing funds for the recumbent figure to lie on top. Kindersley wrote to Bishop Burton saying: 'The present abbot did not think we were called upon to put up an effigy of the man who did so much against us, and that he thought our forgiveness had gone far enough in giving him the tomb, which he was glad he had done'.[2]

Bishop Burton then agreed to raise the money, with the help of the newly-formed Prior Park Association, and appointed an architect, F. A. Walters. Whether Bishop Burton did not know Baines's views on the subject, is not known but Walters clad the recumbent figure of Bishop Baines in the Gothic vestments beloved of Pugin, which were anathema to Baines.

There he lies in the place where he would never have wished to be, dressed in the vestments he hated. Yet the sculptor has given the figure a sense of serenity and calm repose, and one hopes that Peter Baines has found the peace that always eluded him in life.

Notes

1 CDA, Baines Box Files, 19, Abbot Kindersley to Bishop Burton, 2 August 1909.
2 Ibid. 21 September 1909.

Bibliography

Manuscript Sources

Archives of the English Benedictine Congregation, Ampleforth Abbey, Ampleforth, York.
Archives of the English Benedictine Congregation, Downside Abbey, Stratton on the Fosse, nr Bath.
City of Bristol Record Office, Hotwells, Bristol.
City of Bristol Reference Library, College Green, Bristol.
Clifton Diocesan Archives, Bishop's House, Alexander House, Pennywell Road, Easton, Bristol.
St John's Presbytery, Mansel Street, Bath. (The records from here are in the process of being transferred to the Clifton Diocesan Archives.)
The Jesuit Province Archives, Farm Street, London, S.W.1.

Journals

Felix Farley's Bristol Journal
Recusant History: Journal of the Catholic Record Society
South Western Catholic History
Ampleforth Journal
Bath and Cheltenham Gazette
Bristol Gazette
Bristol Mercury
Catholic Magazine and Review
Downside Review
Monthly Intelligence
Morning Herald
The Tablet

Other Primary Sources

Allanson, Dom, 'Lives of the English Benedictines', unpublished material for the English Benedictine Congregation, Ampleforth and Downside, circa 1855.

Annual Laity's Directories to the Church Services, London.

Bath Directories, City of Bath Central Library.

Baines, Peter Augustine, A Letter addressed to Sir Charles Wolseley, Bart, Prior Park 1840.

Baines, Peter Augustine, Sermons preached 1823–1843 in several volumes, CDA.

Catalogues of the sale of Prior Park Mansion and College, Bath 1856.

Cashman, John, Notes on the History of Clifton Pro Cathedral, based on reminiscences of Monsignor Russell, Vicar General.

Theses

Cashman, John, 'Bishop Baines and the Tensions in the Western District', unpublished thesis submitted for the degree of M.Litt, University of Bristol, 1989.

Gilbert, Pamela J., 'In the midst of a Protestant People: The Development of the Catholic Community in Bristol in the nineteenth century', unpublished thesis submitted for the degree of PhD, University of Bristol, 1995.

Hankins, Kenneth, 'The Contention of Power: The Role of the Jesuits in the Catholic History of Bristol, 1770–1830', unpublished thesis, submitted for the degree of PhD, University of Bristol, 1998.

Printed Books

Almond, Cuthbert, OSB. *The History of Ampleforth Abbey*. London, 1907.

Anonymous. *St Benedict's Priory, Colchester*. No name of publisher.

Aveling, J. C. H. *The Handle and the Axe*. London, 1976.

Baines, Peter Augustine. *A Defence of the Christian Religion*: A second Letter to Charles Abel Moysey DD, Archdeacon of Bath. Bath, 1822.

— *Collected Sermons*, Prior Park Press, no date.

— *Public Lectures on the Outline of Christianity*. Bath, 1839.

Birt, H. N., OSB. *History of Downside School*. London, 1902.

— *Obit Book of the Benedictines*, 1610–1912.

Blundell, F. O., Dom. *Old Catholic Lancashire* in three volumes, London, 1942.

Bossy, John. *The English Catholic Community 1570–1850*. London, 1975.
Butler, Cuthbert, Dom. *The Life and Times of Bishop Ullathorne, 1805–1889*. London, 1926.
Boyce, Benjamin. *The Benevolent Man: A Life of Ralph Allen of Bath*. Harvard, 1967.
Caraman, Philip, SJ. *Wardour, A Short History*. Bristol, 1984.
Cashman, John, 'Old Prior Park – The Final Years 1843–1856' in *Recusant History*, vol. 23, no. 1, May 1996.
Challoner, Richard, Bishop. *The Garden of the Soul, A Manual for spiritual exercises and instructions for Christians*. London, 1916.
Chadwick, W. O. *The Victorian Church*. London, 1966, 1970.
Crichton, J. D. *Worship in a Hidden Church*. Dublin, 1988.
Dockery, J. B. *Collingridge: A Franciscan Contribution to Catholic Emancipation*. Newport, 1954.
Fielding, Henry. *Tom Jones, Foundling*. Paper-back edition, Ware, 1992.
Fothergill, Brian, *Nicholas Wiseman*. London, 1963.
Gilley, Sheridan. *Battling Bishop Baines of Bath*. S.W. Catholic History No 3, 1985.
Gwynn, Denis. *Lord Shrewsbury, Pugin and the Catholic Revival*. London, 1946.
— *Luigi Gentili and his Mission, 1801–1848*. Dublin, 1951.
Hayes, Bernard, OSB. *The Via Vitae of St Benedict*. London, 1908.
Hankins, Kenneth. *In my Father's House*. Bristol, 1993.
Hickey, John. *Urban Catholics*. London, 1967.
James, Raymond. *Origin and Development of the Roman Liturgy and Vestments*. Exeter, 1926.
Lancashire Registers, *The Fylde*, vol. 1. The Catholic Record Society, London, 1951.
Leetham, Claude R. *Luigi Gentili, A Sower for the Second Spring*. London, 1965.
Lewis, Michael R. *From Darkness to Light: The Catholics of Breconshire, 1536–1851*. Abertillery, 1992.
Little, Brian, *Catholic Churches Since 1623*, London, 1966.
McLelland, V. A. *English Roman Catholics and Higher Education 1830–1903*. London, 1962.
Marsh, Richard, OSB. *Reminiscences*. Ampleforth, 1995.
Mathew, David. *Catholicism in England, 1535–1935*. London, 1936.
Mowl, Tim, and Earnshaw, Brian. *John Wood, Architect of Obsession*. Millstream Books, 1988.
Norman, Edward. *The English Catholic Church in the Nineteenth Century*. Oxford, 1984.

— *Roman Catholicism in England from the Elizabethan Settlement to the Second Vatican Council*. Oxford, 1986.

O'Brien, James. *Old Afan and Margam*. Aberavon, 1926.

Oliver, George. *Collections Illustrating the History of the Catholic Religion in the counties of Cornwall, Devon, Dorset, Somerset, Wilts, and Gloucester*. London, 1857.

Pawley, Margaret, *Family and Faith*, Canterbury, 1993.

Pius, A Sp Sancto. *Life of Fr Ignatius of St Paul*. Dublin, 1866.

Price, R. J. *Little Ireland*. Swansea, 1992.

Prior Park, *Landscape Garden*. London, 1996.

Pugin, A. Welby, *An Apology for the Revival of Christian Architecture*. London, 1843.

Roche, J. S. *A History of Prior Park and its Founder, Bishop Baines*. London, 1931.

Schiefen, Richard J. *Nicholas Wiseman and the Transformation of English Catholicism*. Patmos Press, 1984.

Shepherd, James. *Reminiscences of Prior Park*. Bath, 1886.

Sitwell, Edith. *Bath*. London, 1932.

Smith, Margaret. *From Victorian Wessex: The Diaries of Emily Smith, 1836, 1841, 1852*. Norwich, 2003.

Smith, John. *Jesuitism and Friarism in Bristol*. Bristol, 1845.

Taunton, E. L. *The English Black Monks of St Benedict*, (2 vols). London, 1897.

Ullathorne, W. B. *An Autobiography*. London, 1895.

Van Zeller, Hubert, OSB. *Downside By and Large*. Downside, 1954.

Ward, Bernard. *The Eve of Catholic Emancipation 1820–1829*. (3 vols). London, 1911–1912.

— *The Sequel to Catholic Emancipation*. (2 vols). London, 1915.

Williams, J. A. *Post Reformation Catholicism in Bath*. (2 vols). London, 1973.

Wiseman, Nicholas, Cardinal. *Recollections of the Last Four Popes*. London, 1856.

Young, Urban. *Life of Fr Ignatius Spencer*. London, 1912.

Index

Printed in the United Kingdom
by Lightning Source UK Ltd.
110795UKS00002B/1-18

9 780852 445921